FILM & VIDEO ON THE INTERNET

The Top 500 Sites

Bert Deivert & Dan Harries

FILM & VIDEO ON THE INTERNET

Published by MICHAEL WIESE PRODUCTIONS, 11288 Ventura Blvd., Suite 821, Studio City, CA 91604 (818) 379-8799 fax (818) 986-3408.
wiese@earthlink.net
http://home.earthlink.net/~mwp

Cover design by Art Hotel, Los Angeles
Book Layout by Gina Mansfield
Final Copy Check by Bernice Balfour

Printed by Braun-Brumfield, Inc., Ann Arbor, Michigan
Manufactured in the United States of America

Copyright 1996 by Bert Deivert & Dan Harries

All rights reserved. No part of this book may be reproduced in any form or by any means without permission in writing from the author, except for the inclusion of brief quotations in a review.

Note: The information presented in this book is for entertainment and information purposes only. The authors are not giving business or financial advice. Readers should consult their lawyers, accountants and financial advisors. The publisher and its assignees are not responsible nor liable for how readers may choose to use this information.

Deivert, Bert, 1950-
    Film & video on the Internet : the top 500 sites / by Bert Deivert & Dan Harries.
      p. cm.
Includes bibliographical references and index.
ISBN 0-941188-54-X
1. Motion pictures--computer network resources--Directories. 2. Television--Computer network resources---Directories. 3. Video recordings--Computer network resources--Directories. 4. Internet (Computer network)--Directories. 5. World Wide Web (Information retrieval system)--Directories. I. Harries, Dan, 1963-
II. Title
PN1998.A1D36 1996
025.06'79143'025--dc20
                                            96-11458
                                            CIP

Books from
MICHAEL WIESE PRODUCTIONS

Film & Video on the Internet
Persistence of Vision
Directing Actors
The Digital Videomaker's Guide
Shaking the Money Tree
Film Directing: Shot by Shot
Film Directing: Cinematic Motion
Fade In: The Screenwriting Process
The Writer's Journey
Producer to Producer
Film & Video Financing
Film & Video Marketing
Film & Video Budgets
The Independent Film & Videomaker's Guide

TABLE OF CONTENTS

Acknowledgements	vi
Introduction by Michael Wiese	vii
Shots in Cyberspace	1
The Top 500 Sites by Category	23
ACTORS	25
ANIMATION	36
DIRECTORS	38
FESTIVALS/EVENTS	44
FILM & MEDIA SCHOOLS	51
FILM REVIEWS	59
FILM & TV ASSORTED	66
FILM & TV INDICES	80
FILMS	87
IMAGES	95
MAGAZINES & JOURNALS	97
MEMORABILIA	108
MOVIE THEATERS	112
MOVIES	118
NEW MEDIA	120
ORGANIZATIONS/GUILDS	126
PRODUCTION & DISTRIBUTION	136
RESEARCH AND DATABASES	147
SCREENWRITING	154
SOUNDS	155
STUDIOS	158
TV NETWORKS	162
TV PROGRAMS	169
VIDEO INFO/SALES	185
Listserv/Usenet	191
Appendix & Cross-References	199
Bibliography	245
Mail in Comments/Review card for readers	246
MWP Books	247

Acknowledgements

One of the exciting aspects of writing a guide "about" the Net is actually using it to harness a wide array of global contacts. This book was literally written "on the Net" exemplified by the hundreds of e-mails in our Eudora folders. This made writing the book swift, exciting, and dynamic. It was a constant hypertextual adventure taking months of exchanging ideas and frustrations in flurries of e-mail between Australia, Sweden, and Los Angeles.

Dan would like to thank Paul Brown (Brisbane-based editor of FineArt Forum and WWW guru) for piquing my early interest in the Internet, Linda Heron, Sarah Barry, Tony May, Gordon Fletcher, Anita Greenhill (Griffith University), Colin Mercer (QANTM-Australia), Nick DeMartino (AFI), Peter Lunenfeld (Art Center College of Design), Andrew Fayé (Georgetown University), and Jeremy Butler (SCREENSite maven) for their constant support, assistance, and feedback over the last few years of my virtual existence.

Bert would like to thank the University of Karlstad's Klas Brohagen for his HTML hack for our database, and John Nilsson for his ongoing techie advice. Jeremy Butler has always been an inspiration for Net idealism and enthusiasm. Eva, Séamus, Finn, and Emmy deserve enormous thanks for putting up with my face being glued to the screen for hours on end. And Dan, thanks for asking me to do this after having met once for 10 minutes at a conference! That was an act of faith.

Both Bert and Dan would also like to thank Michael Wiese for his belief in the possibility of getting this book together over the Internet and without ever seeing either of us face to face or talking on the phone even once!

Introduction by Michael Wiese

The first thing I did when I got hooked up to the Internet was to search for interesting film and video sites. I knew they must be out there but darn if I could find them.

As an new Internet user, I dropped notes in film and video Usenet groups and asked, *"Does anybody know any cool film sites?"* I got two or three responses.

I tried again. *"I am compiling a list of cool film sites; send me yours and I'll send you the list when it is finished."* This yielded several dozen sites but not many were very inspiring. However, one of the tips was to a site called CineMedia where I "met" Web Master Dan Harries.

From then on things moved very fast. Dan and his colleague Bert Deivert in Sweden flooded me with e-mail while we "virtually" designed the editorial approach for the book. For me, this was an exciting period of really testing the Internet's power as a publishing vehicle. I am thoroughly delighted with their results.

So now we open up the process to you, dear reader, and invite you to tell us about sites you've discovered (and like—forget the ones you don't). There is information in the back of the book for you to write your own review. If we use your recommendation or quote, we'll send you free the next edition of this book as our thanks.

To Dan and Bert, I tip my hat. I trusted your instincts, your qualitative insight in reviewing the sites, and most of all, admire and appreciate your enthusiasm about this new medium.

To the reader, you have a treat in store for you. This book will save you hundreds of hours of searching and allow you to blast to the sites that hold the most promise for your particular interest.

Let us know what you think. Happy surfing and successful filmmaking. Now go get 'em.

Michael Wiese

SHOTS IN CYBERSPACE
Accessing Film & Video Resources on the Internet

by Bert Deivert

The Internet, a shot in the dark? Get started!

The reason you are reading this book is probably because you have Internet access and are ready to explore cyberspace for all sorts of exciting film clips, actor bios, film lists, TV schedules, theater times, and pictures of your favorite movie posters. The question you've asked yourself is where and how do I do that?

We will be acquainting novices and seasoned users of the Internet with some of the resources available for film buffs, cineastes, film and video makers, and film students in various domains of cyberspace. A detailed manual of usage is not possible, since this would encompass many volumes in trying to teach the separate programs available. Instead, I would like to briefly introduce some useful ways of using the Internet and to point users in certain directions for information, and leave the rest up to you. Exploration on your own time and at your own pace is the best way to discover the richness and complexity of the Internet. We assume that you have access to the Internet via a commercial online service or through your school or place of work, and that you have a **WEB** browser program such as Netscape. In addition to this, it is best to have the freeware Telnet program as well. This way you may take full advantage of text-based areas on the Internet.

I would like to point out that I am not a computer professional in any sense of the word. I am a film lecturer and musician, fond of using Macintosh computers. Driven by my own curiosity I have explored the possibilities available on the Net during the last five years and have had help from a number of friendly and enthusiastic individuals, primarily in Sweden and the USA. However, my calls for help have been answered from as far away as Japan, Australia, and Venezuela.

The knowledge needed to use the resources mentioned in this book is within reach of anyone who is willing to invest a few hours into learning the basics of a couple of programs and then learn more while working. If you just want to browse the World Wide Web, then you can be up and running in a few minutes with very little study or introduction needed! Do not be put off by all the computer terms. They are just as necessary to the context of computer usage as film terms are to understanding the making of films. They are easily learned and understood. Remember that trial and error is the greatest teacher. Don't be afraid to experiment—you can't break the Net! Any errors in this essay are most likely my own. The Net is constantly changing though, and something there today may be gone tomorrow. If you would like to update anything that you find is erroneous or give us tips about film or television sites not mentioned here, please feel free to contact us. If you wish to use e-mail, please put **FILM and VIDEO BOOK** on the subject line. You may write to us at: *bert.deivert@hks.se*

What Is the Internet?

The Internet is the term used for the network of connecting computer networks all over the world, both commercial and noncommercial. Primarily based on university networks originally established for military and scientific research in the US, other smaller networks have subsequently latched on to use the resources of the larger networks, enabling them to have worldwide access. The terms Internet and Net are used for the same virtual space in this essay.

Since the Internet is like a root system of separate and autonomous networks, some points in this book may be out-of-date by the time it is published. However, we have taken the greatest care to be up to date right up to the time of publishing. Sites on the Internet are constantly changing, moving, being updated, and in some cases, being taken over by commercial forces. Therefore this book may serve as a launch pad for starting points. I will not try to give definitions of all the terms used here in this essay. These can be found in more technical manuals dealing with your specific computer type.

As a net surfer, explorer, and information junkie ever since I learned how to download files using ftp, the Internet has been a place of perusal, chat, serious talk about the meaning of life, work, and the love of film. Certainly, any film buff or serious student of cinema has *every* reason to be roaming the Net in search of contacts, discussions and useful information. The sheer size of the Internet, not really known by anyone, but estimated at about 4.8 million computer host sites (which are in turn serving who-knows-how-many peripheral computers) makes the gathering of information easy, but the sorting of information and narrowly defined searches difficult.[1]

Most computers use programs that are client-server configurations. The client program on your computer gets information from the server program and presents it for you in some readable form. To simplify this with an example, you run Netscape on your computer—this is a client program—and your client asks another computer—a server somewhere—to look at the pictures and text available there. The server replies by letting you download those files to your computer so that you may look at them. As William Dickson says:

You might think of the server software as being a dessert cart; you're not allowed to put your filthy paws on the pastries, so you need a client, a set of tongs perhaps, to obtain that tasty eclair.[2]

For Beginners
One of the great advantages to being a newcomer is that there are many friendly and helpful individuals out there willing to hold your hand (online) through the most rigorous digital exercises in order to help you get to where you want to go. Don't be afraid to say or admit that you are a novice. We all were there at one time, and there is nothing to be ashamed of. Most people take great pleasure in helping newcomers get going. There is an almost evangelical aspect of the Internet that would be worth a sociological study. People extol its virtues and try to get others to get out there and meet people, work, and enjoy themselves.

Commercial Services
Commercial services are expanding rapidly and competition brings lower prices. Though you can get by with only e-mail, I would suggest a full Internet access account that most commercial services like CompuServe and America Online provide, if you can't get access through work or place of study. This allows you the ability to use the graphically oriented programs like Netscape to maneuver the Net.

Most major companies, at least in the USA, seem to have some sort of Internet access or e-mail capability within their organizations. The need to keep the edge over the competition has made companies aware of the immediacy of this type of communication as opposed to "snail mail" and faxes.

Work or School Access
Most universities have Internet access for their faculty, and some institutions have access for students. American universities seem to have the most advanced facilities in this respect at the moment, many of them offering direct Internet connections in student dormitories. However, many European countries are catching on to this. Contact the computer support section at your university or college in order to find out how to get connected.

If you have an account on a computer at your place of work or university, ask your computer support people if there is a PPP or SLIP connection available so that you may connect from home or on the road. If you wish to work at home and use the same programs on your Mac/PC there as the ones you use at work, you need to be able to log in to your account via a SLIP or PPP connection. Simply put, your computer at home makes believe it has a direct line out to the Internet by connecting via the remote server at work or school.

Get the support people to help you set up the software configuration on your home computer, if possible. This can be tricky for novices, though experienced users should have no difficulty. Once this is running, connection is as easy as starting the program you use, which in turn automatically dials the central modem telephone number and connects you.

Commercial Activity
The awareness of commercial possibilities for information brokerage and sales venues online has stimulated many companies to start World Wide Web sites on the Net. The prospects of a totally commercialized Internet is one that I believe is distasteful to the majority of users—that is, the users of today. We can't really predict what future users will want. We are at the brink of a commercial breakthrough on the Internet and if the *majority of users in the future* are most interested in purchasing mail-order products via the Internet, there is a danger that it may become just one more glorified shopping channel monitored and possibly controlled by the watchdogs of certain governmental organizations.

Free Areas on the Internet

The free access for academics, schools, and information seekers of various kinds guarantees a certain democracy on the Internet, and I for one hope it may stay that way. We will have to put up with a certain amount of anarchy and even distasteful activities, such as pornography sites or manuals on terrorism. However that is a small price to pay since this is still a very small part of all the activity that goes on throughout the Net. For those that wish to avoid such sites or keep children away from them, there are a number of software filter solutions available for Web browsers such as Netscape and Mosaic.

Internet and Mass Media

Regular features in newspapers, magazines, and programs like CNN's "On Ramp" have created a demand for more information about the Internet. With commercial online services like America Online, AppleLink, and CompuServe having gateway access for e-mail distribution throughout the Internet, many journalists have expounded on the vast richness of information out there, while *oversimplifying* the easy access to it. A number of specialized magazines, especially dealing with computers, often have well-documented and informative articles on how to get on to the Internet from a home computer over a modem.

I believe the trend for Net support as a compliment to printed media will continue. There are already a number of serious journals, magazines and newspapers available online, and even a number of journals and magazines published exclusively on the Internet. *Time, Filmmaker, Wired, Entertainment Weekly, The San Francisco Chronicle*, and Sweden's *Aftonbladet* are some examples of printed publications with available full-text articles on the Net. There are even a number of academic journals available in this manner. *Postmodern Culture*, a refereed scholarly journal, is published exclusively on the Net by the North Carolina State University, Oxford University Press, and the University of Virginia's Institute for Advanced Technology in the Humanities.

E-zines, which are like fanzines but electronic, exist for small numbers of interested readers on the Internet. There are hundreds, and possibly thousands out there. They were originally distributed by e-mail, but with the advent of the Web, a number of them have become cool graphically oriented Web sites. They address readers from such diversified areas as hacking, sci-fi literature, and cyberfashion. Some of those related to film and video are *FINEcut*, *INDIE*, and *Weltwunder der Kinematographie*.

World Wide Web—Mosaic and Netscape

Hypertext is one of the most heavily touted catchwords in computers, as well as the infamous *multimedia*. Mosaic, a Web client/server program (as well as the Telnet program), was developed by people at NCSA and is now being developed further as an enhanced commercial program in the form of Netscape.[3] Netscape is available free on the Net for educational organizations but has a low cost for commercial organizations. Their strategy is similar to that of the developers of Eudora and StuffIt, the popular Macintosh programs. Originally distributed freely or as shareware, and thereby gaining a large established user base, the upgrade to the commercial version was inexpensive and very much worth it if one wanted the extra capabilities the upgrade provided. Thousands of people have upgraded from free versions to commercial versions, since they wanted the enhanced capabilities. It looks like this may also happen with Netscape, but there are other programs vying for a share of this huge market.

There are other Web client programs available but Mosaic and Netscape are my personal favorites. Netscape has a faster and more easily implemented search capability. It also has a nice filmic feel to the graphics, showing them appearing through a slow fade-in.

At the moment, the World Wide Web system which seamlessly integrates hypertext links, gophers, Telnet, ftp, sound, digitalized movie clips, and graphics is the most popular and fastest growing area on the Net. The graphic interface clients are the most touted ones, though it is possible to use a text-based client through a Telnet connection by logging in as www.

Since we assume that you will be using a Web browser such as Netscape, you will have easy access to graphic and text areas and be able to use the following types of protocols directly in the Netscape program by using the right syntax and prefix. To make use of any of the addresses you will use, you need the correct prefix, and then the address of the site. The latest version of Netscape is so smart about http:// addresses that if you fail to write http:// first in the location field, it will automatically assume that is what you want and put it before the address you have entered when you hit the return key. Here are the most common prefixes.

Hypertext transfer protocol: http://
Gopher: gopher://
Telnet: telnet:// (as long as you have the Telnet program also installed on your computer)
FTP: ftp://

How about some examples? Okay...

http://www.emi.net/repositories.html list of ftp sites
gopher://bpl.org:70/1   Boston Public Library gopher
ftp://ftp.sunet.se   the main ftp site in Sweden
telnet://database.carl.org   the UNCOVER article database in Colorado

To connect to a site, you just need to write in the URL (uniform resource locator), as listed in the book. On Windows or Macintosh interfaces, you may pull down a menu item, which on Netscape for Mac is called *Open Location*. You then write in the URL, such as that for Paramount Studios: *http://www.paramount.com/*
It is also possible to write in the URL near the top of the program window where the location is shown, and then use a carriage return.

Hypertext in the World Wide Web is marked with a recognizable color (on color computers with graphic browsers), often blue (red or purple for previously used connections), and/or underlined. By marking that text with a click or a carriage return in a text-based browser, one is then transported to another site somewhere in the world that has been given a link based upon an association with that hypertext (word).

George Landow describes hypertext like this:

Hypertext, in other words, provides an infinitely re-centerable system whose provisional points of focus depends upon the reader, who becomes a truly active reader in yet another sense. One of the fundamental characteristics of hypertext is that it is composed of bodies of linked texts that have no primary axis of organization.[4]

All Web sites have pointers to other sites through hypertext links. By single clicking on the highlighted text in a graphic browser, the URL is put into action and looks up the address of the clicked text. Home pages, as they are called, are the main fare of the Web, showing pictures, text, and giving the opportunity to listen to audio and see video which is downloaded first to your computer and then viewed or listened to. There are some sites that do offer real-time video images, though slowly updated, and others that have real-time audio being pumped out. The RealAudio program available on the Web supports real-time audio.[5]

Like most major record companies have already done, film production companies are now establishing sites on the Web. These sites support servers that provide information about films being marketed by the studios. Production information, pictures, video clips, and biographical materials are available, for the time being, free of charge.

Clearly, the commercial interests of television and the media in general are increasingly creating sites on the Internet. Though there is a negative side to this—the commercialization—there is one very positive aspect. Film and media scholars, as well as filmmakers and production people with Internet accounts will have a much easier time trying to contact people directly involved with production. Since people involved in production post things online, they will often post e-mail addresses for direct contact, and the dissemination of information from their offices will be expedited easily through electronic communication. I believe that help and information may be easier to come by using this method, rather than by mailing a normal letter of inquiry.

E-Mail
E-mail is the electronic equivalent of a letter with fax and full-text capabilities. This means that you can send digitalized pictures, sounds, and text by e-mail, or just text correspondence. The great difference between fax and e-mail is that with e-mail you can then use the text in your word processing software, and implement the sounds and pictures into your latest multimedia presentation. You can only look at and read a fax or a letter!

E-mail is basically transferring text from one computer to another as a message. The way these electronic letters are sent and received vary, but primarily they are based on the ASCII text table. Hopefully the mail you send will look the same on the computer that receives it as it did on the computer you used to send it. There can be a problem with alternate characters in languages other than English. Most computer support people can help you sort that out, or you can just learn to live with it and get used to substituting certain characters that always seem to appear as other ones!

What Is an E-Mail Address?
You may often be able to guess where people have their e-mail accounts by looking at the suffixes of the address. The **@** symbol means **at**, and a period or dot separating words indicates a new position in the address domain. For example, my full address, **bertd@munin.dc.hks.se**, indicates that my user name is **bertd**. The user name or user id is that which is to the left of the @ symbol. After the @ we can see that the account for the mail address is located at a computer called **munin**. The **dc** part is a network allocation. Though **hks** would be difficult to guess, it is the acronym for Högskolan i Karlstad, the name of my university. The last two letters, **se**, is the international acronym for Sweden. This is what is called the top domain. There are geographical and organizational ones. Some common ones are listed below.6

Geographical:
au - Australia
uk - United Kingdom
org - nonprofit organizations
de - Germany
es - Spain
jp - Japan
us - United States
gov - government

Organizational:
com - commercial organizations

edu - an educational institution
mil - military
net - networking organizations

What E-Mail Program Should I Use?
There are a number of shareware or freeware programs available for download from various ftp sites. I use Eudora, which has been developed into a commercial product but is still available free on the Internet and works on both Macs and PCs. The choice of mail programs is really a personal preference issue, or prescribed by computer politics at your place of work or study. If you don't have a mail program, try Eudora by downloading from one of the many ftp sites available.

A good mail program should make it easy to set up mailing lists with individual addresses or group addresses. For instance, if I wish to mail a letter to a colleague, I have his address in a list. By accessing a menu in the program, I can choose his or her name and the letter will be automatically set up with the address written into the correct area. This saves time. I communicate by e-mail with large groups of students. Some of my main tasks using it are handing out assignments, scheduling changes, and giving feedback on papers. The hardest work in using a mass mailing list is writing in all the e-mail addresses in the list the first time!

Eudora also supports attachments using MIME (Multipurpose Internet Mailing Extensions). This means that when you send a message, you may attach another kind of document which will then be delivered along with the message to the account of the addressee. I regularly send Microsoft Word documents and even programs to people. The larger the file, the more risk there is for corruption of the file along the way, but I have had very good results with this.

What Does E-Mail Look Like?
Below is an example of an e-mail message from Canada. The date and time are recorded on the first line; the second line records the e-mail pseudonym for the address that is filed in a list as described above, or the actual address itself. In this case, it is the actual address. The sender is sometimes listed on the next line along with the actual name of the person. This doesn't always appear, since it depends on what program one uses and what parameters one sets up. The **Subject:** line is very important, though. Because many people subscribe to lists which generate a lot of mail, this is the best way to filter out messages one does not wish to read. It also makes clear what the message is about if you have had ten messages from the same person in one day and are trying to find a particular one. The **To:** line gives the addressee, and MIME is a translation extension to add foreign characters that do not exist in the standard US ASCII table.

One good function in mail programs is one called REPLY. If you are reading a message, you may automatically reply to this message by using the REPLY command in a menu or written command. The message is then prepared with the e-mail address automatically written in to the addressee and the subject line gets RE: and whatever the original subject line said.

Shots in Cyberspace

Date: Sat, 01 Apr 1995 10:58:33 -0500 (EST)
From: SGIBSON@VAX2.CONCORDIA.CA
Subject: Re: films
To: Bert.Deivert
Mime-Version: 1.0

Yo Bert,
Saw "Priscilla, Queen of the Desert" last night.
Have U seen it yet?
It's really very funny. It earned the Academy Award for Best Costumes,
def the most avant-garde costumes I have seen in a while.
We are working hard here, as usual....
What's up with you?
Au plaisir,
Steve

A signature is a little file attachment in the e-mail program where you may create a block of text that always appears at the end of each message. Many people misuse this function and create large text messages with pictures drawn with ASCII text and quotes, all their phone and fax numbers, and so forth. This is not usually appreciated. Keep it short and to the point so that people know who you are and how they may contact you. Since many people write one or two line messages, a signature file with ten or fifteen lines looks absurd in comparison to the content of the message. It also takes up bandwidth on the Internet. Mine looks like this:

Bert Deivert   University of Karlstad   TEL: +46-54-838106
Film Studies   651 88 Karlstad, Sweden
E-mail: bert.deivert@hks.se   FAX: +46-54-838496
ROSEBUD page: http://www.hks.se/~bertd/rosebud.html

Net Tools by E-Mail
There are alternative ways of using advanced Net tools for people who only have e-mail access. For more information about how to use many of the tools on the Net through e-mail, send the following message, *send lis-iis e-access-inet.txt* , as the first line in the body of your letter to the address: *mailbase@mailbase.ac.uk*

Mailbase will then automatically send you an article called "Accessing the Internet by E-Mail." One example of a good e-mail tool is given below.

Sometimes it is difficult to find e-mail addresses of colleagues and friends. There are a number of ways and catalogs, but a very simple way to do this is the following, provided the person in question is likely to have posted to a USENET newsgroup. All addresses of people mailing to newsgroups are logged into a large database which can be searched. Send the message *send usenet-addresses/name* to mail-server@rtfm.mit.edu, and if you need help for this service send the message *send usenet-addresses/help* to the same address. You change the *name* in the message to the name you wish to search for. Here is the answer I received on inquiring about my own last name. The name searched is given as well as the e-mail address in brackets and the date the person posted to a USENET group.

Date: Sat, 1 Apr 1995 09:41:47 -0500
From: mail-server@rtfm.MIT.EDU
To: Bert.Deivert (Bert Deivert)
Subject: mail-server: "send usenet-addresses/Deivert"
Reply-To: mail-server@rtfm.MIT.EDU
Precedence: junk
X-Problems-To: owner-mail-server@rtfm.mit.edu

———-cut here———-
Bert Deivert <Bert.Deivert@HKS.SE>   (Dec 15 94)
Bert Deivert <Bert.Deivert@hks.se>   (Nov 23 94)
bert.deivert@hks.se (Bert Deivert)   (Sep 12 94)
———-cut here———-

Discussion Groups

A discussion group is a subscribable list. Each discussion group has a topic, and many have a moderator or list-owner. These people run the groups, keep them going if there is some computer problem, and inform people if the discussion is getting out of hand. Some lists are unmoderated free-for-all anarchy and others require e-mail applications sent to the list owner to be approved before one may subscribe to the list. Most lists automatically subscribe anyone applying and the same goes when you wish to leave the list.

Shots in Cyberspace

How does it work? Let's look at how we may get started with one group.

My favorite group is Screen-L, a cinema discussion group largely composed of film teachers, some students, and academics in other fields related to film throughout the world. Each discussion group is a list of people that are subscribed.
Let's go through the steps if I wished to subscribe to Screen-L.

- a- I would create a message addressed to:
  LISTSERV@UA1VM.UA.EDU

- b- Leave the subject line blank.

- c- The first line of the message should be:
  Subscribe Screen-L Bert Deivert

- d- Send the message.

You may do this yourself, but substitute your name instead of mine after Screen-L.

The listserv program that receives the message then reads the first line of the message, subscribes you and adds your name to the list, along with your e-mail address, which it reads as sender of the message. You will immediately receive an acknowledgement that you have been added to the list, along with some additional information about how to manage correspondence with the list. As soon as the acknowledgement is sent out you will start receiving all correspondence to the list, except your own, though it is possible to set this option for your system.

You may send a subscription request to *any* listserv, preferably one near you, since it will be automatically forwarded to the right one for subscription. Some people may find it easier to write directly to the address for the listserv running the list. When you write messages to the discussion group, they *must* go to the listserv site that holds that discussion group. You will be informed of that site when you subscribe to the list.

I started the discussion list ROSEBUD for film students for the University of Karlstad Film Studies program in November 1994.

Hopefully this will lead to more international contacts for the department and students, and assist us in the facilitation of exchange programs. More institutions of higher learning should consider the discussion group as learning aid and complement to normal classroom instruction. It may be used as a research aid, a place to try out ideas, and a mode of keeping track of class participation for distance education.

Since it is so simple to set up discussion lists, many organizations might want to use this method to organize informal bulletin boards for their personnel or more specific closed or open discussion groups. The groups do not need to be open to anyone having e-mail. They can be moderated and even censored.

USENET Newsgroups

USENET is a network, in a rather anarchic form, that supports the NEWS, thousands of discussion groups that can be read like bulletin boards with a news reader. Threads, or subjects, are posted to the newsgroup, and then are responded to with replies. There are many different reader programs for different types of computers, and not all academic sites support the NEWS. Those that do have the NEWS don't normally support all groups, since a number of the more bizarre or sexually controversial groups are likely censored by some sites. Other services, like ClariNet, a commercial news service with full-text capabilities from news feeds from services like AP, Reuters, and the like are provided at a fee, and are available by subscription.

When logging on to the local news service and getting a list of all the groups available at your site, you may then choose which groups you are interested in following. The groups are listed under different headings and have naming conventions familiar to many computer users, linking the words with periods instead of spaces after each word. Each heading has a meaning, which you may refer to in the listing below. According to Dave Overoye there are more than 6,000 newsgroups available.[7] Some of the more interesting USENET groups for individuals interested in film, television, and media studies are listed at the end of the article.

This short explanation of these headings for newsgroups is taken from *The Big Dummy's Guide to the Internet* which is published electronically by the EFF (Electronic Frontier Foundation) and is available on the Internet.[8] There are of course local variations as well, such as newsgroups about certain national academic networks.

alt	Controversial or unusual topics; not carried by all sites
bionet	Research biology
bit.listserv	Conferences originating as Bitnet mailing lists
biz	Business
comp	Computers and related subjects
misc	Discussions that don't fit anywhere else
news	News about Usenet itself
rec	Hobbies, games and recreation
sci	Science other than research biology
soc	"Social" groups, often ethnically related
talk	Politics and related topics

Lists of FAQs (frequently asked questions) are usually included in most newsgroups or available at ftp sites. By checking these in advance of reading the group, you can get an idea about what the discussion and content of the group focuses upon. On doing research on vampires for a course I am teaching on horror fiction in film, I found the FAQ for the newsgroup alt.vampyres to be a good resource for the mythology of vampires as well as for films and books available.

Alt. and rec. are the places you will find most newsgroups dealing with film. Most of them are not very academic, but mirrors of some discussion lists are mirrored as newsgroups, such as Screen-L, which is called bit.listserv.screen-l.

Using Netscape you just have to click on the Newsgroups button under the location window, to the right. If you have access to a server that handles newsgroups, this will enable you to read and post without any other specialized software.

Once logged on, you can then browse through the thousands of newsgroup titles and test any that look interesting by reading the latest posts listed. Most software enables you to save lists of the newsgroups you wish to read regularly, so the newsgroup reading software will automatically fetch the latest postings for you when you fire up the program.

Finger
The FINGER program running on UNIX and VAX machines enables one to find out more information on a certain person

through a file called a .plan file that can be used to hold extra information about a person. If you want to try this, log onto your UNIX or VAX machine and write:
finger deivert@munin.dc.hks.se

Since it is increasingly easy to use a Web browser like Netscape to do most of the work several programs did, there are now FINGER sites on the Web so that you don't have to log onto a UNIX machine yourself via Telnet to do this. You use a browser form on a Web site. One such FINGER site is UM Finger Gateway - *http://ftp.cs.umt.edu/cgi-bin/finger_um*

This is what the inquiry looks like from my UNIX machine, named munin.dc.hks.se, when I run it. You should use just the last name and then the domain of the e-mail address.

[bertd@munin]/home/popu/bertd> finger deivert@munin.dc.hks.se
[munin.dc.hks.se]
Login name: bertd   In real life: Bert Deivert
Directory: /home/popu/bertd   Shell: /bin/ksh
On since okt 21 04:52:51 on pts/3, 19 seconds Idle Time
from raxp3.ppp.hks.se
No Plan.

This is information about me that is stored on the computer. Not much at the moment, but before we switched servers I had my address and office hours. Some universities provide extensive information in this regard, and one can find out such useful information as mailing address, home address, home telephone and office telephone numbers for people you need to get in touch with. I recently got film scholar David Bordwell's address by using FINGER on the University of Wisconsin computer where I knew he teaches. He did not have an e-mail address, but this particular university logs students and faculty addresses on the computer, and I was able to get his office address and phone number. This is publicized information, just like a phone book. Below is the exact transcript for the Bordwell inquiry.

DCL > finger bordwell@wisc.edu

[wisc.edu]
qi> 101: query bordwell
102: There was 1 match to your request.
-200:1: name: BORDWELL DAVID J
-200:1: address: 821 UNIV AVE MADISON, WI 53706
-200:1: building: VILAS COMMUNICATION HALL 6039
-200:1: phone: 608-262-7723
-200:1:title: PROFESSOR
-200:1: division: COLLEGE OF LETTERS AND SCIENCE
-200:1: department: COMMUNICATION ARTS
-200:1: title2: PROFESSOR
-200:1: division2: COLLEGE OF LETTERS AND SCIENCE
-200::1: department2: HUMANITIES - INSTITUTE FOR RESEARCH
200:Ok.

To use FINGER for a person, try to use his/her last name and the name of the computer where the information should be stored. If you have the right computer name you will get a list of possible people with the same last name, possible e-mail addresses, and more. If you don't know the computer name, sometimes it will be enough with the domain and country as in the inquiry above. If you have their complete e-mail address, just use the whole thing. Sometimes this will not work though, as in the case of trying Bert.Deivert@hks.se, which is an alias of a real address which is bertd@munin.dc.hks.se. You will get better results with a first or last name instead. Remember that not all computers allow FINGER access.

Telnet
Telnet is a program that allows remote login to another computer, in the next room, or on the other side of the planet. Telnet runs off the local host computer that you log onto, or you may use a tool like the Telnet program written by the NCSA (National Center for Supercomputing Applications) for Macintosh computers. This requires a direct link to the Internet over an Ethernet network. To use telnet, you just write in the address or IP (Internet protocol) number of the computer you wish to log onto.

The Telnet program can be used for a number of logins done on archie servers, gophers, library systems, and World Wide Web text-based

clients. Here are a few examples of Telnet addresses at the prompt by the UNIX computer. On a local client like a Macintosh you would use the menu command *Open Connection* and then write in the address.
YourUnix> telnet library.mit.edu

YourUnix> telnet basun.sunet.se

YourUnix> telnet archie.funet.fi

YourUnix> telnet purple-crayon.media.mit.edu 8888

Using Netscape, an example of the syntax would be:
telnet://purple-crayon.media.mit.edu

Once you are logged on to the remote computer you just need to read directions after the login. Always use a carriage return after writing in a command word or address, unless it says otherwise in the instruction you receive online. Don't use the caps lock key either, since it sometimes sends out confusing characters to the server being called. It is better not to use capital letters since it is not necessary for the computer to understand the address or word.

Gopher
Gopherspace is a searchable, cataloged, virtual space containing files of various types. The gopher program burrows, figuratively, through the space to obtain what you want. You can navigate through catalogs, file folders on remote computers, and do searches for files having a certain word in their titles. You may telnet into some public access gophers, use gopher on your local UNIX machine as your starting point, or run directly from your desk computer and out on the Internet, if you have a direct line out. Just run Netscape and use the right syntax.

For example, *gopher://info.sunet.se* will log you onto the Swedish University Network gopher. Though not having more graphic representation than folders, document icons, binoculars for searches, and computer symbols for Telnet connections, gophers are still places that hold a lot of textual information that may be of use to a large number of people.

After finding a gopher area you are interested in, you may investigate the files there and download them to your computer for reading and saving as text files. There are any number of interesting film files located in various gopherspaces. Like Web sites, gophers have links to other gophers considered to have interesting information. Follow these links and save yourself time searching. You may then make note of spaces you wish to visit again, or save bookmarks or links in the program you gopher with, if that option is available.

You might want to try a test. Try this gopher in Iowa.

- *telnet://panda.uiowa.edu*
- choose *General Information* first
- then *Information on Video Laserdiscs.*

After that you can backtrack and browse around looking at files and different computer and university sites all over the world. You can also use the Veronica tools available in the menus to help search for files that might contain names you are interested in, like *television* or *film*.

What do you find on gophers? You can find information about the government of the USA, course syllabi, research projects, address systems, libraries, and about anything you might be interested in. There are global search possibilities for all gopherspace by using the VERONICA tool available at gopher sites. Look for it in the menus of the site you log onto. JUGHEAD is another search tool that searches a more specific gopherspace, like the sites at a particular university. Information on how to use these tools is available at the gopher site you are logged into.

Archie
Archie is a catalog tool that is able to search all the catalogs for the ftp sites all over the world and find files you are interested in. After you find out where these files are located, it is then easy to download them. There are a variety of ways to access archie. The most direct method is to use a Web site.[9] Use the connection below via your Web browser to try an archie program. If you know of a program available as shareware, you might use that title to see what you come up with.

Interactive ARCHIE GATEWAY
http://www.earn.net/gnrt/archie.html
Archie Guide   *http://www.earn.net/gnrt/archie.html*

Anonymous Ftp

Once you have found your file of choice, you may then download it by using ftp. File transfer protocol (ftp) is a method of moving files from one computer to another. This can be done from your host computer with programs running on the VAX or UNIX systems or on your desktop computer by using special programs like the Macintosh FETCH program or wftp for Windows. Many computers all over the world support anonymous ftp. This enables a user to log on to the computer using ANONYMOUS as the login ID, and then one's e-mail address as the password. This helps systems people keep track of who is using the computer or misusing it. It is good manners to log in using your correct e-mail address if asked by a prompt from the computer. Your Web browser will do all this for you automatically if you have filled in the preferences for e-mail address.

Lists of computers supporting ftp and giving basic information about what kinds of files are located in its directories are available from any number of sources. The most extensive though is Yanoff's list which can be obtained by ftp or through Web browsers. You can also read the READ.ME or INDEX files found in directories on ftp sites. One method of obtaining Yanoff's list is to use your Web browser to get to *http://www.uwm.edu/Mirror/inet.services.html*

One good clearinghouse for anonymous ftp is *http://www.yahoo.com/Computers_and_Internet/Software/ software*

Avoid downloading files from remote computers at peak times for telecommunications traffic. It slows everything down for all users. For example, if I want to download a file from Stanford University in California, I wait until it is in the middle of the night there and there is less traffic going on. The best thing to do though, if downloading from such a site, is to use a mirror site. A mirror is a computer that basically keeps the same set of files updated every night when traffic is light. For example there are various mirror sites all over the world for SUMEX-AIM.STANFORD.EDU, the popular Stanford shareware Macintosh site that has the INFO-MAC directory. *ftp://sumex-aim.stanford.edu/info-mac/*

Conclusion
It does take time to wander throughout the Internet, but the time invested is well worth it, if only for the enjoyment of meeting other people out there with similar interests and bringing closer the dream of a global village. The positive aspects of such a community cannot be underestimated in the troubled world we live in.

[1] You may check yourself by using a Web client and accessing URL http://www1.mids.org/growth/internet/html/hostsl.html

[2] Dickson & Engst, *Internet Explorer Kit*, p. 211.

[3] Read more about Mosaic and its creators in *Wired*, October 1994, p. 116.

[4] George Landow, *Hypertext* p. 11.

[5] Check the RealAudio homepage: http://www.prognet.com/index.html

[6] For a very good explanation of this, see Hahn and Stout, *The Internet Complete Reference*, Chapter 4.

[7] Nightdave (Dave Overoye), *The Video Guide to the Internet*, 1994. Ten minutes into the tape.

[8] Electronic Frontier Foundation, *Big Dummy's Guide to the Internet*, 1993.

[9] More archie sites are http://www.bot.astrouw.edu.pl/archie_servers.html or try YAHOO's archie index http://www.yahoo.com/Computers_and_Internet/Internet/Archie/

THE TOP 500 SITES

ACTORS

Anderson, Gillian
URL: http://gpu3.srv.ualberta.ca/~mlwalter/GAHP.html
Rating: 3
Comments: This page is dedicated to Gillian Anderson, the popular costar of TV's "The X-Files". Loads of links to interviews, pictures, an extensive FAQ, QuickTime movies, and other Gillian Anderson sites. This very current page is maintained by Victor Chan & Mike Walter and seems to be growing daily, helped by the millions of "X-File" fans out there. Best item is Gillian's Class of '86 yearbook photo from Grand Rapids' City High School.

Applegate, Christina
URL: http://www.ifi.uio.no/~steinho/applegate.html
Rating: 2
Comments: This site is devoted to the young star of TV's "Married... With Children," Christine Applegate, and features a hodgepodge of details from her agents' addresses to the names of her pets ("Two Black Cats, Natasha and Jesse; German Shepherd, Sybill"). Problem with this site is that it contains only one link—and that's to an obviously incorrect family tree of Ms. Applegate (as the page states, "Very doubtful that is our own KELLY's family tree!!!"). Still, this site which hails from Norway might grow into a more dynamic page. Better yet, maybe it's time for the ever-enterprising Christine to forge some of her own self-promotion through the WWW.

Bacon, Kevin
URL: http://www.mindspring.com/~mab/kevin/kevin.html
Rating: 4
Comments: It's "Makin' Bacon - Home of the Kevin Bacon Game." This fun page is devoted to actor Kevin Bacon (lovingly referred to throughout this site as "the pig") and features a game revolving around a sort of "six degrees of separation" principle. Here's how the game works: Choose any actor or actress in any American motion picture; pick one of the performer's movies; choose a costar from the designated movie; find a film that costar was in; pick another performer, etc; repeat until the costar is Kevin Bacon. The site also provides a handy list of

all of Kevin's roles and costars as well as a link to the Internet Movie Database to get you started. I tried it using Cary Grant and guess what? It worked! As the page boldly states, the game serves as proof that Kevin Bacon is the center of the universe. Well, maybe...

Barrymore, Drew
URL: http://www.wfu.edu/~david/drew/
Rating: 4
Comments: "Uninhibited, mysterious, gorgeous and unmistakably... Drew" announces this page devoted to the reformed off-screen bad girl, Drew Barrymore. Includes a biography with interesting facts ("Tattoos: cross on ankle, butterfly below naval, one on hand, one on right lower back"), well-mounted filmography and an excellent image database divided by film or Drew's age. The "More Drew" page includes newsgroups, chat lines, and a listing of articles about Drew. Keep an eye on the "What's New with Drew" section for up-to-date info about this fine actress.

Brooks, Louise
URL: http://www.escape.ca/~ianmcc/LB-index.html
Rating: 4
Comments: Louise Brooks inspired generations of moviegoers, and fairly recently, even music video makers. *Pandora's Box* is featured as a music video with Louise's timeless image gracing MTV. Now see what the Net has. High quality photos, available here for the idol worshippers, plus history, movies, and books make this a wonderful silent movie site. Since I haven't read her book, I became very interested in it after reading the review of it here. A very simple but well-done homage to Ms. Brooks.

Carter, Helena Bonham
URL: http://www.io.com/~mjf/helena.html
Rating: 2
Comments: There aren't many pages on this actress out on the Web, but the people that have them seem to know each other. A slightly less hysterical tone abides here than when dealing with pages on Anna Nicole Smith and other media wonders. In fact, I believe the fellow that created this site actually respects HBC as an actress! A

number of photos of varying quality, bio, and filmography and links to other pages are here. Okay if you want to check up on this actress and her work, though it is not very extensive.

Cates, Phoebe
URL: http://pages.prodigy.com/AL/kellerra/Phoebe.html
Rating: 2
Comments: The site of homage to this actress is comprised mostly of photographs in thumbnails which can be expanded. Links to other Phoebe sites as well. Not terribly informative or exciting. How many of these places will exist in the future? It is great if you just want fan photos of Phoebe, but is this all there is? Check out Audrey Hepburn's site for a little more content. Get back to work Phoebe fans.

Dangerfield, Rodney
URL: http://www.rodney.com/rodney/index.html
Rating: 4
Comments: From the man who can't get no respect, it's Rodney Dangerfield's very own Web site! Nonstop fun as you navigate through Rodney's philosophical musings ("The Way I See It"), his recent denial for entry into the Academy of Motion Picture Arts and Sciences (including a copy of the rejection letter from Roddy McDowall), loads of pictures of Rodney and his friends, and a Joke of the Day page. Be sure to check out his "How Ugly Is He?" link ("Once I stuck my head out the window and got arrested for mooning!"). And don't pass up on the chance to e-mail Rodney directly. Loads of fun!

Ford, Harrison
URL: http://www.mit.edu:8001/people/lpchao/harrison.ford.html
Rating: 3
Comments: "The Unofficial Harrison Ford Stuff Page" is stuffed full of images and audio clips ("It's not wise to upset a wookie") as well as very up-to-date information about Ford's future projects. One tidbit of gossip states that "rumor has it that the first version of an Indy 4

script has been written and both George Lucas and Steven Spielberg like it and are making adjustments." Be sure to check out the picture titled "Harrison Ford in a Good Mood." No wonder this guy is one of the hottest actors in town!

Foster, Jodie
URL: http://weber.u.washington.edu/~jnorton/jodie/jodie.html
Rating: 4
Comments: Jodie's own autograph is the background picture for the opening page of this site. Images, mailing list for discussions, interviews, and all the rest make this a typical fan site, yet a more intelligent one. Other Jodie pages on the Web are linked up. For a fan site, it is well done.

Grant, Hugh
URL: http://ucsub.colorado.edu/~kritzber/new/hugh/hugh.html
Rating: 4
Comments: Poor Hugh. First he gets caught in a rental car with his pants down and now his Web site gets a shakedown from us! Blake Kreitzberg's site is definitely "I LOVE HUGH." You can't help noticing with an e-mail address like slacker@hughophiles.net ! I love the link to "Couple of the Year." Saucy critique of Andie MacDowell, and wry comments in general make this an amusing pit stop while looking for serious actors. Rated high on the chuckle scale.

Harris, Ed
URL: http://www.fishnet.net/~decadent/edharris.html
Rating: 2
Comments: The "Definitive Ed Harris Page" is chock full of everything you would ever need to know about this star of such space blockbusters as *The Right Stuff* and *Apollo 13*. The site includes Harris's filmography complete with links to the Internet Movie Database as well as a few interesting interviews. A big plus for the section on upcoming projects. The page opens with the proclamation that "Ed Harris is an actor of unmitigated physicality and presence. His trademark intensity, an uncanny combination of piercing emotivity and understated stubbornness, never descends to staginess." Well, maybe this site is a bit stagy itself, but if you are a big Ed Harris fan, then you won't be disappointed.

Hepburn, Audrey
URL: http://grove.ufl.edu/~flask/Hepburn.html
Rating: 3
Comments: A number of Audrey Hepburn's admirers and their comments are listed here as well as some of the films she made. Quotes attributed to her are listed as well, but with no source. A number of black and white images from the films listed are available in decent quality, and there are links to the Internet Movie Database for the films mentioned here. Filmography and a few links to other Hepburn sites are listed. Meager but nice pictures of a great but quickly forgotten star who devoted the latter part of her life to humanitarian efforts. Here is one of the quotes on this home page. "The world has always been cynical, and I think I'm a romantic at heart. I hope for better things, and I thank God the world is also full of people who want to be genuine and kind."

Herman, Pee Wee
URL: http://www.seanet.com/Users/weazel/peewce.html
Rating: 4
Comments: "I know you are, but what am I?" It's the "Pee Wee Herman Worship Page!" A kooky site with sound clips, images, and an episode guide. Enter the play house, and click on any of the characters to hear them say something zany. There's even an "Ask Globey" link for posing questions. Check out the "Paul Reubens is God" page for a truly syrupy declaration of love for Pee Wee's other persona. "Today's secret word is GLUE" (complete with linked audio "Ahhhhhhhhhhh")! Well worth a visit!

Hopkins, Anthony
URL: http://www.mit.edu:8001/people/douglas/sirtony.html
Rating: 4
Comments: "The Sir Anthony Hopkins Home Page" is maintained by the founder of the Hopkins Mailing List and includes an extensive array of information about "Tony"—a few biographies, a filmography (linked to the Internet Movie Database), digitized images and audio clips, interviews, and film reviews. For die-hard fans of the man who

played Hannibal Lecter, this site even includes a Hopkins WWWBoard to post messages to other die-hard fans. Always up-to-date and growing, this site provides a fun browse.

Kilmer, Val
URL: http://www.tc.cornell.edu/~cat/pages/
Rating: 4
Comments: Val Kilmer, heartthrob star of *The Doors* and *Batman Forever*, is featured at this extensive site which includes a biography, an excellent filmography (credits and reviews as well as links to the Internet Movie Database), sound clips, and the "Val Quiz." Be sure to have a look at the hilarious "I Met Val Kilmer" essay ("He had his back to me, and I said, 'Um, Mr. Kilmer, would you please sign my hat?' He turned just his head to me and said, 'Er, sure, as soon as I'm done taking a leak.' I was MORTIFIED. I looked down and saw this yellow stream. ahhhhh! I couldn't look away"). Applause to Catherine Starkey for maintaining this wonderful site.

Lewis, Juliette
URL: http://netspace.net.au/~tpropert/jl.html
Rating: 2
Comments: What can one say about the abundance of actor and actress sites? The usual bio info, magazine articles and covers, pictures from movies interviews, and adulatory text abound here too. The one mystery link that I just had to take was the "Unknown Sources" one. It just led to some photos that could not be identified by source! These clickable thumbnail shots had good quality larger photos attached to them. The newly formed alt.fan.juliette.lewis had a link, but nothing was discussed there according to my news server. For being on the top 5% list, this seemed pretty limited to me.

Locklear, Heather
URL: http://uptown.turnpike.net/garyfs/index.htm
Rating: 4
Comments: From "Dallas" to "Melrose", Heather has surely made a splash! This has a pretty good graphic layout and use of images for the fan. All the things you want to find. This is really a very comprehensive site with interviews, a lot of information, photos,

filmography, TV series listings, fan club, and the works! There are even pictures from Heather's high school yearbook. An obvious labor of love lies behind this site.

Martin, Steve
URL: http://www.dundee.ac.uk/~dcyork/steve.htm
Rating: 2
Comments: Just think, a Scottish site for American comic Steve Martin. What does the single malt crowd think of the wild and crazy guy? Well, this guy David had some photos he snapped of the star at the Edinburgh film festival and couldn't help sticking them out there along with the scanned autograph. Hope Steve's cat doesn't get hold of it and forge more checks to order cat toys. There is also an interview with Steve, a movie of Steve doing a card trick, and some reviews of his films. Neither elegant nor well done, this is a puppy love page. Still, maybe you want some stuff that is here…

McNichol, Kristy
URL: http://coos.dartmouth.edu/~elnitsky/Kristy.html
Rating: 2
Comments: Serge Elnitsky's Kristy McNichol site is a fun, no-frills page devoted to the star of TV's "Family". There are a few pictures, a number of transcribed articles ("Kristy McNichol Answers 57 Questions" from "Teen Bag"), and a couple of cute e-mails from other fans of Kristy. My favorite part, though, is Serge's own "two cents' worth" section which includes such critical gems as "Her real beauty is *in motion.* The little expressions—grins, frowns, sighs—that's what's incredible about her, not just a pretty face…" By the way, where *is* Kristy these days?

Monroe, Marilyn
URL: http://ux1.cso.uiuc.edu/~jarrett/marilyn.html
Rating: 3
Comments: The biographical information is really sparse, basically a few lines with some dates, but the 30 films and plot breakdowns and their links to databases make up a bit for that. Six song lyrics are included so you can sing along with Marilyn while watching the films. Most of the images are scanned black and white photos from newsprint and don't have very good quality, but a few of them are quite okay.

Monroe, Marilyn
URL: http://www.ionet.net/~jellenc/marilyn.html
Rating: 4
Comments: "The Marilyn Pages" is a beautifully designed and well-organized site which features an extensive biography (interspersed with quotes by Marilyn), a filmography, image collection, and links to other "Marilyn" sites (including links to the U.S. Postal Service's Marilyn Monroe stamp site as well as GEM International's Marilyn phonecard information. These pages are graphic-heavy, so make sure to have your images turned on. Diamonds might be a girl's best friend, but a Web page sure doesn't hurt the path to continued immortality!

Pitt, Brad
URL: http://web2.airmail.net/~jimhoffa/bradpitt.html
Rating: 3
Comments: Talk about meat market! I checked out four sites for Brad Pitt and found not one of them that mentioned anything about what he did or who he is, but had 90% images. So, if you want pics, come here. Do not get to know about Brad as a person, just a *thing*. Another Brad Pitt webmaster explained, "I've been told that Brad Pitt is adored for two reasons (besides his acting ability). These are his smile and his stomach." This site will break your telephone line if you use a modem!

Reeves, Keanu
URL: http://www.users.interport.net/~eperkins/
Rating: 4
Comments: KeanuNet is devoted to that budding Shakespearean actor and Dogstar bassist, Keanu Reeves. You find here an FAQ ("Does Keanu have a scar? He has several. The most prominent scar runs from chest to navel and is a result of the time he crashed his motorcycle into a mountain in 1987(?)"), biography, photos, magazine covers, and separate sections for each of his most recent films.

Ricci, Christina
URL: http://login.dknet.dk:80/~klaus/ricci/
Rating: 3
Comments: "The Christina Ricci Fan Club Page" is devoted to the young star of *The Addams Family* and *Casper* and includes a biography ("Her first school production was The Twelve Days of Christmas at age 6"), a limited filmography, and links to other Ricci sites. The fan club archives contains a large database of images ("of Christina alone," "from her movies") which are quality rated as well as a number of sound and movie clips. This site comes from a server in Denmark, is maintained by a Canadian, and is augmented by an Australian. Only on the WWW…

Ryan, Meg
URL: http://web.cs.ualberta.ca/~davidw/MegRyan/meg.cgi
Rating: 3
Comments: The opening page is quite pleasant with a nonexploitive picture of Meg and a nice background. Fans of romantic comedy can enjoy this page with bio, image links, sightings, fan discussions, and "Why are you a fan?" section. One of the minus points here is the use of italic text which is difficult to read on any screen, but legible when printed. "Why are you a fan?" has too many italics. Considering Meg's success, the following quote is quite interesting. "Dennis is a romantic. I'm not. I'm not big on Valentine's Day. Romance novels — yuck. Sickeningly romantic films — no way."

Ryder, Winona
URL: http://www.auburn.edu/~harshec/WWW/Winona.html
Rating: 4
Comments: I think this actress has ranges from the brilliant to boring, but she never leaves me feeling cold. Some nice photos and Winona's autograph being written greet you upon landing here. This site is interested in her work as an actress, not in her glorification as some pinup, and it reflects that atmosphere. This is very well done and features nice graphic montages of photos, a link to the Polly Klaas Foundation which, according to the author, is close to Ms. Ryder's heart. Eric Harshbarger, the Web Master here, said in correspondence with me: "In numerous magazine articles Winona Ryder states that her involvement with PKF went far beyond 'celebrity involve-

ment.' Having grown up in Petaluma (PK's hometown), Ms Ryder took a genuine interest in the young girl's disappearance and still, today, has close involvement with the Polly Klaas Foundation." Interviews and the like abound all over this excellent resource.

Shearer, Harry
URL: http://pobox.com/harry/
Rating: 3
Comments: "Spinal Tap" hero Derek Smalls is this actor's alter ego and one role he will probably never live down, if he wants to, that is. He plays a number of roles on "Simpsons" like Mr. Burns, Smithers, and Ned Flanders. Sound samples, photos, and movies of various highlights of his career are on tap here. His "Le Show" radio show is also made playable through RealAudio over the Net. He has a lot to say about O.J. Simpson....

Thompson, Scott
URL: http://204.225.234.1/
Rating: 4
Comments: "Welcome to ScottLand"—Scott Thompson's (of TV's "Kids in the Hall") wonderful virtual world. New visitors are invited to proceed to the Royal Palace for an audience with the Queen while citizens of ScottLand (registration required) are asked to proceed directly to ScottLand. A fun and dynamic site featuring such tongue-in-cheek locales as the Bottoms Up Cafe, the Rim Room, and the Lid Lounge. Keep an eye out for many new additions to this site by a very funny comic.

Van Damme, Jean Claude
URL: http://www.shef.ac.uk/uni/union/susoc/cass/homes/pm/pm933303/vandamme.html
Rating: 3
Comments: "The Shrine to Jean Claude Van Damme" is a decent looking site devoted to the Belgian-born star of *Universal Soldier* and *Street Fighter*. There's a nice selection of pictures for downloading (magazine covers, a young teenage pic, and various other Van Damme poses) as well as an informative article titled "Four Weddings and a Front Kick" by Alan Richman. Bonus links point to Van Damme's other hobbies: martial arts and body building!

W.C. Fields
URL: http://www.louisville.edu/~kprayb01/WC.html
Rating: 4
Comments: Kevin Rayburn has set up an extensive site (actually a "cyberbook") devoted to the great comic W.C. Fields, which features amazingly intelligent items related to Fields' career. Included is a chronological W.C. Fields Biography 1879-1946, a Quote of the Week, a filmography with brief reviews, a "Fieldsian Dictionary" (full of Fields' oft-used words: "beezer," "drat," "scalawag"), and a reference list for further reading. With an Internet often filled with trivial data, this site is a most welcome relief. Makes you want to run out and rent a few videos of the "Great Man."

Walken, Christopher
URL: http://www.brunel.ac.uk:8080/~mapgsat/movies/walken/
Rating: 4
Comments: This is one of the better sites around for actors. An attempt at a very definitive filmography, theater production list, bio, personal information, and including links to film databases and photos puts this one near the top of the list. Walken is one of the creepiest actors out there, and he is good at it. When one looks at his credits, you can see why.

Weaver, Sigourney
URL: http://www.pt.hk-r.se/student/di94vno/ripley.html
Rating: 2
Comments: This easily navigable page is devoted to Sigourney Weaver and includes some biographical details, a filmography linked to the Internet Movie Database, some pictures and interviews. Sigourney is probably most famous for her roles in the *Alien* films, but did you know that she is a fluent French speaker and that her favorite perfume is Eau de Charlotte (which is made from black currants)? Ahh, the pleasures of such pages!

ANIMATION

Animation Journal
URL: http://www.chapman.edu/animation
Rating: 2
Comments: This excellent academic journal on animation has a Web site listing subscription information and articles included in issues. I asked Maureen Furniss, editor, about the possibility of full-text articles on the Internet but she explained that no such possibility had been planned. For the time being we will have to be satisfied with abstracts and issue listings. Graphics related to the journal articles, links to other journals, call for papers, and other information for scholars are readily available. Some of these pages are still under construction at this time. This is a good initiative but has a long way to go to reach other standards set by journals like *Postmodern Culture*.

animation usa
URL: http://www.usa.net/ausa/
Rating: 1
Comments: animation usa is a firm which sells animation art, such as original cartoon cels or production drawings. Too bad there aren't any images of the artwork (mere descriptions). Not much here, really, except a lot of text for reading about how to collect animation art and how to order some of their pieces. There's a limited "Milestones in Animation" section which details some of the big moments in cartoon history, which I guess is something.

Animator's Mailing List
URL: http://www.xmission.com:80/~grue/animate/
Rating: 3
Comments: The "Animator's Mailing List" Web page provides information on how to subscribe to this lively discussion group. Topics often revolved around the use of certain animating equipment, programs, education, and techniques. This site also provides a handy booklist with quick reviews as well as *big* lists of production houses, freelancers, and animation schools. This is a good starting point for those interested in animation as a profession. No images on the site, though, which is a shame!

Animation

Cartoon Factory
URL: http://www.cartoon-factory.com/
Rating: 3
Comments: This is an online animation art gallery where one can browse and decide which item might be interesting to purchase. Cel animation originals from the studios of Warner Bros., Disney, Hanna-Barbera, and others grace this site. Saw a great cel that I loved, which was a mix between a lot of different characters and the price was only $1,475 dollars! Well, there are cheaper ones but most will be about the price of a bad used car. Have a look.

CartooNet
URL: http://www.pavilion.co.uk/cartoonet/
Rating: 4
Comments: CartooNet, out of the UK, is the gateway to European cartoon arts and is an excellent professional resource for those involved in animation. The site features over 200 examples of cartoon art, Cartoon News (an informative newsletter detailing festivals, competitions, exhibitions, and press releases), and a decent collection of links to various European cartoonist organizations. The Marketplace pages provide invaluable listings of agencies, collectible dealers, and a small ad section.

@cme Page (WB Cartoons)
URL: http://www.io.com/~woodward/@cme/
Rating: 1
Comments: This page began as a homage to old Warner Bros. cartoons—that is, until their lawyers got on the case. All of this is well chronicled on this useful jumping-off point for other animation sites. There is a listing of the 50 greatest cartoons, a variety of newsgroup links, and a nice selection of other animation hotlinks. Too bad there are no images on a site devoted to cartoons—but what would those lawyers think???

Felix the Cat
URL: http://wso.williams.edu/faculty/psci335/gerstein/felix.html
Rating: 4
Comments: "Felix the Cat, the wonderful, wonderful Cat...." David Gerstein's "Classic Felix the Cat Page" is a wonderful, wonderful assortment of images, reviews, and sounds. Includes a very comprehensive 1919-1936 filmography as well as Felix's first newspaper strip. There's also a good deal of information about the new "Twisted Tales of Felix the Cat" series. Many links and a sure bet to keep growing.

Shizuoka University Animation Page
URL: http://www.lib.shizuoka.ac.jp/animaw1.html
Rating: 3
Comments: The Shizuoka University Animation Page is an odd site with some very interesting pointers. Highlight of the site must be the Animation Database featuring short credits for American Animated Short Cartoons in the sound era (1928-1972). Click on the face of Tex Avery on the cover drawing to access "Moc's Tex Avery Page," complete with an excellent filmography and a wonderful collection of original cels and drawings. Also contains link to the Anido Animation Museum.

DIRECTORS

Allen, Woody
URL: http://www.idt.unit.no/~torp/woody/
Rating: 4
Comments: This excellent site devoted to director Woody Allen is well organized and full of interesting information. There are tons of images, audio samples, favorite lines as well as other information about Woody (books, albums, trivia, other net resources). But the real treat of this site is the filmography. Each film page has nicely mounted credits in a table format, a list of favorite quotes with accompanying sound clips, and links to images (often including the film's poster). This ever-growing site hailing from Norway can only get better and better. A must for Woody Allen fans!

Directors

Almodóvar, Pedro
URL: http://www.netpoint.be/abc/pedro/
Rating: 3
Comments: The King of Kitsch, Pedro Almodóvar, is featured on this fairly simple site. You get a biography (textual, no links) and a filmography (with a few links). But, the three films that are linked have all sorts of information critique, and any awards won by the film. Let's just hope for this site to be fleshed-out further by Bruno Bollaert.

Cameron, James
URL: http://www.soton.ac.uk/~pdc194/cameron/
Rating: 4
Comments: Famous for directing *The Terminator* and *Aliens*, James Cameron is featured on this comprehensive WWW site. Information includes a worthy biography, a very clever "Directorial Trademark" page ("films frequently involve nuclear war or nuclear explosions" or "likes to show close-up shots of feet or wheels"), and clean filmography pages. There's even a link to Digital Domain, James Cameron's computer effects company.

Griffith, David Wark
URL: http://ernie.bgsu.edu/~pcharle/gish/dwg.html
Rating: 4
Comments: D.W. Griffith, the innovator of early motion pictures, has a number of texts, images, and links to other related areas on the Web. Images of production stills from *Birth of a Nation* and of his actresses make this an interesting site for the film student or cineaste. The author of the site is a research fellow in photochemical science from the UK. I guess he has something in common with Griffith—a thing for Lillian Gish.

Hartley, Hal
URL: http://www.best.com/~drumz/Hartley/
Rating: 4
Comments: There is Hal in front of his 35mm Panavision camera as

we land here in cyberspace. The tastefully designed and minimal page carries a mailing list, reviews, quotes, images, and so forth. A variety of informative articles and interviews are listed here, so this is a great research start for people writing about Hal Hartley. Students, cineastes, and academics may unite here and commune.

Hitchcock, Alfred
URL: http://www.primenet.com/~mwc/
Rating: 3
Comments: The Master of Suspense, Alfred Hitchcock, is featured on this well-designed WWW page. This site contains a short biography, filmography (nicely tabled by decade with links to the Internet Movie Database), awards listings, and a list of cameo appearances by Hitchcock. You can even cast your vote for the top five Hitchcock films. Be sure to check out the link titled "Pure Cinema" which provides an interesting shot-by-shot breakdown of the famous shower scene from *Psycho*.

Hitchcock, Alfred (French)
URL: http://hitchcock.alienor.fr/
Rating: 4
Comments: This French site devoted to Hitchcock, the favorite of the French auteurs of the New Wave, daringly uses only French language. I think it deserves praise for that very reason. There are too few native language sites out there. Even with rudimentary French one can navigate around and look at the pictures, check the links to other sections on actresses, a page on composer Bernard Herrmann, film synopses, and even French film posters! The little scans of original posters are a very nice addition to this charming and devoted shrine to the late director. Sound bites from the film and some great photos of young Hitchcock and the man himself in various poses, including playing on some instruments, make this a must to visit.

Kieslowski, Krzysztof
URL: http://www-personal.engin.umich.edu/~zbigniew/Kieslowski/kieslowski.html
Rating: 4
Comments: Since Kieslowski's films are some of my personal

favorites, I looked forward to seeing what was published on the Web. Biographies for Krzysztof Kieslowski, his partner in writing Krzysztof Piesiewicz, and musical collaborator Zbigniew Preisner are hyperlinked to the main page. I consider Preisner to be one of the finest composers in "art film" today, and it was nice to find out more about him and his music. Filmography, reviews, interviews, articles, contact addresses for Kieslowski and others involved with his films, and hyperlinks to other related pages fill out the remainder of this site. There are things done on this site that are normally not seen on other director sites, and that is why it is rated highly. Included is a very good multilingual bibliography.

Kubrick, Stanley
URL: http://www.lehigh.edu/~pjl2/kubrick.html
Rating: 4
Comments: The Kubrick Multimedia Film Guide is a wonderful site for exploring the films of this enigmatic director. Each film has a page which includes a selection of images (stills and promotional material), sound clips, and links to other related sites. One of the highlights of these pages is their use of interesting backgrounds which each reflect that particular film. There's also a few nuggets here, such as images from a cut scene in 2001 or an audio clip featuring General Jack D. Ripper in *Dr. Strangelove* explaining the International Communist Conspiracy. A true pleasure to wander about.

Lynch, David
URL: http://web.city.ac.uk/~cb157/Dave.html
Rating: 2
Comments: This UK based site features links to various screenplays, other Lynch-related home pages and a number of interviews, discussion areas, and the like. I tried to take the David Lynch interactive Web form quiz, with questions like "In 'Twin Peaks,' who played Sheriff Harry S. Truman?" Unfortunately, the old 404 came up, indicating no pages after the first one was accessed. Needs fixing, I assume. Most of the material here is related to Twin Peaks.

Marker, Chris
URL: http://www.ss.rmit.edu.au/miles/marker/Marker.html
Rating: 4
Comments: Arising out of his Ph.D. thesis at Monash University, Adrian Miles has set up an exquisite site centered on director Chris Marker. Included here is a very detailed filmography, a bibliography (wonderfully divided into "General," "Review," and "Theoretical"), a large listing of Marker's own texts (words, photographs, scripts) and image collection. And a huge site this is containing approximately 22,000 words consisting of around 185 pages with 1,600 internal links!

Ray, Satyajit
URL: http://math.umbc.edu/~arghya/satyajit.html
Rating: 3
Comments: "Someday I'll make a great film!" remarked Satyajit Ray in 1948 to his friend Chidananda Das Gupta. This great Indian director, famous for his APU trilogy, is featured in this informative site with bio information, stills from films and newspapers, and awards Ray received. Unfortunately a number of the stills are of rather bad quality, faded and overexposed.

Tarantino, Quentin
URL: http://www.GANet.Net/~pg0/quentin/greatbig.htm
Rating: 2
Comments: The official title of this site is "The Great Big List Of Quentin Tarantino Magazine References And Articles." And indeed, that is exactly what it is! Very up-to-date with many of the articles hyperlinked to their electronic version. The site is organized in terms of an introduction, new articles, new links, and "The Great Big List." With the upsurge of scholarly work being done on Tarantino, this site will undoubtedly help many undergraduates get their papers finished.

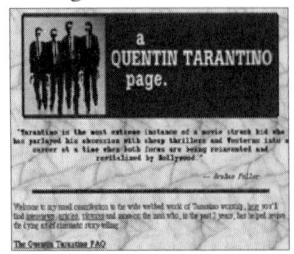

Tarantino, Quentin
URL: http://www.webcom.com/~kbilly/
Rating: 4
Comments: A top-notch site focused on the "man who, in the past three years, has helped revive the dying art of cinematic story-telling," Quentin Tarantino. Beautifully designed, there's virtually everything here that a Tarantino fan could desire: biography, FAQs, interviews, pictures, newsgroups, transcribed articles, scripts and links to the many other Tarantino sites on the Web. For my money, this is where you should start. Also be sure to check out the hilarious photo of Tarantino and John Travolta at the bottom.

Woo, John
URL: http://underground.net/~koganuts/Galleries/jw.main.html
Rating: 4
Comments: These are a collection of images featuring stills from Woo films and images of John Woo and Chow Yun-Fat. There are links to more info about Hong Kong films and Woo's productions. Very good if you dig Hong Kong films.

Wood, Ed
URL: http://garnet.acns.fsu.edu/~lflynn/edwood.html
Rating: 3
Comments: A page devoted to the newly resurrected "worst director of all time," Ed Wood. Lovingly compiled by Leisa R. Flynn, this site provides a good deal of information about the director and his notoriously bad films, from *The Bride and the Beast* to the classic bomb, *Plan 9 from Outer Space*. Although there are only a few images of Wood here, the real treat comes in the form of credits and brief reviews for each of his films as well as where to locate video tapes of them. There's even a "Hot News Flash" about Johnny Depp (who played Ed Wood in the Touchstone film of the same name) buying Bela Lugosi's former home! Now THAT'S news! A good giggle for anyone familiar with Ed Wood and his films.

FESTIVALS/EVENTS

AFI Los Angeles International Film Festival (USA)
URL: http://www.afionline.org/SCREEN/AFIFEST/index.html
Rating: 3
Comments: This festival, held in October, is a huge film festival. In 1995 it celebrated the "100th anniversary of cinema, featuring approximately 80 feature films, including new work by Michelangelo Antonioni, Jean Luc Godard, Henry Jaglom and many others." There is also a link to their video festival, which will be held for the 15th time in 1996. The synopses for the featured films are present, but it would have been nice with more production stills. There were just a few, but of very high quality.

Berlin Film Festival
URL: http://fub46.zedat.fu-berlin.de:8080/~frs/bff-index.html
Rating: 1
Comments: A list of hypertext links to production info and reviews of all of the films listed in the main section for the festival is here. This is in turn connected to the Internet Movie Database. Good to know about the newest films at the festival, but otherwise, rather bleak.

Cannes International Film Festival (France)
URL: http://franceweb.fr/Cine/Cannes/
Rating: 4

Comments: This French language site for the Cannes Film Festival is designed around the different awards of the festival and provides detailed information about each film screened. If you feel like listening to the Palme d'Or ceremony, there's an audio clip to download. The festival calendar operates from a useful button-interface, and the link to the city of Cannes itself is worth a browse. Even if you don't speak French, this site still evokes the excitement and energy of this annual film festival.

Festivals/Events

Chicago International Film Festival (USA)
URL: http://www.ddbn.com/filmfest/
Rating: 3
Comments: Upon arriving at this site, you are greeted by the following question: "What's the only difference between Cannes and Chicago?" Answer: "You can pronounce Chicago without sounding like a jerk." The festival offers free wallpaper—for your computer desktop—of the festival poster. If I am not mistaken, those are Theda Bara's eyes looking at you. The festival started in 1964 and is devoted to "seek and discover films representing the highest level of artistic excellence; to utilize cinema as a tool for education and discourse; and to promote international communication and celebrate cultural diversity through film." Besides the program, there is a festival store and poster gallery.

Chicago Lesbian and Gay International Film Festival
URL: http://videos.com/gandl/
Rating: 3
Comments: This film festival Web site is a volunteer effort and nicely done. Though the information on the festival has only some of the films reviewed or featured, the screening dates and times are there. The most interesting feature here is a great resource listing information on lesbian and gay films on video, with a link on how to buy some from Vanguard, a video retailer.

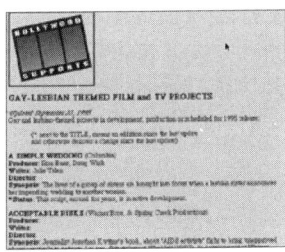

Denver International Film Festival
URL: http://www2.csn.net/DenverFilm/
Rating: 2
Comments: This site from the Mile High City drowns a bit in its text, but offers a good deal of information about the festival and its program (i.e., there's "validated festival parking available" and the festival gang all seem to meet at Cadillac Ranch after late night screenings). Film program includes credits, some stills and some descriptions. Kudos to the festival staff for recognizing New Media in its screenings.

Filmfest München
URL: http://filmfest.spacenet.de/
Rating: 4
Comments: This film festival has a site that is primarily in German, though there are some English language areas, including the excellent "Loving Life Is Loving Cinema" section. Discussion lists for films and the program are available, and the program titles with synopsis in German and English, including production information, are online for most films.

London Film Festival
URL: http://www.ibmpcug.co.uk/lff.html
Rating: 2
Comments: The London Film Festival site is full of relevant information about the festival with a few perks, such as a program diary in table format, images of the festival poster for downloading, and a linked listing of all the celebrities who will be attending the festival. There's also a wonderful personal guide to the 1995 festival written by Alan Jay. Still, these pages could easily do with a design overhaul to make them look snazzier and more navigable.

Montreal World Film Festival
URL: http://www.ffm-montreal.org/
Rating: 4
Comments: One of the nicest and most inexpensive metropolises around is Montreal, and I hope to get to this festival sometime. This bilingual (French/English) site looks very nice and features a Multimedia symposium discussing new media and multimedia during the festival. Except for hotel bookings, all you need to get ready is here.

Oberhausen Short Film Festival (Germany)
URL: http://www.uni-duisburg.de/HRZ/IKF/home.html
Rating: 2
Comments: Quite the Spartan site, but still offering some useful information about the festival and those who run it. In both German and English, these pages also mention last year's award winners and the rules for entering short films for this year's festival. There's also a short history of the Oberhausen Short Film Festival for those who want it. Yet, frankly, compared to the many innovative sites out there promoting various film festivals, this one falls quite...uh...short.

Portland International Film Festival (USA)
URL: http://www.film.com/film/filmfests/portland.95.html
Rating: 2
Comments: The small city of Portland, Oregon, hosts this festival which is the "Northwest Film Center's annual invitational survey of new world cinema." The Web site is modest, with no graphics, but with most of the information you need about the program, schedule, and prices. The festival looks interesting, but the site could use some face-lifting to grab attention, and a little about Portland to make you want to come.

Rotterdam International Film Festival
URL: http://www.luna.nl/~iffr/home.html
Rating: 4
Comments: Since 1972, the Rotterdam International Film Festival has evolved into one of the hot tickets on the film festival circuit with over 200 feature films screened and over 250,000 spectators last year. The full festival catalogue is online with ample descriptions of each film and, if you are interested, there's even a form sheet for submitting film entries. I also liked the section on Dutch film news which grounded the page into its host country.

San Sebastián International Film Festival
URL: http://sarenet.es/iffss/
Rating: 4
Comments: This Spanish event, held in September every year, will have its 44th festival in 1996. Special sections on little known Spanish films, new films from Spain and Latin America, animator and director Gregory La Cava, and films recently restored by the European Community's Media Programme Lumière make this a wonderful alternative to the glitzy media circuses of some of the other festivals. Not all the graphics are imaginative, but the information and presentation is well done. The goal of the festival is "... Internacional Film Festival of Donostia-San Sebastian aims at promoting better understanding between nations and making a positive contribution to the development of art, culture and the moving image industries." Information is available in three languages.

Seattle International Film Festival
URL: http://www.siff.film.com/
Rating: 3
Comments: Wacky site for the Seattle International Film Festival with loads of kitsch and fun. Check out the film program by title, director, country or screening date and read the extensive notes. The "Custom Program Guide" allows you to personalize your attendance schedule based on the types of films you want to see and the days you can attend.

Stockholm Film Festival
URL: http://www.filmfestivalen.se/
Rating: 4
Comments: This is definitely one of the most exciting and fun cities of Europe, at least during the summer when Swedes take to the outdoors. This festival comes at a time when people start moving indoors for the weather's sake, but don't let that scare you away. The Venice of the North has a great festival and guests, and their site is excellent in content and form. This is one of the best festival sites I have seen. No garbage, and no fill. This has what you want and need, and didn't even know you needed!

Festivals/Events

Sundance Film Festival
URL: http://plaza.interport.net/festival/intro.html
Rating: 4
Comments: You'll find the festival program, reviews, awards at the festival, QuickTime movie trailers, photos of the events, gossip, which restaurants to eat at for this unique and unusual festival devoted to quality filmmaking. The Restroom Report was one of the highlights of the Sundance local town info. "Bathrooms in the Prospector Inn do not get high marks...unbelievably tacky."

Sydney Film Festival
URL: http://www.ozemail.com.au/~sff/
Rating: 3
Comments: Huge background GIF takes centuries to come up, but once it is there, an informative site unfolds. Each film has a very brief description and there are details about venues and attendance as well. A new feature of the site is the Traveling Video Festival which "offers you a film festival in your own home...[with the aim] to offer quality films (on video) to people without ready access to cinemas or video hire—in country and remote areas or in the city." Great idea, folks!

Toronto International Film Festival
URL: http://www.bell.ca/toronto/filmfest/
Rating: 4
Comments: This festival has a wonderful Web site, though it is a smaller film festival in international circles. I love their logotype! Ambitious, entertaining, and tasteful.

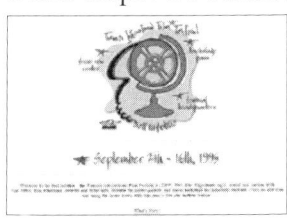

Vancouver International Film Festival
URL: http://www.viff.org/viff/
Rating: 4
Comments: Not only one of the *best* film festival sites on the WWW, but quite possibly one of the best sites period! Snappy features ranging from the searchable screening program (title, director, country, and date) to the hilarious "Nosh-O-Meter" (Kino Klassen's official VIFF party rating system). Additionally, there's a 3D map of the festival's venues and online box office information. Web designers: take note of this beautiful virtual space.

Venice Film Festival
URL: http://www.portve.interbusiness.it/wetvenice/biennale/cinema/cinema.html
Rating: 4
Comments: Information about the festival, directors, screenings, films, and very high quality promotional stills can be viewed here. There are a number of images listed as "LIVE" that are documentary photos of people arriving at the festival, talking to other film personalities, and gossip-type photos with paparazzi everywhere. Check out the unlikely dynamic duo of Kenneth Branagh and Joan Collins! The awards offered and lots of production information on the entries are also online.

FILM & MEDIA SCHOOLS

American Film Institute
URL: http://www.afionline.org/
Rating: 4
Comments: The American Film Institute has courses, advanced studies facilities, grants, and much more. Dan Harries, one of the authors of this book, has just taken over as Director, Online Media at AFI, and has moved his massive CineMedia site there. See tours in QuickTime VR of the campus, check out the meetings of special interest groups, and see who is giving the latest talk. This is the Web site to tune to for American film research and production.

Art Center College of Design (Pasadena, CA)
URL: http://www3.artcenter.edu/
Rating: 3
Comments: A maze of murky images and cryptic symbols, the Art Center's Web site is an artistic experience in itself. After you get past the tedious initial instructions, explore the various programs offered by the college. Lots of graphics (as expected), so make sure you have both a fast connection and a bit of patience!

Australian Film Television and Radio School
URL: http://www.usyd.edu.au/~graham/aftrs.html
Rating: 3
Comments: Filmmaking is alive and well Down Under and the AFTRS is at the forefront of training new filmmakers. Check out their course handbook or download any of the school's "Film and Television Technology Updates" or bibliographies which are excellent reference documents about new developments in media technology. Hopefully in the future this site will develop into a showcase of student projects and achievements.

Bowling Green State University—Department of Telecommunications
URL: http://www.bgsu.edu/departments/tcom/
Rating: 2
Comments: You can find information about the telecommunications department here and their various programs. The university has a number of interesting projects, including a journal called *Popular Music and Society*, which features articles on music in different medial contexts. They also have a film studies program, but there is no information on the Web about it. Academically I would say the material is okay, but rather boringly presented. Gopher-type text is lifted up to be viewed on a Web page, and there are no faculty photos.

Brown University—Department of Modern Culture and Media
URL: http://www.modcult.brown.edu/
Rating: 4
Comments: The Modern Culture and Media Department at Brown is noted for its distinguished faculty members, including Robert Scholes, Mary Ann Doane, Philip Rosen, and Nancy Armstrong. Here you can e-mail each of them and find out about some of their current projects. Look at the student-based Dog Video Collective section and see images from their first installation. There's obviously lots happening at Brown these days.

California Institute of the Arts—School of Film/Video
URL: http://itchy.calarts.edu/FV.html
Rating: 4
Comments: This very interesting school offers a variety of courses related to the film industry. Want to direct animated films and do it using computers? This is probably the right place for you then. Some of the programs offered are: LIVE ACTION, EXPERIMENTAL ANIMATION, CHARACTER ANIMATION, DIRECTING FOR THEATRE, VIDEO AND CINEMA. Tim Burton (*Batman, Ed Wood*) and John Lasseter (*Tin Toy*) are a couple of the alumni. The school seems great, and probably expensive, and this Web presentation is very informative and sparse on heavy graphics.

Chapman University—Department of Film and Television
URL: http://www.chapman.edu/comm/ftv/index.html
Rating: 4

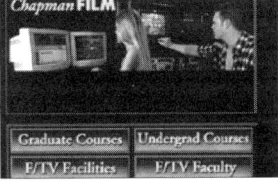

Comments: Chapman is home of the *Animation Journal*, which also has a Web site reviewed in this book. This film program is primarily geared toward production, and has a nice-looking studio picture of a digital editing suite on the main page. "Chapman University—located just 30 miles from Los Angeles—boasts a nonlinear post-production center, a state-of-the-art television studio, and an extensive array of film production gear." They offer undergraduate and graduate programs and one can use the Web browser to send them an inquiry for a hard copy catalog. Good use of the Web.

Florida State University—Film School
URL: http://www.fsu.edu/~film/
Rating: 3
Comments: The FSU Film school is an up-and-coming program and their Web site is highly informative, including enrollment details, course requirements, a newsletter, and press releases. The posted list of alumni activities is amazing considering the school was only established in 1989! Let's hope we soon see some of this great work in the form of stills and QuickTime flicks. Roll 'em Seminoles!

Johns Hopkins University—Department of Film and Media Studies
URL: http://www.jhu.edu/~english/film_media/film_media.html
Rating: 2
Comments: Film and Media Studies is a relative newcomer to Johns Hopkins, yet their pages suggest a fresh outlook to the discipline with compelling links to various forms of new media. The film and media hotlist is also quite useful and they are expecting to mount examples of student projects in the near future. Still, fairly simple in its infancy.

London International Film School
URL: http://www.tecc.co.uk/lifs/index.html
Rating: 4
Comments: This film school is based in London and has a two-year diploma plan. Some very interesting names in British and European film have attended the program, and the list of films related to the school is impressive. Let's drop a few directors' names: Bill Douglas, John Irvin, and Mike Leigh (one of my favorites). The fees for the school during the 95-96 school year was just under 4,000 British pounds, which is a bargain by any standards for international students. Similar programs in almost any area of the world would command a higher price. The comprehensive information on the school, FAQ, how much you need in the real world to get by in London, and illustrated brochure make this an excellent site for the student or semiprofessional wishing to look into further possibilities of study in the world of film.

Minneapolis College of Art and Design—Media Arts
URL: http://www.mcad.edu/academic/mediaArts/mediaArts.html
Rating: 4
Comments: Great looking site from the Twin Cities with one of the coolest front pages on the Web! This hip college has photos of the faculty members as well as examples of their own projects. Curriculum listings for both BFA and MFA. Check out the student art exhibits.

New York University—Cinema Studies
URL: http://www.nyu.edu/gsas/dept/cinema/
Rating: 2
Comments: Thinking of doing a degree in cinema studies? NYU is one of the top film schools in the world and its Web page outlines requirements, course offerings, and faculty members. Unfortunately, that's all that's here.

Northwestern University—Department of Radio/TV/Film
URL: http://www.rtvf.nwu.edu/info/Info.html
Rating: 4
Comments: A heck of a lot is going on at Northwestern these days and this site doesn't miss an opportunity to showcase it. Not only is

there the usual course and faculty information, there's also course syllabi, a page for Studio 22 (a student-based production company), and a link to the always impressive Marjorie I. Mitchell Multimedia Center. Be sure to check out grad student Dayna Cernansky's funky homepage. Look up Northwestern's other main sites in this book under "Magazines & Journals" (|T|E|L|E|C|I|N|E|), "Movies" (!PIXIN(*)COMPENDIUM! Project), and "Film & TV Indices" (OMNIBUS:EYE).

Queen's University—Film Studies
URL: http://www.film.queensu.ca/
Rating: 4
Comments: Since I have done a syllabus page myself, I was very impressed to see the use of tables to connect to syllabus pages for courses offered at Queen's University. This is just one implementation of good sense and design that pervades this whole film studies site. If you are a student, you would probably like to go here, and if you are a teacher, this is a good place to compare reading lists and course outlines. The student production QuickTime film archive is a nice touch, offering the outsider a chance to see what goes on at this educational production facility. They also offer multimedia interactive projects done by students. This rather unusual service is something that should be implemented into more educational sites working with new media.

Radio & Television Institute—Finland
URL: http://www.yle.fi/rti/rtiengl/rtihome.htm
Rating: 2
Comments: In either Finnish, Swedish or English, you can find out what's happening at the Helsinki-based RTI. Here you can join to utilize their databank which contains "Finnish language information on educational institutions around the world that provide further and in-service training in the field of radio and television." You can also access the table of contents and covers from their journal, *MediaVIRTUOOSI*. Other than that, not much else here, really.

San Francisco State University—Cinema Department
URL: http://www.cinema.sfsu.edu/
Rating: 4
Comments: Having visited this department a few years ago, I was very curious as to how they would deal with the Web treatment. The head of the department at the time had an Academy Award for a short film on his office wall, and Francis Ford Coppola's brother was the dean of the Arts College. A tasteful graphic of written text on white background and links to faculty, newsletter, student projects and related sites made this an aesthetically and brain pleasing experience. The Media Lab at the department connects screenwriting students to others in Berkeley for joint writing experiences.

Temple University—Film and Media Arts
URL: http://blue.temple.edu:80/~fma/
Rating: 2
Comments: Still under construction, Temple University's Film and Media Arts page is developing into a reasonable resource for anyone interested in attending the school. Currently, there is an excellent link to a showcase of projects created by students and faculty. Still, little else here at this time, although we expect this to flesh out in the near future.

University of Barcelona—Centre for Cinematic Research
URL: http://www.swcp.com/~cmora/cine.html
Rating: 2
Comments: The Centre for Cinematic Research at the University of Barcelona has launched a fairly limited WWW page detailing their work in conducting seminars, organizing film festivals, and promoting Spanish cinema culture. Also here is information about the journal they publish called *Film-Historia*. More of an electronic brochure, there are some useful contact details here.

University of Copenhagen—Department of Film and Media Studies
URL: http://www.media.ku.dk/
Rating: 2
Comments: This Danish site has limited information about its programs and faculty. The real treat here, though, is the student Web pages. My favorite is definitely Timme Bisgaard's wonderful "The Baudrillard Scene" at
http://www.media.ku.dk/students/timme/index.html
Hopefully more intriguing student projects will follow.

University of Iowa—Film Studies
URL: http://www.lib.uiowa.edu/proj/film/
Rating: 3
Comments: Nicely designed film program at Iowa presents courses, faculty (no pictures), degree information, application and admissions info, and guides to local cinemas, local student film club, and links page. It looked like an interesting program so I was sorry that there were no pictures of the facilities and campus. It is always nice to see what the faculty look like as well. *Iris*, a journal of film and sound, is published here.

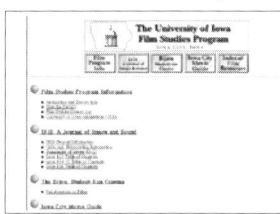

University of Karlstad—Film Studies
URL: http://www.hks.se/~bertd/toc.html
Rating: 4
Comments: The University of Karlstad's Film Studies Pages are an excellent example of how to showcase student work on the Web. Not only are there the obligatory details about the degree itself (quite innovative with hyperlinked syllabi and reading lists), but also a growing collection of student essays. The Film Studies program here is also home to the ROSEBUD discussion group, which was established for film studies students around the world. Check out the "Shots in Cyberspace" section for an excellent directory of other film sites. Oh, by the way, co-author Bert Deivert is head of the Film Studies Program here!

University of Texas at Austin—Department of Radio, Television, Film
URL: http://www.utexas.edu/coc/retf/
Rating: 2
Comments: With a stellar faculty including Tom Schatz, Janet Staiger, and Horace Newcomb, the R-T-F department at UT Austin is becoming one of the top institutions for film and media studies. Their Web page includes full course descriptions (with some syllabi), faculty listing, and requirements. Still a no-frill site, let's hope we see some sample student essays and other highlights of this excellent department in the future.

University of Toronto—Cinema Studies
URL: http://www.utoronto.ca:80/innis/cinema/
Rating: 4
Comments: Well-organized and nicely designed site guides you through such courses as "Quebecois Novel into Film" or "Semiotics of Visual Art." Some of the faculty members are currently getting up their own home pages and the schedules for their Free Friday Films are posted. I also like the explanatory sections titled "What Do We Mean by Cinema Studies?" and "What Can I Do with an Undergraduate Degree in Cinema Studies?" Uh, probably a lot of people would like to read these sections.

University of Waterloo—Film Studies
URL: http://arts.uwaterloo.ca/FINE/juhde/film.htm
Rating: 2
Comments: Course descriptions and curriculum required for studying film as well as the schedule for the local film society are available. One good feature of the site is *Kinema*, their local film journal which has certain full-text articles available online. Also has link to the local cinema which lists synopses for current films. This one is okay but not that interactive. Best part is the course info and the *Kinema*.

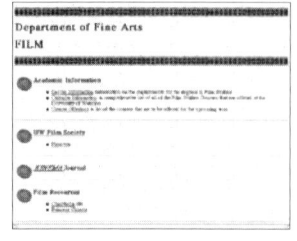

Vancouver Film School
URL: http://www.multimedia.edu/
Rating: 4
Comments: The Vancouver Film School's site is designed for Netscape 2.0 and really utilizes it with Shockwave "pong" and sliding windows. There are wonderful animation and multimedia galleries showcasing student work as well as other nifty items relating to their course offerings. This is one of the best sites currently on the WWW, so check it out.

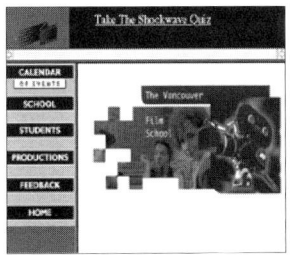

York University—Department of Film and Video
URL: http://www.yorku.ca/faculty/finearts/fv/fvhome.htm
Rating: 3
Comments: For the most part an excellent effort in posting comprehensive information about their program. Course details, faculty member bios, and facility listing. Still seems to be wanting for more content arising from the department's own people. And I won't mention a couple of the HTML no-no's I came across (...other than the black lettering on dark chocolate-brown background...?).

FILM REVIEWS

100+ Movie Reviews by Joan Ellis
URL: http://movie.infocom.net/
Rating: 4
Comments: The Joan Ellis reviews are entertaining to read and can be a good alternative to a synopsis put out by a major studio on their latest film. She said this about *The Brothers McMullen:* "Raised in a Catholic Church that still clings with bloody fingernails to dictates that contradict human nature, the brothers ponder the forbidden sins of premarital sex, birth control, abortion, and masturbation—and then get right on with it." No graphics, but a search function and easy maneuvering through the many reviews. After reading her bio information, I was suspicious and sent a letter to the WebMaster. His reply assured me that "Joan Ellis is a real person. She was just reviewed by *Newsweek* magazine as 'The Pauline Kael of the Internet.'" Joan's bio contains a little blurb about her spy materials and their use during her stint in the CIA. Read it!

As the Reel Rolls
URL: http://www.fcs.net/maclark/
Rating: 2
Comments: Malcolm Clark says here, "I write a review when I see a movie, and I see a movie when I feel like it. Low pressure, right?" I counted 21 reviews written over a couple of years, and most were mainstream multiplex flicks. Just another source for movie reviews by a volunteer that felt the call. There are better places around.

Detroit News Movie Page
URL: http://www.detnews.com/SHOWTIME/movies/index.html
Rating: 3
Comments: Detroit being one of the great cities for crime and violence, check out something to keep you off the streets at night! You can see what is going now in first-run movie theaters, grosses for the films, and what is coming next week. The Limited Run section mentions some of the theaters showing alternative or art films. Capsule reviews of first-run films by *Detroit News* critic Susan Stark are also online.

Entertainment Extra!
URL: http://www.ddc.com/extra/
Rating: 1
Comments: This entertainment Web zine has film and music reviews and related links to entertainment sources. According to the intro blurb, they are not a "fanzine," but devoted to publishing high quality articles. There were a variety of first-run films reviewed (linked to Mr. Showbiz) as well as the standard "old-run" and "rerun," but nothing that seemed very different than any other film site doing reviews. In fact, if the *Mask* review I read is indicative of most of this, avoid this place like the plague!

Film.com Reviews
URL: http://www.film.com/film/reviews/
Rating: 4
Comments: This is the film review and discussion area of current releases. There are usually several reviews written for each film, which makes comparison a natural part of the game without having

to move to another site. Good move by Film.com, and it is part of their Web site which is reviewed on another page of the book.

Mandel & Patrick's Movie Corner!
URL: http://www.fyi.net/~andre/mand&pat.htm
Rating: 3
Comments: Kid critics on the Net. (Andre) Mandel and (Jay) Patrick review newly released and video films as well as rate them with cute little drawn stars. If you hate intellectual movie critics, you'll love these reviews. Sample from the review of *Seven*: "The seven deadly sins...Gluttony, Greed, Sloth, Pride, Lust, Envy, Wrath. This movie deals with these and the philosophy of a murderer who uses the seven sins as a reason for his killings." Okay, it's not Siskel and Ebert, but each review does give you an idea about the film (even though these guys actually rattle on a bit much about the plot). Check out each of their 101 best film lists and compare.

Middlesex News Film Reviews
URL: gopher://ftp.std.com:70/11/periodicals/Middlesex-News/movies
Rating: 2
Comments: Save three bucks a week and read the *Middlesex News* film reviews free! This hometown newspaper catering to MetroWest, the high-tech region west of Boston, Mass., decided to post news and other features on the Internet. Beginning in 1993, they say themselves that "It marked the first time a general-interest newspaper committed itself to an active presence on the Net." The reviews are not very exciting, nor do they cover particularly low profile films, but for media types who want to see what is around on the Net, it is one more available source. Some sample headlines from the reviews: BRADY BUNCH IS ONE NEAT-O, FUNNY FILM; BUNGLED IN THE JUNGLE: CONGO AN ADVENTURE IN STUPIDITY; TOO MANY HACKS IN HACKERS.

Movie Mom's Guide to Films and Videos
URL: http://pages.prodigy.com/VA/rcpj55a/moviemom.html
Rating: 3
Comments: This is the attempt at being the PC, parentally correct site, of movies on the Web. Isn't it amazing that five of The Movie Mom's Top Web Sites are: "The Movie Mom's Guide to Family Movies Recommendations on Current Theatrical and Video Releases; The Movie Mom's Movie of the Month This Month—a Guide to All the Versions of *A Christmas Carol*; The Movie Mom's Guide to Watching Movies with Children—What to Do with Kids Who Won't Watch Anything but PG-13 Movies with Lots of Explosions; The Movie Mom's List of the Best Movies for Families—No One Should Grow Up (or be a grown-up) Without Seeing These; The Movie Mom's Guide for Foster Families Recommendations for Families Facing the Special Challenges of Connecting to Foster Children." "I've been wondering about this one.... Anyway it is a first stop for parents with small children, though I wouldn't want to hang out here or take all of this *too* seriously. No graphic(s) violence or otherwise.

Movie Review Query Engine
URL: http://www.cinema.pgh.pa.us/movie/reviews
Rating: 4
Comments: This search engine queries the rec.arts.movies.reviews archive and checks on reviews posted there and on other parts of the Internet. On searching for *Toy Story* I received a very good number of reviews, varying from professional ones in *Time* magazine to volunteer reviews for the Internet Movie Database. This is an excellent resource. No images, just quick searches!

Film Reviews

Mr. Showbiz
URL: http://web3.starwave.com:80/showbiz/
Rating: 4
Comments: You can ignore the commercials running at the tops of pages if you want, they are not that disturbing. This commercial site offers some news on showbiz, which changes every day or so. Pictures, sound bites, RealAudio, archives of earlier articles and reviews make this a very large resource for show business gossip, profiles, and box office information.

Out Magazine Movie Reviews
URL: http://www.out.com/out/entertainment/movies.html
Rating: 4
Comments: Hip movie reviews from one of the top gay and lesbian magazines on the newsstand. Most of the featured films have gay themes or might appeal to a gay audience and the reviews reflect this slant. For example, the review for *Showgirls*: "A racy romp through the lives of Las Vegas showgirls. The camp quote of the season , 'I'm a dancer!' offers some insight into the movie's depth." Ahh, Rex Reed couldn't say it better!

Pathfinder Movie Reviews
URL: http://pathfinder.com/@@N4f1msEDRQIAQPdo/pathfinder/hitcity/movies.html
Rating: 3
Comments: Very short reviews of films reside on this very commercial server housing *Time*, *People*, *Entertainment Weekly*, and a number of other magazines. The latest hit films in this likely titled area called *Hit City* is about as amusing as reading the local rag's critic's ten line rave about *Basic Instinct*. There is a chance to compare your own ideas with syndicated critics and put in a vote for the films listed in the "Critical

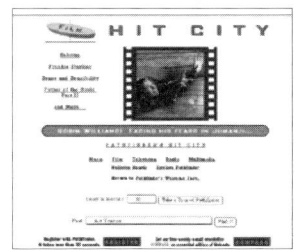

Mass" area. Not my favorite pastime surfing here, but it will be enjoyed by most, at least for a while.

San Francisco Chronicle Film Reviews
URL: http://www.sfgate.com/chronicle/pink-section/film.html
Rating: 4
Comments: Up-to-date film reviews from the "Pink Section" of the *San Francisco Chronicle*. Each film gets a short review, running time, Bay Area theaters running the movie, and a funny rating icon of a man in a chair. I always check these pages before seeing a flick since these reviews don't give most of the plot away.

Teen Movie Critic
URL: http://www.skypoint.com/members/magic/roger/teencritic.html
Rating: 4
Comments: The darling of Netscape's "What's Cool" link page, Teen Movie Critic (Roger Davidson) has been a hit ever since it began wandering around the Web. Yet fame becomes blinding (notice HUGE first link titled "Interviews, Honors, Etc."). Roger writes: "The reviews I give are not for one type of teen, but for every teen that you can possibly imagine." Wow, what a feat! Still, the reviews are insightful and fun to read and the ratings (from 1-4) seem spot on. Roger adds that "I will do a page every week, but it will not necessarily include movies in theaters, since I can't afford to go that often." Cute.

The Third Thumb
URL: http://www.microscopolis.com/thirdthumb.html
Rating: 3
Comments: Sophisticated database of very brief movie reviews (by Patrick Brenner) allows you to search by title, review date, rating, and review verdict. Sample review for *Leaving Las Vegas*: "Probably Nicholas Cage's best movie so far. The two characters are overstated, but so is the city in which they find themselves. An excellent, thoughtful tale." I probably could have gotten that review off the film's poster.

Film Reviews

Tucson Weekly's Film Vault
URL: http://desert.net/tw/film/index.htm
Rating: 4
Comments: This place is a good set of reviews from the *Tucson Weekly* newspaper with added links to various databases, picture files, and so forth. You may search for a film or name or just browse alphabetically through their archive. You first find a synopsis of the film and are then led to the review by a hypertext link. As we went to press, I got to see a preview of the new version supporting frames and it looked very promising, and above all, more navigable for finding film reviews.

USENET Movie Archives
URL: gopher://ashpool.micro.umn.edu/77/fun/Movies
Rating: 3
Comments: rec.arts.movie.reviews has a good database going for movie reviews from 1987 to 1993 which is cataloged with index words. Search for *Sunset Boulevard* and you get all reviews that mention *Sunset Boulevard* , including addresses on that street that are listed for a reviewer, or mentions of the film or play. Useful for people that would like to see how the average film viewer reacts to film. Not academic, though a lot of students write reviews. It gets three slates because it only covers reviews to 1993.

Video & Movie Review Database
URL: gopher://isumvs.iastate.edu/1~db.VIDEO
Rating: 1
Comments: This review database is made up of films released on video that have been reviewed by interested parties. The searchable database allows searches by several categories, as well as a few others. Good idea, but very terse reviews, if you could even call them that! A sample review follows:
Ace Ventura: Pet Detective
Rated: PG13
Rating: ****
Year Released: 1994
Directed by: Josh McDowell
Starring: Jim Carrey
Review: Extremely funny. Jim Carrey is a great comedian.

Women Studies Film Reviews
URL: http://www.inform.umd.edu:8080/EdRes/Topic/WomensStudies/FilmReviews
Rating: 3
Comments: Feminist film reviews of both popular and little-known movies out of the University of Maryland. A simple A-Z listing of film titles contain short and insightful reviews. Most of the reviews come from Linda Lopez McAlister's "The Women's Show" Tampa, Florida radio program and film scholar, Cynthia Fuchs. Easy to use and worth a look.

FILM & TV ASSORTED

Amazing Clickable Beavis
URL: http://freedom.nmsu.edu/~jlillibr/ClickableBeavis.html
Rating: 4
Comments: Hilarious picture of Beavis of "Beavis & Butt-head" fame which you can click on to hear the voice of yours truly. Click on his head and he replies: "It's cool to…uh…try to think of stuff" or tap on his knee and hear: "aaaahhhhh!" Very clever!

As Seen on TV
URL: http://www.asontv.com/
Rating: 3
Comments: One of the "Cheesiest" sites on the Web! A page devoted to those wonderful products hawked on the tube: "Blue Shield True-Vision Eyewear" ($8), "Mega Mop" ($12.50), the "Orthopedic Comfort Pillow" ($7.50), etc. You get the picture. Best part is you don't even have to lift up the phone any more to order. Kitsch at its best!

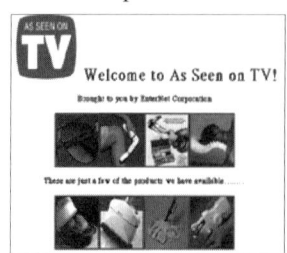

Film & TV Assorted

Australian Television Guide
URL: http://www.sofcom.com.au/TV/index.html
Rating: 4
Comments: Want to know what's playing tonight on Melbourne TV screens? Want to find out when Seinfeld is on in Brisbane? This wonderful TV guide allows you to browse up-to-date television listings through word searches ("cricket"), time segments, and channels in most of Australia's capital cities. A truly civilized way to plan your TV viewing.

Bagpipes Go To The Movies
URL: http://www.ems.psu.edu/~fraser/PipesMovies.html
Rating: 3
Comments: If you want the ultimate bagpipe list in movies and discussions pertaining to it, this is *the* place. For that reason, this gets (almost) top ratings! Here is a quote from the site: "Backdraft—1991... the movie tells the story of firefighters in Chicago. It contains a funeral scene with massed police/fire pipers. The pipers were from the Chicago Emerald Society Pipe Band."

Balcony
URL: http://balcony.com/
Rating: 2
Comments: In their own words, "Balcony is the name of a private, unmoderated discussion group dedicated to cinema-related topics." The Head Usher gives his favorite Web site of the month, one can join the discussion group, which is "chatty" but has some interesting threads, and there is a link page which is rather short and of limited interest to people familiar with film resources. For example, CineMedia's site is listed three times in different categories. The Concessions Stand is one of the low points of the Web. Buy a virtual hot dog with virtual money and get a receipt, but you don't get to eat it! You see some pictures of the snacks on sale. Save the bandwidth for the discussions, please!

Cable Online
URL: http://www.aescon.com/cableonline/
Rating: 4
Comments: This site offers a source of information for what is going on in the cable and telecommunications industries. News releases, changes in company heads, and assorted information may be of great use to researchers, industry pros, and curious consumers. The cable yellow pages for the the entire USA looks like one of the really good information resources online here. Educators may be interested in the "Cable In Education" section. This is an excellent and valuable source of what is going on in the information technology business.

Cathouse British Comedy Pages
URL: http://cathouse.org/BritishComedy/
Rating: 4
Comments: The British Comedy pages has everything from revues to TV programs. There are transcripts from shows, skits, and links for featured performers like Rowan Atkinson of "Black Adder" and "Mr. Bean" fame. The *Carry On* film series has its thirty titles listed here with a brief story line. Britcomedy Digest e-zine is on the same server and offers a monthly dose of British humor. This site is not graphics intensive, but does load rather slowly due to the server's limitations. However, it is worth its wait in gold.

Celebrity Pages
URL: http://emporium.turnpike.net/~daniel/Alicia/celebs.html
Rating: 3
Comments: Celebrity hunting? Want the latest page and pictures of your favorite actor, actress, supermodel, singer, or TV host? If it is out there, you may find it on Celebrity Pages. It will also help you to connect to a few of the USENET groups that discuss such things. As a link page it is okay, but not much information right here at the site. The Yahoo directory offers more.

CNN Showbiz News
URL: http://www.cnn.com/SHOWBIZ/index.html
Rating: 3
Comments: This lightweight showbiz program on CNN has its own Web area on their server. I like the Web presentation better than the

television version, since I can easily skip things that don't interest me. If you like showbiz news, add this to your bookmarks or hotlist.

Contemporary Chinese Cinema
URL: http://www.citri.edu.au:8888/ccc/index.html
Rating: 4
Comments: This site wishes to keep people all over the world up-to-date about contemporary Chinese cinema, the people behind the scenes and in front of the cameras, and what films are currently being shown around the world. One of the goals is to provide a history of the Chinese film, though this is still under construction. Hong Kong has the most postings at the moment, but Taiwan and China are on the march. This is suited for both academics and cineastes.

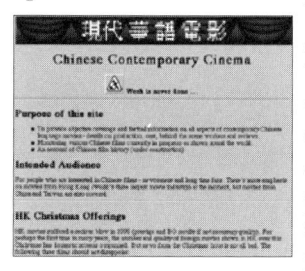

Cosmo's TV Guide
URL: http://home.ptd.net/~cosmo/
Rating: 2
Comments: A Web page devoted to the American *TV Guide* magazine? "1953—*TV Guide's* first national issue (April 3-9, 1953) with Desi Arnaz, Jr., hits the stands." Cosmo collects TV Guides and lets us know what he has in his collection. "The very first *TV Guide* I ever collected was the *Inauguration Day* issue from January 1981, with Ronald Reagan on the cover." Some of the older ones he has are from the 1970s! The links here are as good as the page content, with his cybermom high on the list, and *TV Guide* itself up in the running. Kind of low on content.

Cult Film Page
URL: http://sepnet.com/rcramer/index.htm
Rating: 3
Comments: Ronnie Cramer's Cult Film page is a commercial page for Scorched Earth productions and an indirect homage to cult films of various types, notably horror and exploitation films of the 1950s to 1970s, though there is more than just this for sale. The choice reflects the

author's own taste in films, but it is a fun place to look for the bizarre and non-mainstream stuff for purchase. Ronnie's own films have incredible titles like his *Even Hitler Had a Girlfriend*, which is hailed by drive-in expert Joe Bob Briggs as "best drive-in movie of the year!" Here is a little example from the catalog: *"The Prime Time* (1960) a.k.a. *Hellkitten*—Herschell Gordon Lewis (*Blood Feast*) produced and directed this story of a young girl who leaves home only to get mixed up with a demented beatnik artist who forces her to pose nude. Features skinny dipping parties, clothes-tearing girl fights and more. Karen Black (in her screen debut) plays a painted woman."

Cult Shop
URL: http://lasarto.cnde.iastate.edu/Movies/CultShop/
Rating: 4
Comments: Current movies by cult figures in the entertainment industry prevail here. Cinema releases, video releases, television, and more info about featured cult personalities can be found here. Adam D. Bormann, who runs this site, is a major in advertising, and that is the first thing you notice—simple but nice graphics. Some of the directors and writers featured are John Carpenter, Joel and Ethan Coen, Peter Jackson, Dan O'Bannon, and Adam Rifkin. Offbeat content, though not repulsive, and a variety that is not often featured on other Web pages. I will be going back to this one a lot.

Cult TV Episode Guide
URL: http://www.ee.ed.ac.uk/~jmd/CultTV/
Rating: 3
Comments: From "Absolutely Fabulous" to "The Zoo Gang," this recently created directory pulls together the many episode guides out on the net relating to cult TV programs. So far, you can only grab links alphabetically, but hopefully other searching elements will be added later. This site also houses the "Cult TV Episode Guide Top 20" listing.

Film & TV Assorted

Drew's Script-O-Matic
URL: http://home.fish.net.au/~drew/scripts.htm
Rating: 4
Comments: Sassy site for getting copies of screenplays on the Net. This directory serves up scripts in three flavors: "1. Marlon Brando Style (with table): The best, be patient; 2. Kathleen Turner Style (no table): Meaty, but can still move; and 3. Kate Moss Style (bare bones): Everything you need, but nothin' extra." Much needed resource.

Film Censorship Archive
URL: http://fileroom.aaup.uic.edu/FileRoom/documents/Mfilm.html
Rating: 4
Comments: This collection of film-related censorship incidents is part of an overall site on censorship involving different media. The films listed on this page have links to more info on the case and why the film was censored. Everything from the NAACP's opposition to *Birth of a Nation* to *Schindler's List* being banned in Jordan is covered here. This material doesn't seem readily available anywhere else. Cross-referenced lists based on censorship reasons also make for richer comparison of contemporary works.

Film Personality Deaths
URL: http://catless.ncl.ac.uk/Obituary/movies.html
Rating: 4
Comments: If you are looking for mondo exploitation pictures of Hollywood deaths, this is *not* the place. Recent actors, directors, producers, and journalists who have passed away end up in this collection of links to information about deceased cinema personalities. The links are usually to the Internet Movie Database which supplies more biographical information, as well as filmographies. There are even some links to interviews. Check out the Randy Shilts interview about gays in the military and the 1950s and 1960s code word "friends of Dorothy." Fascinating reading.

Flicker
URL: http://www.sirius.com/~sstark/
Rating: 4
Comments: Flicker is a home page centered on the "alternative cinematic experience." Sections of this site include film artists, filmmaking resources, images (with heaps of thumbnails), and venues (divided by location). No actual flicks online here, but the maintainer, Scott Stark, hopes to get some on in the future. Flicker also serves as host to *Beyond*, a serial QuickTime film by Zoe Beloff which explores the paradoxes of technology and imagination. A nice-looking site which serves an important function.

Gay-Lesbian Themed Film & TV Projects
URL: http://www.datalounge.com/hsupports/development-projects.html
Rating: 3
Comments: This is just a list of film and television productions with gay and lesbian themes produced in the past year, but is good as a start for research on finding these films and productions.

Great Comedy Movies
URL: http://www.sccs.swarthmore.edu/~dansac/movies/comedy.html
Rating: 2
Comments: "Great Comedy Movies" is a list created by Dan Sacha who guarantees that "you will laugh your buttocks off watching the following films." Laughfest flicks include *The Naked Gun*, *Hudsucker Proxy* and *Midnight Run*??? Boy, Dan, doesn't take much to get a hoot out of you, I guess. Nice try, though.

Grolsch filmpagina
URL: http://www.riv.nl/grolsch/film.htm
Rating: 3
Comments: A movie page sponsored by Dutch beer brewers, Grolsch? Go figure, but a great site to wander through, even if you don't read Dutch! Includes a "Movie Top 10" with some decent graphics and a form for you to send in your own mini-film reviews. By the way, there is also a link to their beer pages as well!

Hans Zimmer Worship Page
URL: http://www.ugcs.caltech.edu/~btman/hanszimmer/
Rating: 2
Comments: This page, devoted to Hans Zimmer, movie composer best known for his Oscar-winning score to *The Lion King*, is a very worthy collection of information—that is, once you scroll down pages of nonstop text! Links go out to biographies, filmographies, and anything thing else which has to do with the man himself. There's also a very interesting selection of soundtrack reviews by various fans of Hans as well as by MovieScore Magazine critic, Peter Holm. Don't let the text-laden pages scare you away.

Hong Kong Movies
URL: http://www.mdstud.chalmers.se/hkmovie/
Rating: 3
Comments: The Hong Kong Movies Homepage, hailing from Gothenburg, Sweden, has tons of information about the films of Hong Kong. Items available include FAQ's, long lists of films, weekly Hong Kong box office reports, movie awards, and a searchable Hong Kong movie and actor database. Fans of Jackie Chan and films such as *Royal Tramp* will go nuts over this site.

Lumo - Finnish Film Page
URL: http://www.kaapeli.fi/~lumo/English/
Rating: 2
Comments: The Lumo Pages contain everything you would ever need to know about Finnish cinema. Sections include the Finnish Film Archive, cartoon forum, festival listing, and the Finnish Film Foundation. With many pages still under development, we hope construction continues along these lines. Currently available in Finnish, Swedish, and English versions.

Martial Arts Films
URL: http://www.digiweb.com/webm/chris/
Rating: 2
Comments: Jet Li, Jackie Chan, Bruce Lee and other favorites jump out at you with a scream and a kick on this page. Though other stars, both female and male, as well as directors are listed, the first three are the only ones so far with hyperlinks to more info. There is one page of information on each actor, and then at the bottom of the text there are links to other pages on the Web or to image files. Okay, but there are better and more complete sites in the Hong Kong realm.

Marvin the Martian
URL: http://eeisun2.city.ac.uk/~ftp/maw/marvin.html
Rating: 3
Comments: Remember this little guy? This page features sound clips and pictures of the star of many Warner Bros. cartoons. Favs: "I'm going to blow it up" audio file and image of Marvin shooting his ray gun. More to be added soon!

MORSE: Movie Recommendation System
URL:
http://www.labs.bt.com/innovate/multimed/morse/morse.htm
Rating: 4
Comments: Funded by British Telecommunications, the Morse site is actually quite interesting. What it does is "recommends films to you after comparing your tastes with other people's." Links to the Internet Movie Database also make it easy to get quick access to film information. Give it a twirl.

Movie Cliches List
URL: http://www.well.com/user/vertigo/cliches.html
Rating: 3
Comments: With its mission clearly stated, this site maintains "a list of the most annoying and common logic flaws and stereotypes found in movies, compiled from various sources." Cliches are arranged by topic (Airplanes to Wood) and merely spell out the cliche. For example, "When there's an intruder somewhere in the house, the thing that jumps at the heroine in the dark turns out to be her cat, even if it comes from places cats wouldn't be, like inside a cupboard! As soon as she relaxes, the killer will show up and strangle her." So true! Good for a fun half an hour or so.

Nielsen Media Research
URL: http://www.nielsenmedia.com/
Rating: 2
Comments: Yes, those Nielsen Families are now online and informing advertisers of what we access. Check out the much talked about Internet Demographic Survey they conducted. Sorry, but TV ratings aren't available here, although you can order them at the standard cost.

Samuel French Theatre and Film Bookshops
URL: http://www.hollywoodnetwork.com:80/hn/shopping/book-store/sfbook.html
Rating: 3
Comments: The Samuel French Theatre and Film Bookshops, one of the great places to get hard-to-find cinema books, now have a section on the Hollywood Shopping Network site to sell their books. Although there are currently only a few titles listed on their online catalog, the real benefit is their direct e-mail address (samfrench@earthlink.net) for book queries. They have yet to set up a secure online order form, but will hopefully do so in the future.

Science Fiction Film Archive
URL: http://www.primenet.com/~laurus/scifi/sffilm/sffilm.htm
Rating: 3
Comments: As the opening page announces, the Science Fiction Film Archive is "for those with a lust for lasers, a passion for interstellar fashion, an appreciation for a rebellion nation!!!" Not terribly pleasant to look at, these pages have a nice appreciation of what makes sci-fi films so good. Case in point is their rating system of the films which is as follows: "+10 = This is the stuff legends are made of !! So great you must see it; -10 = This is the stuff legends are made of !! So bad you must see it; 0 = This is worthless." Each film title (in table format) gets a rating, brief description, and some even an image of the poster.

Soundtrack Web
URL: http://alfred.uib.no/People/midi/soundtrackweb/
Rating: 4
Comments: This is the homepage of the rec.music.movies newsgroup. It has the FAQ file here, database, and links to other pages, like the composer Bernard Herrman's Web pages. Herrman did the music for *Psycho*, *Taxi Driver*, and *Citizen Kane*, among others. Devoted to the composers and soundtracks for films, this site is a great starting point for the neglected audio portion of films.

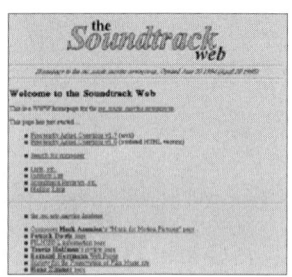

Ticket Booth
URL: http://www.cipsinc.com/spot/
Rating: 3
Comments: Discount movie tickets for any Loews/Sony, Cineplex, or United Artists theaters may be purchased through this site. Good service, though these are not stunning or mind-boggling pages.

TV1
URL: http://www.TV1.com
Rating: 3
Comments: Can we really make an intelligent decision when deciding what program to watch on television? Well, we have an interactive guide here to help us do just that! The former "What's On Tonite" has been updated to TV1. This is a television guide to end all for interactive choice. Unfortunately, this guide is only for the continental US, so it may be awhile before Europeans, South Americans, and Asians get to use it. This is a service that sends e-mail according to your specifications about what you wish to see. According to the contact I had there, the service will always be free of charge. In that case, it is a good idea and a bargain for North Americans. This is also a good place to turn for executive television producers who want exposure for their coming attractions. This commercial service looks like one of the most interesting for television viewers and choice.

U.S. National Film Registry - Titles
URL:
http://www.cs.cmu.edu:80/afs/cs.cmu.edu/user/clamen/misc/movies/NFR-Titles.html
Rating: 4
Comments: "In 1988, the (United States) Library of Congress established the National Film Preservation Board, to preserve film deemed 'culturally, historically, or aesthetically important'. Each year, the board selects 25 films to add to the National Film Registry. Herein is the complete list of those films so honoured to date." This is the text that opens this page at the Library of Congress. Each film has a hypertext link that joins it with the Internet Movie Database. That this IMD has been accepted by such a revered facility as the LOC means it has arrived! You may actually submit films to the Library of Congress for inclusion in the National Film Registry. Film scholars will find the Library of Congress an important resource. I believe that more digitalized media will be available in the near future.

Urdu/Hindi Film Music Page
URL: http://www.lehigh.edu/sm0e/public/www-data/sami.html
Rating: 3
Comments: Sami's Urdu/Hindi Film Music Page is a lovingly produced page devoted to Indian music on film. Much of the material here is culled from the newsgroup RMIM (rec.music.indian.misc) and has been archived according to specific threads. The page includes an essay titled "An Introduction to Indian Film Music" by Renu Thamma as well as lists of notes and chords of certain film songs. A fascinating exploration for fans (or not) of Indian cinema and music.

Vampyrs Film List
URL: http://ubu.hahnemann.edu/Misc/Vamp-Mov.html
Rating: 4
Comments: This is *the list* of vampire films! Though not all the films have posts in the Internet Movie Database, the list of titles is connected with the search engine there. Though I have seen a lot on vampires, this is a valuable resource if you don't want to shell out for the "complete" vampire film books out there. No images are here, but you get high value content.

VCR Q&A
URL: http://bradley.bradley.edu/~fil/vcr.html
Rating: 4
Comments: Video Cassette Recorder Questions and Answers should help the majority of VCR owners who don't know how to stop that blinking clock at 12:00, want to program the thing to tape a movie, want to copy coded tapes, and other assorted user problems associated with this necessary accessory in our electronic cottages. Philip Kuhn, an engineer at Bradley University in Peoria, Illinois, reckons he has worked on more than 1,000 different tape machines in the last years and offers his considerable experience to bewildered VCR owners. A great help site and wonderful way to share information with the non-techie.

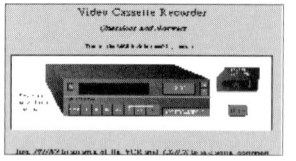

Weekend Box Office Report
URL: http://cellini.leonardo.net/aasen/topbox.html
Rating: 3
Comments: The Box Office takes for the top ten films as provided by *Daily Variety*. This weekend and the past six months is online for reading. No graphics, but the information is important for people following the industry, from students to marketing types.

World TV Standards Guides
URL: http://www.ee.surrey.ac.uk/Contrib/WorldTV/
Rating: 4
Comments: PAL? NTSC? SECAM? Confused by these acronyms often found on video labels and VCRs? This helpful page explains the different TV standards, discusses why there are different standards and what countries have what standards, and spells out the pros and cons of each. Excellent section offers some solutions to bridging these different standards.

WWW.FilmMusic.Com
URL: http://www.filmmusic.com/
Rating: 4
Comments: Though this site is useful for entertainment value, I see its primary audience as serious students and researchers of film and music. There are hundreds of great links and resources, critique of film music, and interviews and portraits of composers. This is a gold mine and one of the best Web sites around for academic quality information. This is easily the best Web site on film music.

FILM & TV INDICES

AIRWAVES Television Page
URL: http://radio.aiss.uiuc.edu/~rrb/tv.html
Rating: 3
Comments: A great meeting place of links to broadcasters all over the world. They are arranged according to radio, TV, and cinema. Frank Zappa's memorable song about the slime in the video opens the page. This is not the most comprehensive link page, but a good start.

Broadcasting Link
URL: http://www.algonet.se/~nikos/broad.html
Rating: 3
Comments: The three main broadcasting links at this Swedish site are for lists of sites all over the world, separated in European, other countries, and other broadcasting resources. Very simple but pleasantly structured layout with white background. Pleasing to tired eyes!

Cinema Connection
URL: http://www.webcom.com/~3e-media/TMC/cineprax.html
Rating: 3
Comments: A huge directory of cinema-related links including historical studies, production resources, and film festivals. Updated often, this site also has Italian translations for many of its descriptions. This directory is particularly noteworthy for its division of production resources. Always growing.

Cinema Sites
URL: http://www.webcom.com/~davidaug/Movie_Sites.html
Rating: 4
Comments: David Augsburger's Cinema Sites directory has been around for some time now and is always up-to-date with new additions to the WWW. Although the cover page and index are less than glamorous, its annotated film links are well worth it. And the lists go on and on and on. A solid film and TV directory.

CineMedia
URL: http://www.afionline.org/CINEMEDIA/CineMedia.home.html
Rating: 4
Comments: Dan Harries, formerly WebMaster at Griffith University's CineMedia site, has assembled an impressive collection of links to film, media, and new media on the World Wide Web and beyond. It is most likely the largest and most extensive collection available and is now based at the American Film Institute's Website in California. Harries has moved to California and taken over the responsibilities for further development of Internet resources at AFI. We can expect much more for cineastes, academics, and general film people at the AFI site. CineMedia has a focus on useful sites for students and researchers but does not forget the "fun" aspect of film sites. There really is something for everyone here. Highly recommended!

Clamen's Movie Information Collection
URL: http://www.cs.cmu.edu/afs/cs.cmu.edu/user/clamen/misc/movies/
Rating: 3
Comments: Clamen's collection was one of the first ones I saw on the Web a couple of years back when I first started collecting resources. It is still a very good resource which is free of graphics, making it fast loading. This is "clean" as skateboarders would say. No frills, but rather an abundance of intelligently arranged links preside on one main page. It is not as comprehensive as CineMedia, but then what could be? Since it is located in Pittsburgh, there is even information on movie theaters and what is playing. Put this on your hotlist.

Film.com
URL: http://www.film.com/film/
Rating: 4
Comments: The motto of this site is "Bringing a critical perspective to the world of film," and it tries to live up to this difficult task on the glitzy cybertrail of film sites on the Web. This is an excellent site that has interviews and profiles of a number of actors, directors, and film people. There are even video sales places like Scarecrow Video portrayed in interesting articles. This is a gold mine and it isn't hard to find the gold. Maneuverable and great reading all the way. Definitely one of the best. Low key graphics make this look cheap, but it is not!

GEWI Film Page
URL: http://gewi.kfunigraz.ac.at/~puntigam/
Rating: 4
Comments: Primarily a listing of links around the world, this German based, and German language site has a very nice photo on the main page. You can use the site to some degree without understanding German, but this is a good place to see what is going on locally in Austria, where the site is based, and check what European film magazines are available. Electronic journals in several languages are also listed. Overall, this is a good European resource.

Guide to Film & Video Resources
URL: http://http2.sils.umich.edu/Public/fvl/film.html
Rating: 3
Comments: This document was originally a text document which could be viewed online or downloaded. The conversion to a hypertext document made this guide much more valuable for academics and film researchers. The only problem here is that it doesn't seem to be updated since 1994, and therefore a number of sites have moved. The author leaves no e-mail address for contact and additions. It

is still a very good place though to get a feel of what is out there and where it is located on the gophers and discussion groups.

Hollywood Online
URL: http://www.hollywood.com/
Rating: 4
Comments: This site lives up to its name, a glitzy flashy, graphically based movie site devoted to new releases. Hollywood Online is arguably *the* place to go to see multimedia promotional materials for current films out of Hollywood. The designers have come up with a logical interface that works in all modes and makes easy jumps between films, video clips, sounds, images, and the like. Each film section typically includes image clips (around 15), sound files, QuickTime movies, trailers, and production notes. The real treasures here, though, are the cool interactive press kits which are fun to download and navigate through. Caution: these are very big files averaging 1.5 megabytes! These multimedia interactive programs are for both Windows and Macintosh platforms and free for downloading. Although most of these files are also located at their respective studio sites, Hollywood Online allows for quick access to what you really want without having to jump through the multitude of hoops often found at their original locations. Check it out for total mainstream enjoyment.

Media-Link
URL: http://www.dds.nl/~kidon/media.html
Rating: 3
Comments: Here is a Dutch site in English, one of the few I have encountered in my film and video site reviews. It is part of a bigger site called "The Digital City" and contains information in Dutch and English about this site and related projects. An exciting media conference called "The Next 5 Minutes" is one of the announced activities. Relations with other digital cities, like the one in Berlin, is one of the interests explained in

the manifest here online. The Media-Link has newspapers, film, television, radio, and other related media links divided into section pages, and then by countries. Though there are other places like this on the Web, this one places small flags next to each country title, and the bent is definitely not slanted toward North America.

OMNIBUS-EYE
URL: http://www.rtvf.nwu.edu/
Rating: 4
Comments: Gigantic site hosting efforts by Northwestern University's R/TV/F Department including the !PIXIN(*)COMPENDIUM! Project, digital rag |T|E|L|E|C|I|N|E|, and the Chicago Moving Image Scene. But most people stop by this site to visit its huge Mega-Media Links Page with over 3,000 links. Many of the links are annotated with brief descriptions and these can also be searched. Definitely a site which will be growing, and growing, and growing, and...

Queer Media Resources
URL: http://abacus.oxy.edu/qrd/media/
Rating: 3
Comments: Queer theory is a fast growing and popular discipline in cultural studies for film theater, media, and other areas. This resource list is from the Queer Resources Directory, but unfortunately the interface is pretty primitive, and you just get up file names. It is definitely worth exploring though. There are articles, call for papers, film reviews, and related movie and sound files. A better interface would make this a gold mine of information.

RML's Movie Page
URL: http://netspace.net.au/~haze/
Rating: 3
Comments: RML Production company's page explains their motives like this: "The RML Movie Page is designed to cause you to waste lots of time finding out lots of useless facts about MOVIES... (and CINEMA for you purists)." It is really just an Australian based link page, though the links are good. My favorite link section is Magazines and Essays page. There is something for the browser, academic, or film student here.

SCREENSite
URL: http://www.sa.ua.edu/TCF/welcome.htm
Rating: 4
Comments: Launched in October of 1994 by Jeremy Butler, SCREENSite is *the* resource center for film and TV scholarship. There's an ever-growing archive of course syllabi, a massive e-mail listing of media scholars, up-to-date conference information, school listings, and the SCS job list. Designed for people with little Internet experience, this very helpful site gingerly guides you through its resources. Very comprehensive!

Take TWO
URL: http://www.webcom.com/~taketwo/
Rating: 2
Comments: Don't know if this site is even active any more since the last update was over six months ago. Still, once you get past the less-than-appealing front page, you'll find "some" information which is useful, like the decent listing of newsgroups—that is, if they are still around.

Television Pointers
URL: http://www.cs.cmu.edu/afs/cs.cmu.edu/user/clamen/misc/tv/README.html
Rating: 3
Comments: Clamen has a cinema page on the same site. See the review for that one for comparison. This is a link page with TV shows, lyrics for songs from television, production companies, links to FAQs and discussion lists, and more. For those with American television, there is an interesting link to the alt.tv.commercials USENET group. Check out the Sofasphere Project link for info on how we can manage with 500 channels in the future.

TV Net
URL: http://www.tvnet.com/
Rating: 4
Comments: TV Net bills itself as your starting point for television-related hot spots across cyberspace and worldwide and I think that's good advice. Very smart looking site with an amazing menu of items to choose from: huge listing of network and program sites, various chat areas, the "virtual agent," job listings, and large Internet directory of TV sites. Looking more and more slick and branching out like mad. Keep an eye on this site.

WebOvision
URL: http://www.catalog.com/cgibin/var/media/index.html
Rating: 4
Comments: WebOvision provides media links all over the world. This is a merging of lists of different link categories and may be chosen in a graphic or text version. It looks very comprehensive. Worth some serious browsing.

Yahoo Entertainment
URL: http://www.yahoo.com/Entertainment/
Rating: 4
Comments: The monster Internet directory. Zillions of entries. Searchable. Everything seems to be listed here. Essential bookmark. Period.

FILMS

Basketball Diaries
URL: http://underground.net/BDiaries/
Rating: 4
Comments: The official Web site for this movie with screening dates in many states, film clips, and much more. The story and photos are intriguing enough to get you to go see the film, which is the idea in the first place. Here is what the film is based on. "The unflinching and articulate story of a teenager's descent into drug addiction whetted the appetite of publishers and readers alike when excerpts from Jim Carroll's diaries first appeared in *The Paris Review* in the late 1960s." Jim Carroll served as consultant on the film and actually has a cameo role. This site features more about his person and sound bites with his spoken word from the book. Looks like a great film and an important one.

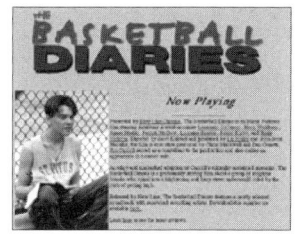

Batman Forever
URL: http://batmanforever.com/
Rating: 3
Comments: Even if you are not a *big* fan of the flying rodent man you may enjoy this fun site. Lots of commercial-type graphics (don't do it over a modem at less than 28.800). My telephone bill went up radically waiting for this to load. This place celebrates the release of the video and offers video clips and trailers in French or English.

Blade Runner
URL: http://kzsu.stanford.edu/uwi/br/off-world.html
Rating: 4
Comments: Since *Blade Runner* is on my Top Ten list of great films, I was excited about getting to this off-world.html. The site abounds in links on the Net, but has a lot of very good information right here, primarily their "Blade Runner File" and "Blade Runner References." Whether you want to grab some pictures of Sean Young, Harrison Ford, or Rutger Hauer, or do some research on the Net by reading articles published, this is the place. They even have their own online discussion board!

Bloodlust
URL: http://www.ozemail.com.au/~jswjon/
Rating: 4
Comments: Known as the only Australian film ever banned in Britain, *Bloodlust* is the subject of this home page. Read reviews of the film and download lewd images and movies from the film. But, of course, this site is really here to sell the film—on video now! You can even purchase a copy of the "Director's Special Edition" video which includes deleted scenes of "diabolical dismemberment and gruesome graverobbing." Pleasant.

Blues Brothers
URL: http://matahari.tamu.edu/bluesbrothers
Rating: 3
Comments: The Ultimate Blues Brothers Web Site has links galore for our wacky duo! Want a transcript of the movie, biography of Jake and Elwood, poster of Jake and Elwood, or trivia? This is the place. They also have a link to other Brother pages on the Web as well as alt.fan.blues-brothers USENET group. Black and White first page is cool. Some trivia—"Listen closely, each time after a number of police cars crash into a pile," someone says "They broke my watch."

Casablanca
URL: http://users.aol.com/VRV1/index.html
Rating: 4
Comments: Though this is a one-page presentation with some links and some photos, movies and the like, it somehow captures the

enthusiasm for the film in a very delightful way. Lines from the film, cast list, critical review of the film, the French poster, and even links to Morocco for learning more about the country make this one a beauty. "I came to Casablanca for the waters."

Cry the Beloved Country
URL: http://os2.iafrica.com/ve/cry_menu.htm
Rating: 4
Comments: This site presenting a film about an aging priest living in a Zulu village in South Africa has one of the most aesthetically pleasing designs I have seen in my years on the Web. The film is based on a novel by Alan Paton, which is critically acclaimed according to the site. *Sarafina!*, the film with Whoopi Goldberg, was directed by the same person, Darrell James Roodt. "Videovision Entertainment is a multifaceted entertainment business based in South Africa, with strong international relationships in production and distribution." This presentation has a lot of information of high quality and is minus the hype of a lot of commercial film sites.

Desperado
URL: http://cinemascape.comtecmedia.com/chris/desperado.html
Rating: 4
Comments: This is an unofficial DESPERADO/EL MARIACHI site, but well worth a visit. Graphics intensive, and intelligently structured, this is a product of pure love! The usual fare is present here, reviews, links, good pictures and information about Robert Rodriguez and his meteoric rise to fame as an independent filmmaker. Really well done.

Dr. No
URL: http://www.dur.ac.uk/~dcs3pjb/jb/drno.html
Rating: 2
Comments: Ian Fleming would have loved this one. This first movie started the whole thing rolling and turned Bond into one of the favorites of tongue-in-cheek spydom. A short synopsis of the film,

trivia, a little about the theme song composer, and links to other Bond places on the Net make this place short but sweet. Not graphics intensive, this can be easily used with a clunky 2,400 kbps modem! There is a picture gallery though with downloadable pictures, and you can get the whole Bond theme from the movie.

Dune
URL: http://www.princeton.edu/~cgilmore/dune/
Rating: 4
Comments: Boy, some of these *Dune* fans really get into the world of the story. This site is called "Museum Arrakeen" and hosts FAQs, a copy of the screenplay, quotes from cast and crew of the film, a *Dune* timeline and a gaming chamber with links to the Dune II *Mush*. Clean and detailed site which is obviously a passion for its maintainer, Christian Gilmore.

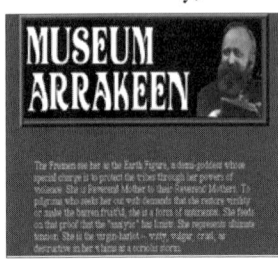

Fast Times at Ridgemont High
URL: http://wizvax.net/truegger/fast-times.html
Rating: 4
Comments: This is one of the most comprehensive sites about a single film that I have seen on the Web. There is a complete cast and film information section, excerpts from the novel and screenplay, an exam about the movie, alternative versions of the film, and reviews and press clippings. The images are of very good quality, even the ones digitalized from the video. Pretty cool, but graphically it isn't that slick.

Godfather Trilogy
URL: http://www.exit109.com/~jgeoff/godfathr.html
Rating: 3
Comments: This set of movies must have generated the most amount of critical written texts of any film of this century. Now there is even a Web site! The Christmas greeting was the following quote: "Have yourself a very happy holiday or I make you suffer! —Don Santa Corleone" Good quality graphic images are displayed, but not of the highest quality. A lot of trivia about where, how, and by whom things were done for the movie are listed, though not always in a very

structured and intuitive way. The sounds on these pages are *only* playable with Internet Wave, which is a proprietary player for Windows only. Mac browsers need not push any sound downloading buttons. It will just be a waste of time. In general, this is not a very well-designed site, but it has a lot of interesting info. You have to do a lot of browsing to pick up the gold nuggets, though.

Godzilla
URL: http://www.ama.caltech.edu/users/mrm/godzilla.html
Rating: 4
Comments: I just loved the Godzilla movies as a kid, and this was a flash from the past, to say the least. Enjoy the images, thrills, and cult quality of these Japanese monster movies in the privacy of your own home! The 22nd movie is on its way, according to this Web site. Not for the faint of heart. High ratings for its cult quality. Layout is so-so.

Hoop Dreams
URL: http://www.well.com/user/srhodes/hoopdreams.html
Rating: 2
Comments: Amazing how much is out on the Internet about this highly acclaimed documentary. This "unofficial" page is primarily all text and links (lots of 'em). Also info about the film's two subjects, William Gates and Arthur Agee. If you want to know more about this film or keep up with the careers of Gates and Agee, check this page out.

Indiana Jones
URL: http://dialin.ind.net/~msjohnso/
Rating: 3
Comments: The Indiana Jones fan has interviews, pictures, movies, sounds and more present on this site. Scripts for Raiders and Last Crusade reside here as well. Some of the more amusing parts present are the Spoof and Trivia section and the wonderful Ark Theories files. Did you know that the Ark is presently located at a church in Ethiopia? Find out how to get there and beat the Nazis to it!

Jeffrey
URL: http://www.digitopia.com/jeffrey/
Rating: 3
Comments: Jeffrey is a gay romantic comedy set in New York. This site covers production aspects of the film, film clips, and reviews and quotes about the film. This is a cheery site, and when reading the production notes, it turns out that the filmmakers tried to portray New York in a cheery, bright way, rather than our usual expectations of gritty, dirty, dark, and stinking (excuse me New Yorkers) urban landscape. Jeffrey is linked to another Orion production, that of *Bar Girls*, a lesbian romantic comedy. It is nice to see other portrayals of different kinds of people in the gay community. The stereotypes and token gay or lesbian is hopefully a thing of the past.

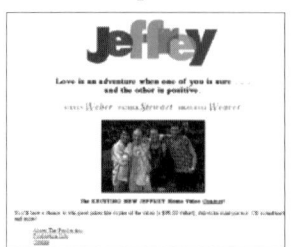

Leon
URL: http://www.ltm.com/dinan/leon/html/leon.html
Rating: 3
Comments: This 1994 film (a.k.a.: *The Professional*) by Luc Besson is well represented here with synopsis, credits (cast and technical), reviews, production notes, JPEG files and QuickTime movies. They have just begun placing sound clips from the movie online, so keep an eye out for further additions.

Lion King
URL: http://www.ugcs.caltech.edu/~btman/lionking/
Rating: 4
Comments: Mufasa, Simba, Nala, and Scar - they're all here on this absolutely stunning home page devoted to Walt Disney's animated blockbuster, *The Lion King*. Images, sounds, scripts and a lovely little storyboard combine for the next best thing to watching the film itself. A *Washington Times* article describes the site's cocreator: "Brian Tiemann at Cal Tech either needs to get a life, or he already has one. Simply put, he has devoted his existence to *The Lion King* (TLK to insiders)." And it shows. Prime WWW site.

Monty Python and the Holy Grail
URL:
http://cathouse.org/BritishComedy/MontyPython/HolyGrail/
Rating: 3
Comments: Scripts, pictures, and an illustrated script with small thumbnail pictures in the text is online here. The JPEG thumbnails can be expanded to large versions by clicking on them. As always, if you love Monte Python, you'll want to look at this.

Norwegian Films 1995
URL: http://www.dnfi.no/nf/nf-indx.html
Rating: 4
Comments: This is the electronic version of a brochure produced by the Norwegian Film Institute for upcoming films produced in 1995. I assume that films for 1996 will be used in the next version. Synopses of the films, production information, and release date give a head start on knowing what kind of material is used and made in Norway. Useful addresses are also included. Every national cinema should do this. Some of the material is even available in Postscript format for printing quality documents. Pictures are included in those film documents with an asterisk beside the title.

Phantasm
URL: http://www.phantasm.com/
Rating: 4
Comments: Enter the Tall Man's Mausoleum to find every item you could "die for" related to this highly successful series of cult films. FAQs, casts and credits, quotes, images and sound clips. Visit the Crypt Collectibles section for *Phantasm* memorabilia. Great looking and humorous site with quick-downloading images.

Psycho
URL: http://www.geopages.com/Hollywood/1645/
Rating: 4
Comments: You may be wary to take a shower again after visiting the *Psycho* home page. This site has *everything* about this classic Hitchcock film: heaps of downloaded articles critiquing the film, images, MPEG films (featuring no less than three examples from the

famous shower scene), sound clips including the opening credit music composed by Bernard Herrmann, and even a special Psycho 3D VRML space. Fun exploring here!

Rocky Horror Picture Show
URL: http://www.nforce.com/~rhps/
Rating: 4
Comments: "Let's Do the Time Warp Again!" By far the best of the *Rocky Horror* sites on the Internet with the huge "The Rocky Horror Picture Show Theater List" and various versions of the script (with and without audience participation). The links to other resources on the net is comprehensive and useful. This site is maintained by George Burgyan, cast member of the local *Rocky Horror Picture Show* in Cleveland, Ohio.

Sex, Drugs & Democracy
URL: http://www.cc.columbia.edu/~arb33/
Rating: 3
Comments: Using a quote from the *New York Times*, but spelling Newt's name wrong, this poster and headline reads "Newt Ginrich's Worst Nightmare." - Dave Kehn, *New York Times*

This site is dedicated to the film of the same name and describes the work: "The film takes an uncensored look at the unconventional approach to morality and politics in Holland." Dutch attitudes towards sex education in schools, legalized drugs, sexuality in general, and political radicalism are portrayed in a film with a supposedly great soundtrack by Dutch and American bands. Black and white photos from the color film are presented to give you an idea of some scenes. An alternative film site and nicely portrayed, though one wishes for more critical info from both sides of the ocean. Here is a quote from the movie: "The Amsterdam police had a beautiful ad in a gay publication. They said, 'We like young men as much as you like them!'"— Dr. G. Hekma, Prof. of Gay Studies, Univ. of Amsterdam

Star Wars
URL: http://www.princeton.edu/~nieder/sw/sw.html
Rating: 4

Comments: With over twenty new *Star Wars* home pages being launched every month, this major directory of links serves an obvious and welcomed function. This neatly designed directory is divided into New Links, Information Sites & FAQs, Company & Merchandise Sites, Thematic & Character Specific Sites, Games, Entertainment, and Collecting Sites, Pictures & other Multimedia, and finally Miscellaneous Sites. If it's *Star Wars*- related and on the Internet, you'll find it here.

TRON
URL: http://www.aquila.com/guy.gordon/tron/tron.htm
Rating: 3
Comments: One of the first of the slew of cyberpunk films, because of its fantastic premise of being alive and miniaturized inside a computer, this site is a homage to the film. Video clips, sounds, PC arcade game, trading cards, and more are here for the clicking. All images are in JPEG format and original black and white press kit photos are also available. This is high on imagery but low on background and production info.

IMAGES

Dystopian Visions Image Galleries
URL: http://underground.net/~koganuts/Galleries/
Rating: 4
Comments: "Now Showing (Off)" is the opening line here! Featuring a really great logo that takes a fast connection and time to download, this site presents images galore of actors and actresses from various films and series related to *Star Trek*, *Star Wars*, John Woo films, and Quentin Tarantino. There are some very nice scanned sketches by animators in the industry, production stills and info for the films listed, and is a generally cool site for images. Well done, but oh so slow in loading!

Hollywood Sign Live
URL: http://www.rfx.com:80/hollywood/index.html
Rating: 2
Comments: This page takes a picture of the famous Hollywood sign at regular intervals. Fun the first time, silly after that. I often use it to see what the weather is like in Los Angeles or how bad the smog is that day.

Hong Kong Movies Picture Library
URL: http://kaarna.cc.jyu.fi/~tjko/hkmpl/
Rating: 4
Comments: This Finnish site devoted to the likes of John Woo, Jackie Chan, and Chow Yun Fat offers JPEG pictures of excellent quality, links to other Hong Kong film resources, and biographies for actors, directors, and synopses of films. This is a nice resource for a marginal but increasingly popular national cinema. Remember that Hong Kong cinema is not just action and choreographed violence. There is a lot more beneath the surface.

Image Finder
URL: http://arachnid.cs.cf.ac.uk/Misc/wustl.html
Rating: 3
Comments: The Image Finder is a searchable database of pictures. This particular address is the UK mirror site. Many of the categories deal with movies and cartoons, but there are many other types as well. I did a combo search for Movies, People, Art, and came up with only one, a quite okay original color drawing of Humphrey Bogart. The screen grabs of films were not as high quality though.

Movie Poster Web Page
URL: http://www.musicman.com/mp/mp.html
Rating: 4
Comments: This must be one of the ugliest Web pages with a huge bank of buttons staring straight at you when you arrive but it also has some of the best content available: Movie Posters! Lots of them. Each poster has a downloadable image, description, dimensions, and condition rating. You can even buy the real paper-based thing if you want to. And they even offer a "movie poster encapsulation service" for preserving your own poster collection. Good stuff here!

Spanish Movie Flyers
URL: http://eliza.netaxis.com/~cbird/spain/spantext.html
Rating: 2
Comments: While visiting Spain in April of 1995, CBird acquired a collection of film advertisements from the 1960s and 70s. He has scanned them and made them ready for downloading in JPEG format. Thumbnails of them appear on the page. My favorite is El Panuelo Asesino (The Murdering Handkerchief).

Three Colors - Pictures
URL: http://www.mty.itesm.mx/~dch/centros/cinema16/tres_colores/texto/tres_colores.html
Rating: 2
Comments: Beautiful scans from Krzysztof Kieslowski's *Three Colors* film trilogy. Well presented and organized from the Cinema 16 club in Monterrey, Mexico.

Twin Peaks Pictures
URL: http://www.uaep.co.uk/pages/tpph1.html
Rating: 3
Comments: Twin Peak stills from UK TV channel, Bravo. Most images are available in either GIF or JPEG formats as well as in high- or low-resolution. And can I have a piece of the apple pie, please?

MAGAZINES & JOURNALS

Biz
URL: http://www.bizmag.com/
Rating: 4
Comments: The entertainment industry now has an e-zine as flashy as anything in print. Nice layout, interesting articles and lists like "The Top 10 Lawyers Working in the Film Industry." A number of movie trailers and tongue-in-cheek comments about them are some of the fun things you can latch onto here. Good source for hard facts, news, gossip, and details about industry players.

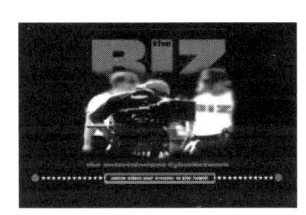

Bright Lights Film Journal
URL: http://www.crl.com/~gsamuel/bright.html
Rating: 4
Comments: This journal has a few of its articles online, and just enough to make you want to buy the paper version. I plan to subscribe after checking out the latest issue on superstars in the horror genre, one of my research areas. Good-looking, interesting articles, and people that do this magazine for the love of it on the side of their day jobs. There are book reviews, film links, and all the things you want in a specialized magazine. Definitely worth a look!

Buzz
URL: http://www.buzzmag.com/
Rating: 4
Comments: *Buzz* is a media magazine about Los Angeles. It costs 15 bucks, or just read it free here. If you are going to LA to hawk your script or to get cast in the latest Burton flick, read this to find out where to be seen and not to be seen. Find out who or what is cool for the next five minutes.

CONNECT Magazine
URL: http://www.connectmag.com/connect/
Rating: 4
Comments: This is India's first online magazine in the entertainment industry. Since it can be difficult to find information on entertainment produced in India, this is a wonderful source for starting out. I found this e-zine very entertaining and international, with an Indian perspective on the issues presented. Make the world smaller. Read *Connect*.

Cosmic Landscapes: Film & Video Review
URL: http://users.aol.com/cosmicland/cl1.htm
Rating: 3
Comments: "News, Reviews and Commentary of Hollywood and the Film Industry." Originally this started out as a Star Wars-Star Trek-Sci-Fi 'zine 10 years ago, but grew into an electronic version that was based on the general film industry. For one dollar, you can receive all issues for one year, up to about 52 of them, since they say the Web site is updated every week. Top stories, recent reviews, blockbusters and other articles abound. All the articles and reviews are pretty short, but cover current happenings, and may be interesting for that reason.

Critical Inquiry
URL: http://www.uchicago.edu:80/u.scholarly/CritInq/
Rating: 3
Comments: Top scholarly journal goes digital—almost. Here you'll find searchable excerpts and table of contents from past and present issues. Cover images as well. Fun to check out back issues and future articles.

CTHEORY
URL: http://www.freedonia.com/ctheory/
Rating: 4
Comments: "*CTHEORY* is an international, electronic review of books on theory, technology and culture" and is one of the foremost critical journals on the Net. Edited by Arthur and Marilouise Kroker, this review features writings by such luminaries as Jean Baudrillard, Paul Virilio and Kathy Acker. Many of the articles contain hyperlinked footnotes and e-mail addresses to the authors. Louise Wilson's "Cyberwar, God And Television: Interview with Paul Virilio" has already become essential reading in techno-culture.

Dis 'n' Dat Newsletter
URL: ftp://ftp.wang.com/pub/lar3ry/dnd/dnd-HOME.html
Rating: 2
Comments: The top of this home page on fictional news about the Disney empire reads "All Disney news fitted to print." Larry Gensch satirizes the Disney community and business world, as well as referring

to things in the USENET group—rec.arts.disney If you are Disney savvy or curious, take a look. Larry says, "The actual story behind its starting is just about apocryphal nowadays. So instead, I'll use the truthful story that I like to do parody, and that I felt that Disney is a good enough target."

Entertainment Weekly
URL: http://pathfinder.com/ew/
Rating: 4
Comments: This magazine is interconnected with the Pathfinder Movie Reviews, but offers articles on popular stars, TV shows, cultural heroes, and more. Lots of good-looking graphics. High cholesterol, low fiber *Entertainment Weekly* is just entertainment, but can be a fun read at times without shelling out for the paper version.

Fade In
URL: http://www.best.com/~market/fadein/
Rating: 3
Comments: This paper magazine has some of the material online in full text as a come-on to buy the real thing. If you are a struggling screenwriter, you might want to subscribe, but I would prefer to check this out on the Web and keep in tune with other industry organs.

Federal Communications Law Journal
URL: http://www.law.indiana.edu/fclj/fclj.html
Rating: 4
Comments: The Indiana University School of Law at Bloomington's legal journal is now online providing access to past issues containing both articles and notes in a fully hypertext format. Best feature is the ability to conduct full-text searches of the journal.

Film International
URL: http://gpg.com/film/
Rating: 3
Comments: Film International, a Cross Cultural Review, is a quarterly magazine that has a cyberversion in the English and Persian languages. Based in Teheran, it also has offices in the US, Dubai, UK, and France. The focus of concentration is Iranian filmmaking, but viewed in an international context. Iranian film entries in screenings and festivals in places like Bosnia-Herzegovina and Japan are reviewed and listed. In the issue I read, the first Iranian modern music video was released!

Filmmaker Magazine
URL: http://found.cs.nyu.edu/CAT/affiliates/filmmaker/filmmaker.html
Rating: 4
Comments: This magazine of independent film has a very nice layout but takes awhile to load. A few of the articles are downloadable from the Internet, but most things must be read in the paper version. There is also a resource guide with links for filmmakers to other sources on the WWW. The articles range from lighting history to Terry Zwigoff's "Crumb."

fps: The Magazine of Animation on Film and Video
URL: http://www.cam.org/~pawn/fps.html
Rating: 3
Comments: fps is a journal on animation. As they say themselves, "we cover Japanese animation, cutout animation, big-budget commercial productions, independent works, the old, the new, the famous, the infamous, the obscure." There were some very interesting articles on anime, Japanese animation, in a few of the issues. Guidelines for submitting material and favorite sites for animation on the Web are present here. This gets a plus for the full-text articles. Not many graphics, but tasteful use of them.

GLAAD Newsletter
URL: http://www.digitopia.com/glaad/news/news-index.html
Rating: 4
Comments: Gay & Lesbian Alliance Against Defamation is the whole name for this acronym. The Media awards presented by the organization "honor and congratulate those individuals and programs in the media and entertainment industries for their inclusive and accurate representations of lesbians, bisexuals and gay men and the issues which affect our lives." One of the 1995 awards went to FRIENDS. Here is the excerpt: Outstanding Television Comedy Series—Friends.

This refreshing series, from the creators of 'Dream On,' includes among its cast a lesbian mother-to-be, her girlfriend and the baby's father, a situation providing much comic fodder and food for thought." There is a Media Alert and Media Contacts section for aiding people in reaching the right people in charge while practicing media activism. This is a good resource for the gay/lesbian community and anyone interested in gay and lesbian issues.

HotWired
URL: http://www.hotwired.com/
Rating: 4
Comments: *HotWired* is the online version of the hip computer culture rag, *Wired*. Great feature articles, movie reviews, an online mall, and a number of online chat groups. This is a must visit for anyone cruising the net these days. Unfortunately, registration is required (free, but a bit of a hassle).

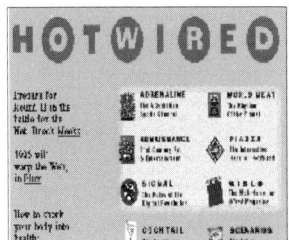

Inquisitor Magazine
URL: http://www.inquisitor.com/
Rating: 4
Comments: "*Inquisitor* is the logical end result of the 'soupification' of various media, art, culture, and technology." This is the description by the magazine's Web pages. Covering artistic projects on the Net, technology and aesthetics, and similar issues, this magazine has some short but rather good articles for use in academic research or artistic investigation. For fun, you can get episode breakdowns, in detail, of 90210 at the 90210 Weekly Wrapup, by Daniel Drennan. Neither subtle nor PC, these are rather funny to read. There are the usual links at alternative Mediarama, but these are rather unusual! This is one of the better offbeat, but not too bizarre spots.

Journal of Norwegian Media Research
URL: http://macmedia19.uio.no/Prosjekt/nmt/index.english.html
Rating: 3
Comments: The Institute for Media Research at the University of Oslo has a very interesting Web site, and graphically well designed. In both English and Norwegian, the site features a number of projects, articles, and information about the people behind them. Some of the Hyperfoto projects are very interesting, and probably controversial by US standards. Take a look at Jan Stenmark's. This particular section of the site features the journal articles and authors with abstracts in English, but with the articles all online. This is the way all journals should be presented online, though it could use some more pictures or illustrations with the author presentations and abstracts. Unfortunately, it seems that only issue number 1/94 is in the directory.

KINEMA
URL: http://arts.uwaterloo.ca/FINE/juhde/kinemahp.htm
Rating: 4
Comments: *KINEMA*, a Journal of History, Theory and Aesthetics of Film and Audiovisual Media, is published at the University of Waterloo, Ontario, Canada. The few feature articles with full text seem interesting enough to make this a good addition to academic hotlists. Subscription info for the hard copy version is listed here too. Some of the articles listed were on Asian Cinema, Sexual Antagonism in Early Bergman, and an Interview with Akira Kurosawa. A quality journal, but would be better if one could read everything online. That would probably not stop everyone from buying it but rather encourage one to have the glossy version. Good content, but low on flash.

London Calling
URL: http://www.demon.co.uk/london-calling/filmmus.html
Rating: 4
Comments: London calling is a what-is-happening zine for that great cinema city. News about screenings, like the restored version of *Pandora's Box*, new video releases in Britain, and competitions, make this a welcome site for European users. Since the availability of PAL video titles is rather hard to keep track of, it is important to have a clearinghouse for some of this information. Other than film magazines, like *Sight and Sound*, this seems to be one of the few European video listings sources I have seen.

Media 3
URL: http://www.deakin.edu.au/arts/VPMA/Media3.html
Rating: 3
Comments: Well, these Aussies have a sense of humor with a slogan like "Media Talk and Analysis from the Arse End of Cyberspace"! Peter Greenaway is the WebMaster, and presumably not the famous one. This site is for students, professionals, teachers, and other interested parties by the third year and postgraduate students in

Media Arts at Deakin University in Victoria, Australia. One of the students, Paul Boswell, has a nicely done mangamania site devoted to Japanese animation. Though the text is very dense, the content is fine. Another article in this particular issue is Katrina Dale's "Women in Comics." This time the text was easily read and had a pleasant layout. The texts are very short and feature links to other related sites. Nice try by some students, with a pretty varied editorial content.

Media Magazine
URL: http://www.adelaide.edu.au/5UV/MM/
Rating: 2
Comments: Like the Australian Broadcasting site, this one is committed to public service. "*Media Magazine* is Australia's National Community Radio Program on media and communications. *Media Magazine* is committed to providing information, analysis and entertainment to those who are often marginalised in these debates—the community." This site is not finished yet but intends to feature links, articles, and sound bites. Some sound bites are available now. Looks good when there is more on offer. This is just a presentation at the moment.

Mediamatic
URL: http://www.mediamatic.nl/Magazine/
Rating: 4
Comments: Hip online media rag from the Netherlands. Excellent hypertext articles on new media and technoculture.

Millennium Film Journal
URL: http://www.sva.edu/MFJ/
Rating: 3
Comments: Since 1978, *Millennium Film Journal* has published engaging articles and dialogues revolving around independent cinema and the avant-garde. Now they are online with table of contents for every past issue as well as some fully digitized articles in the more recent issues. Let's hope they continue integrating their fine journal into cyberspace.

Postmodern Culture
URL: http://jefferson.village.virginia.edu/pmc/contents.all.html
Rating: 4
Comments: This is my favorite e-journal, and one I have used for several years. Great reviews, interesting articles, discussion list, chat areas, a MOO, and distribution free over the Net make it one of the premium sites for intellectual discussion related to the sometimes elusive "postmodernism." My favorite essay is a comparison of *Terminator 2* and *Blue Velvet* by Fred Pfeil. This e-journal is published by North Carolina State University, Oxford University Press, and the University of Virginia's Institute for Advanced Technology in the Humanities. Originally available only by e-mail, the Web presentation makes the material easier to find and use. If I could give it a 5, I would!

Premiere
URL: http://www.premieremag.com/
Rating: 4
Comments: Online presence for leading entertainment magazine. Slick, concise, and snazzy. Entire texts of many feature articles. Be sure to pop into the chat area, appropriately called "Schmoozing!" I think this is even better than their paper-product version at the newsstand!

|T|E|L|E|C|I|N|E|
URL: http://omnibus-eye.rtvf.nwu.edu/telecine/
Rating: 4
Comments: T|E|L|E|C|I|N|E is The Journal of New Media Authoring in the Digital Domain out of Northwestern University with excellent essays by such scholars as Robert Scholes and Chuck Kleinhans. Great feature of this electronic journal is that the essays themselves are typically housed elsewhere, like on the author's home page. Oddly presented layout (with too much text) shouldn't distract from its engaging content.

Time Out
URL: http://www.timeout.co.uk./
Rating: 4
Comments: One of London's top entertainment guides is now online providing up-to-date info about events and happenings in many of the world's major cities. Click on the world map and get ready to search for cool cafes or find out what film events are occurring. Registration is required, but easy.

TV Guide
URL: http://www.delphi.com/tvgo/
Rating: 4
Comments: This is the online version as a digital backup to the revered granddaddy of TV program listings in the US. Hated by some, but bought by millions, this best-selling magazine offers previews, reviews, new shows, pictures, digital clips, and sometimes information about the old, lost, obscure, and cult shows of the past. There is a special section on "Returning Favorites." Day-to-day listings for the current season are online now. If you watch TV in the US, surf to this site. As a cross-listing, you might look at Cosmo's TV Guide site which pays homage to *TV Guide*! It is also reviewed in this book.

Videomaker Magazine
URL: http://www.videomaker.com/
Rating: 4
Comments: *The Videomaker Magazine* site is more than just a place to sell their published rag. Along with almost totally digitized versions of their magazine are sections for classifieds, professional forums, events, and offered products. The "Fundamentals of Video" section contains helpful FAQs and glossaries. Also available for immediate downloading is a decent collection of videomaking goodies. Chunky, but useful WWW site.

Weltwunder der Kinematographie
URL: http://www.snafu.de/~dgfk/WDK_Iverz.html
Rating: 3
Comments: Because some scholars do speak German, French and Spanish, this German language journal seems to be a good access for reading what is going on in critical circles for film and related digital techniques. Film technique is the major interest.

MEMORABILIA

Addresses of the Rich and Famous
URL: http://www.infohaus.com/access/by-seller/Addresses_of_the_Rich_Famous
Rating: 2
Comments: For only $9.99, you, too, can get an address list of the rich and famous without having to drive up and down the streets of Hollywood! This page reminds you that "Stars love to acknowledge their fans with notes, photos, and personalized autographs! This list is an invaluable tool for anyone who loves celebrities of any type." It's your money, I guess.

Aspen Moon Grafika (Polish Posters)
URL: http://www.mjwebworks.com/webworks/amg/
Rating: 3
Comments: Talk about an odd site! As the front page announces, "We're here to provide you the easiest access to one of the world's largest collections of Polish poster art dating from the 1940s thru the

Memorabilia

1980s." Oh, and each poster is for sale as well (most costing over $100). With a large portion of those posters being of the movie variety, there's plenty of great images to feast your eyes upon.

C*stars Cinemagic Art
URL: http://www.3i.com/cstars/cinemagic/cinemagic_top.html
Rating: 1
Comments: Buy a variety of film memorabilia via the Internet! At the moment I looked, there were no animation posters for sale, two classic lobby cards, two western lobby cards, and one lobby card from *Forbidden Planet* for $150. E-mail contacts for selling and buying are on the page. The movie poster information was interesting, but why none for sale?

CBS Store Online
URL: http://www.cbs.com/blackrock/store.html
Rating: 2
Comments: Can't find that "Late Show With David Letterman" T-shirt at the local dry goods store? Is Sears out of CBS Sports Golf Caps? Well then get on over here to the virtual store and stock up. Just a few items on tap and prices are listed, but there will surely be more.

Hollywood Shopping Network
URL: http://www.hollywoodnetwork.com:80/hn/shopping/index.html
Rating: 2
Comments: The Hollywood Shopping Network is a huge site full of various Hollywood-related products sellers, software vendors, and dead links. Eager to try out their interactive sections, I entered the Price Is Right chat lounge only to find information on where to write for show tickets and publicity photos! There is some good stuff here, if you can find it. My personal favorite product to buy here is the authentic "Cop Cap" for $19.95. Keep working at it, guys!

109

Hollywood Toy and Poster Company
URL: http://www.hollywdposter.mb.ca/hollywdposter/
Rating: 3
Comments: This site housed in Canada, not Hollywood, is a very extensive place for purchasing movie-related memorabilia. Their movie poster photo gallery contains images of over 50 films and there's even a form to search the company's entire holdings. Also on sale is a large selection of Star Wars merchandise (including the Hamilton Collection series of 8 plates entitled "Space Vehicles of Star Wars"). If you are in the market for movie stuff, then this online catalog will be of help.

Iconographics: Movie Poster Gallery
URL: http://www.newmexico.com/icon/
Rating: 3
Comments: Massive collection of movie posters for sale here. Although the catalog merely lists the available posters in text form, the gallery currently features over 50 JPEG images of posters ready for your downloading pleasure. Online ordering for your convenience. An attractive and functional commercial site.

Jess and Carl's Theater Posters
URL: http://www.atw.fullfeed.com/~huster/
Rating: 2
Comments: Carl and Jess are husband and wife. Find out why they sell film posters over the Net. There are nice JPEG images of the posters for viewing. This is just a sideline for two electrical engineers, so you know they are not just in it for the money. Take a look. Some nice posters, otherwise this is not on the cutting edge.

Memorabilia

Movie Madness
URL: http://www.moviemadness.com/
Rating: 2
Comments: Tons of movie and TV-related merchandise on sale here with online ordering. Autographs, posters, scripts—you name it. When I entered the site, the one minute "movie" which the pages trap you in malfunctioned, so I went and made some coffee while they kept loading up graphics of "coming attractions." More like WebPage Madness!

Movie Poster Warehouse
URL: http://www.io.org/~mpw/
Rating: 2
Comments: When I logged on to this site, I was expecting to see some cool images of movie posters. But amazingly, I couldn't find *any*. I did find a very ugly welcoming page and countless decade-by-decade lists of their poster stock with prices. One of the only images I could find was a map to their store—in Toronto! And why is the "server stats" button at the top of the page???

Nightmare Factory
URL: http://www.io.com/~nightime/trek.html
Rating: 2
Comments: Attention Trekkies: here is a WWW site offering "quality, official, Star Trek Uniforms, masks, and accessories!" No more searching for those hard-to-find Next Generation uniforms ($45). Typical catalog page with images of their goods and online ordering. Bonus: one link to another Star Trek Web site.

Warner Bros. Studio Stores
URL: http://batmanforever.com/welcome/stores.html
Rating: 1
Comments: As a sideline of the Batman Forever site, there is a listing of a few products available at the Warner Bros. Studio Stores. How about the "Batman Forever" baseball cap featuring the printed movie logo? Or what about Riddler boxer shorts? You can't buy these

online; just look at some pictures and check prices, but there is a good listing of stores in the US and internationally. Low content—why is there not a whole listing of products available?

MOVIE THEATERS

Amsterdam Film Guide
URL: http://www.dds.nl/~filmhuis/ladder.htm
Rating: 3
Comments: Practice up on your Dutch. The times and titles for films playing in Amsterdam are only a mouseclick away. There are hyperlinks to some reviews of the films which are accompanied by a high quality black and white production still. The links page has the usual two or three big international sites, but also a couple of Dutch sites of importance for distribution of film and a database of reviews. This is a pleasantly designed site with very little in the way of graphics.

Atlanta WWW Movie Guide
URL: http://www.echonyc.com/~mvidal/atlanta-movies.html
Rating: 3
Comments: This is just one more listings calendar for movie theaters, this time in Atlanta, Georgia. It does give you the offbeat and independent theaters, art houses, and less than mainstream areas as well as the totally commercial offerings. Seems like a good bet for Atlanta.

Berlin Cinema Guide
URL: http://www.netcs.com/Kino/
Rating: 3
Comments: One of the first decent cinema guides on the WWW, this one from Germany, allows you to see what's playing by way of film title, day of the week, undubbed movies, and even Berlin neighborhood. This site looks very low-tech now and could use some serious design updating. Still, a gold medal for blazing the trail and still existing! In German.

BigScreen Cinema Guide
URL: http://www.execpc.com/~sjentsch/cinema/PCG.html
Rating: 2
Comments: "Your hypertext guide to what's playing in the movie theaters." Well, that is exactly what they deliver too, but only for the Milwaukee, Wisconsin, area. The guide for the movies and theaters is good, but don't bother with any link areas. The major comprehensive lists are much better and worth the time.

Boston Local Movie Listings
URL: http://www.actwin.com/movies/index.html
Rating: 3
Comments: This listing is for independent and nonprofit cinemas in the Boston area, northern suburbs, and some up in southern New Hampshire. A good but very local resource. The database for theaters, dates, and movies seems very good and is easy to search. No graphic interface to speak of, but this is still a good one.

CINEASC - UK Internet Film Guide
URL: http://www.gold.net/users/ae37/cineasc/index.html
Rating: 3
Comments: Smart, imageless guide to film screenings throughout the UK. First select a region, then browse by film title or venue. Amazingly up-to-date and useful. Not a pretty site, just pure functionality. Quick and easy to navigate.

Dublin Cinema Guide
URL: http://www.maths.tcd.ie/pub/films/dublin_cinemas.html
Rating: 2
Comments: Clean and basic movie guide to what's playing on Dublin screens. Fairly limited navigability, with only current day's films displayed by theater. Each film is linked to the Internet Movie Database as well. One frill, though: this site keeps track of how many weeks each movie has been playing. Updated daily.

Hawaii Movie Page
URL: http://aloha.com/~ia/wallace.html
Rating: 2
Comments: An unofficial listing of current shows at the Wallace Theatres in Hawaii. Some QuickTime trailers are available. Good if you live in Hawaii, otherwise.

Los Angeles Webstation Online Movie Guide
URL: http://198.147.111.7/movies/
Rating: 4
Comments: Complete Los Angeles movie listings of current films. Also contains movies on TV for the current and following weeks, and current and future video releases. The currently playing movies also have connections to reviews and to the Internet Movie Database. Quite a number of reviews are available on the site, signed by Scott Renshaw. Renshaw does intelligent and entertaining reviews showing a knowledge of film history and production not present in the average newspaper review. There is even a small section for foreign and revival movies. A rich spot for the LA moviegoer, or people wanting to check out the flick before it gets to their hometown. Don't miss the studio link page for new releases.

Manchester Cinemas
URL: http://www.U-net.com/manchester/cinemas/home.html
Rating: 2
Comments: Handy listing of movie theaters in Manchester, England, with addresses and phone numbers as well as current movie times. This site additionally contributes its Web pages to the online CINEASC UK Internet Film Guide, also reviewed in this book. Nothing fancy, but worth a quick visit to see what films folks are watching in Manchester.

Movie Theaters

Metro Movie Guide (Halifax-Canada)
URL: http://www.isisnet.com/mm/movieguide/
Rating: 4
Comments: Folks up in Halifax, Canada, are really lucky to have this site serving up movie times for the area's six cinemas. Each theater's film page has screening times as well as links to other sites connected to the film. The explanation of movie classifications and movie hot links pages are also well presented. Extra points for inclusion of local reviews.

Movie Link
URL: http://www.movielink.com/
Rating: 4
Comments: Seems like only a couple of years ago when people were jumping up and down about being able to order movie tickets from little electronic teller machines outside of the theaters. Now, you can get your tickets over the Internet. Clickable maps get you to your neighborhood to see exactly what's playing at the local cinema. Pick a film, click on your preferred time, and order your tickets (with correct admission amount) via an online form. Updated every hour. Too cool.

Movienet (Goldwyn/Landmark Theaters)
URL: http://www.movienet.com/
Rating: 2
Comments: Movie times and infobase for the Goldwyn/Landmark Theaters in North America. The Film Finder's Buzz is a section providing gossip about the industry, and there is a mailing list for finding about what will be playing at this theater chain. This site is okay, and the Buzz section might be interesting in the long run, but I found it only mildly amusing since I couldn't go to any of the shows!

Movietimes.com
URL: http://www.movietimes.com/
Rating: 3
Comments: Movie guide for the San Francisco bay area is pretty basic with text–only listings by neighborhood. Check out the "Classic Theatre Series" section featuring a wonderful photo essay by Marcie Richie. There are plans to load up more files in Adobe Acrobat Reader format in the future, which will be nice.

Mr. Woof's Drive-In Theater Information
URL: http://www.wInternet.com/~mrwoof/driveman.html
Rating: 3
Comments: A bizarre and entertaining place on the Net. A page devoted to that icon of 1950s American film culture: the Drive-In. The page reminds us how "there is nothing quite like the experience of enjoying a movie from the comfort of your own vehicle or supplemental lawn chair." Check out the listing of Midwest Drive-Ins under "Ticket Booth" or view kitschy photos of food under "Concession Stand." But for the truly adventurous, click on "Intermission" and view eleven different projected intermission messages. Gosh, it's *almost* like the real thing! But why???

Nederlands Filmmuseum
URL: http://shaman.dds.nl/~nfm/index.html
Rating: 3
Comments: This Dutch film museum's Web pages have some information on screenings and location in English but most of the text is in Dutch. This lovely museum, which I have visited in person, is located in a fantastic building in Vondel Park, Amsterdam. It is a great place to visit in person. The screenings and film club are of very high class, and there are projects for visiting artists. The Web page is a place to get preliminary information about times and programs. The Dutch version also features cinema lists for Amsterdam which has a fantastic restored art deco cinema and some very good alternative ones. This site could use some more information about Dutch filmmakers and film in Holland.

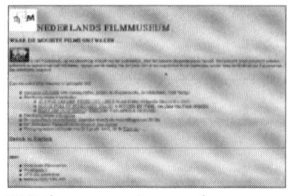

Rocky Horror Theater List
URL: http://www.cis.ohio-State.edu/hypertext/faq/usenet/movies/rocky-horrortheatres/faq.html
Rating: 2
Comments: What must be the cult movie of all time has its own Web site to show which theaters around the US are showing our favorite movie, some of them with a cast of their own on stage. Prices, locations, and the like are in this FAQ text document, last updated in 1994.

Toronto Movie Guide
URL: http://www.hype.com/toronto/movies/home.htm
Rating: 4
Comments: This site is a regular feature of the HYPE! Toronto City Guide and offers very extensive details about what's playing on Toronto's cinema screens. You can access this information through film titles or film house (with wonderful graphical map) and even read their mini-reviews of the movies. Use their "online usher" to search titles, cinemas, or show times.

Vancouver Movie Listings
URL: http://www.iceonline.com/icedocs/resources/icemovie.html
Rating: 2
Comments: ICE Online's movie listing for Vancouver allows you to browse through film titles and venues. Nothing very fancy here except up-to-date movie times and locations. ICE Online also maintains cinema schedules for Victoria, Canada.

MOVIES

Comedy Central Flicks
URL: http://www.comcentral.com/loads.htm
Rating: 3
Comments: You can find a number of QuickTime movies for downloading at this site run by Comedy Central. The caption at arrival is "Fill up your hard drive." Everything from Benny Hill to Madonna on "Saturday Night Live". Seventeen clips were present on my visit. You will have to decide yourself if you think Howard Stern for governor is funny or frightening.

Movies on the Net
URL: http://www.el-dorado.ca.us/~homeport/Internet_movies.html
Rating: 3
Comments: This is a large collection of digitalized movie clips that can be downloaded and shown on your personal computer. They are listed in QuickTime or Windows format. There are music videos, film clips, classical concerts, and just an eclectic grab bag of stuff here. The largest file was about 12 megabytes, but there were many smaller ones too.

MPEG Movie Archive
URL: http://w3.eeb.ele.tue.nl/mpeg/index.html
Rating: 3
Comments: This is the first time I have ever seen a site with a disclaimer. "I, the individual downloading a movie, promise to delete the downloaded MPEG-movie after two weeks from my harddisk. The maintainers of this site do not accept any responsibility for persons not obeying this rule. If you do not agree, please leave without downloading anything." Everything from "Simpsons" to Schwarzenegger resides here. MPEG requires certain types of software, and these are available via links on the home page. The content of the few movies I downloaded to test were okay, though not as good as QuickTime. On the other side of the coin, I didn't find the content very interesting.

MTV Animation
URL: http://www.mtv.com/animation/
Rating: 4
Comments: The Maxx, Beavis & Butt-head, Aeon Flux, and The Head are featured in this section of MTV's site on the Web. View the high quality images, listen to the sounds, and check out the digital movies. After you have done that, try to make sense of it all with the episode synopses. Who would expect less from MTV? The Brady Bunch with Beavis and Butt-head video clip is a killer.

News Reels Archive
URL: http://192.253.114.31/D-Day/News_reels/News_reels_contents.html
Rating: 3
Comments: World War II MPEG or QuickTime movies concentrating on D-Day are available from this server located in Stuttgart, Germany, at the Patch American High School at the United States European Command. Some of the other movies available deal with Harry Truman and the atomic bomb, Adolph Hitler, and V1 attacks on London. A new ftp server available has more movies and photos available.

!PIXIN(*)COMPENDIUM! Project
URL: http://omnibus-eye.rtvf.nwu.edu/compendium/
Rating: 4
Comments: A dynamic journal-style collection of "transpixins" (or digital Internet movies) out of Northwestern University featuring works from around the world. Most of the flicks are hefty (around 5MB), but you can also find a few charmers with less downloading time. I especially like Volume 2 and John Brattin's "Fat Heart Video." So far they are managing about two volumes a year, but expect that to expand soon.

webdog's Movies
URL: http://www.webdog.com/movies.html
Rating: 4
Comments: QuickTime movies, QuickTime movies, and more QuickTime movies. Little ones (40k) and big ones (4.5 MB). Feature film clips and TV cartoon clips. New movies added often. Good boy, webdog, good boy...

NEW MEDIA

Adobe Systems
URL: http://www.adobe.com/
Rating: 4
Comments: Since Adobe is one of the leading software producers in the world and most famous for its Postscript typefaces, one expects a high standard of presentation. Well, you get it too. There is free software, tips on using their variety of products, and press releases. This is well worth the visit. Learn more about what you can do with Photoshop, PageMill, and all the other things here. You need about a full day to go through this one! I downloaded a fantastic tip on using Photoshop as a QuickTime movie. Great resource.

Apple Computers
URL: http://www.apple.com/
Rating: 4
Comments: Apple's main Web page highlights products and support, developer services, technology and research, outside resources, and special communities, like the Apple Education Program. You can check out the latest developments and new releases before your local Apple rep gets them in, and of course you may download certain demos and free software. Well designed and implemented.

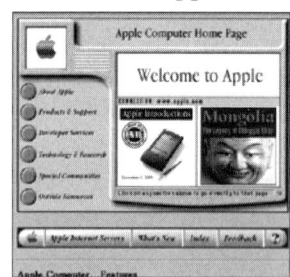

Apple Multimedia Program
URL: http://www.amp.apple.com/
Rating: 4
Comments: Apple has always had a reputation for R&D, design and content. This multimedia program may be just what you are looking for if you want to get into new media development. Join here to develop for Apple software, some of which is multiplatform, like QuickTime. Great looking Web site with content.

Digital Planet
URL: http://www.digiplanet.com/
Rating: 3
Comments: Loaded with graphics and films enhanced for Netscape with the Shockwave plug-in, this commercial presentation is unbearable over a modem. The time taken to load pages would be better used to make a coffee. Since their customers are obviously execs or academics with fast ISDN or T3 lines, the mortal Internet user can just as well stay away unless totally enraptured by watching pages load. One employee page, with no hyperlinks, just a list, took about 3 to 4 minutes to load. Talk about disappointment! Looked nice, but what could I do with it?

Director Web
URL: http://www.mcli.dist.maricopa.edu/director/
Rating: 4
Comments: A "must-carry" hotlist item for anyone fiddling around on Macromind Director. Full of information and resources devoted to this cool software package. The searchable "Director Tips n' Scripts" is worth its weight in gold! Go into the Demos section to see what others are creating on Director. You'll spend a lot of time downloading these babies, but fun to watch on your screen.

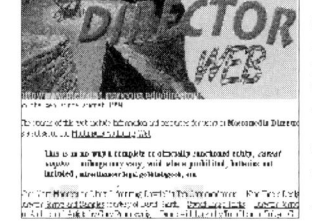

Edge Interactive Media
URL: http://www.well.com/user/edgehome/
Rating: 3
Comments: The *Edge* is one of the longest established developers and publishers of interactive entertainment games and their site is full of all kinds of goodies to purchase (games, software, magazine), but little else to offer a Net visitor. This should hopefully change soon when they launch their games online page in the near future.

Howard Rheingold
URL: http://www.well.com/user/hlr/
Rating: 4
Comments: Howard Rheingold, mind power maven and author of *Virtual Realities*, has set up a groovy site titled "Brainstorms," which he describes as an "experiment in community futurism… something more like a jam session than a magazine." Take a peek at Howard's digitized oil paintings or keep track of his nonstop travels around the world. There's even a few of his out-of-print books online in full text and ready to download. Dream on, Howard!

Interactive Systems Inc.
URL: http://www.teleport.com/~isi/
Rating: 2
Comments: Interactive television seems like one of those things which comes and goes in conversations, but never really materializes. This company would beg to differ and their Internet site offers many reasons why. Bone up on this ever-developing technology and see what test trials are currently going on in the world. Plenty to read here, but, ironically, little interactivity for a WWW page.

LucasArts Entertainment
URL: http://www.lucasarts.com/menu.html
Rating: 3
Comments: From the man who brought us *Star Wars*, the LucasArts site is full of interesting stuff. Most people come to this site for the free, downloadable demos of their games, but you should also take a peak into the pressroom to find out what's happening at the company. Also be sure to check out their online, behind-the-scenes magazine, *The Adventurer*, or purchase some of the Star Wars/Indiana Jones merchandise available from the company store. Beware of their *huge* image map—could take hours over a slow line!

New Media

Microsoft Corp.
URL: http://www.microsoft.com/
Rating: 4
Comments: With Microsoft joining up with NBC to produce another 24-hour news channel, Bill Gates inches closer and closer to entertainment delivery (and total world domination). Fun place to hunt for new PC products. Believe it or not, their Web page even looks like Windows 95!

Multimedia World Online
URL: http://www.mmworld.com
Rating: 4
Comments: Popular computer magazine, *Multimedia World*, is online and offers more than just an electronic version of their paper version. Articles, hotlinks and chat forums make this a worthwhile monthly visit. Very handy for keeping tabs on new software releases.

Nintendo
URL: http://www.nintendo.com/
Rating: 4
Comments: Nintendo Power is the name of this site set up by the electronic game giant. And as expected, everything Nintendo is here: Donkey Kong to Super Mario. Lots of image dumps from their games to download and press releases about new games. If you play Nintendo, you'll love this site.

Philips Media On-Line
URL: http://spider.media.philips.com/media/
Rating: 3
Comments: This is a pretty good-looking commercial site showcasing Philips and their developments in technology and software for multimedia, music, CD videos, educational applications, and pure entertainment. This site offers a free "Secret Agent" subscription to some software they use to scour the Net for those who have a hard time finding things themselves. "Smart Agent On-Line is your personal digital assistant to the Internet and beyond." According to Philips, this agent will find places you are interested in

and send e-mail to you with information specified in your profile. I am a sucker for this kind of stuff and signed up right away. Information wants to be free, and I like it that way.

QuickTime Continuum
URL: http://quicktime.apple.com/
Rating: 4
Comments: QuickTime is the standard for digital video developed by Apple Computer. It is cross-platform for Mac and Windows and gives high quality digital video in a variety of sizes for screens. New developments include support for musical instruments in the hardware of the Mac and MIDI implementation. QuickTime VR is the newest development and one that should ignite the QT market. This site has downloadable software, news, tips, and links to exciting QT areas. You can even buy QT clothes, but I think the software is much cooler. Lots of movies on tap here.

San Francisco Digital Media Center
URL: http://www.well.com/user/sfdmc/
Rating: 4
Comments: Joe, Nina, and Dana bring you the San Francisco Digital Media Center, a nonprofit community arts production company offering a variety of digital media courses. Many of the student projects are online and worth a look. There's a calendar of events and classes to keep you posted on their doings. Rumor has it that they want to develop this WWW site into a really wild experience. Cool.

Sega Online
URL: http://www.segaoa.com/
Rating: 4
Comments: Games, Games, and more games are spotlighted on Sega's WWW site! Keep up on new game releases and read about the "history of sega." As expected, cool graphics and easy to navigate. Clear about its demographics, this site also has a "comic of the day"

New Media

and three chat rooms featuring kids saying "hi" to each other and testing new swear words. Lots to explore here!

Silicon Graphics' Silicon Surf
URL: http://www.sgi.com/
Rating: 4
Comments: This computer company has been an important player in making the Internet a user-friendly environment and is blazing the way for the future. In fact, I'd say this is the place to explore if you are interested in where the Web is moving toward. Look under "Serious Fun" for a bunch of QuickTime movies, freeware, and 3D images.

TeleCircus San Francisco
URL: http://www.well.com/user/tcircus/
Rating: 4
Comments: Check out the San Francisco new media scene at TeleCircus. See what The Residents are up to lately or take a comic book tour conducted by Flathead. Lots of QuickTime movies to download here. For really funky stuff, look at CyberLab 7's "Planet Change Projects." You can explore this site for a long time. Enjoy!

Voyager Co.
URL: http://www.voyagerco.com/
Rating: 4
Comments: The Voyager Co. has always been at the forefront of new media with their electronic expanded books and flicks on CD-ROMS. Their Web site is new media in itself with lots of downloadable images, sounds, and movie clips. Don't miss the hilarious "This is Spinal Tap Home Page." Their events calendar is always worth a look with information about current exhibits at the American Museum of the Moving Image as well as other venues.

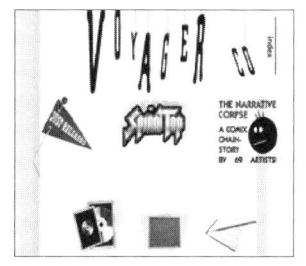

WAXweb
URL: http://bug.village.virginia.edu/
Rating: 4
Comments: Is this entertainment, information, or academic research? I will let this site describe itself - "WAXweb is the hypermedia version of David Blair's feature-length independent film, '*WAX* or the discovery of television among the bees' (85:00, 1991). It combines one of the largest hypermedia narrative databases on the Internet with an authoring interface which allows users to collaboratively add to the story." Sponsored at the Institute for Advanced Technology in the Humanities at the University of Virginia, the server holding this 1.5 gigabyte project also houses the e-zine Postmodern Culture. It has German, French, English, Japanese, or English options, VRML (Virtual Reality Modeling Language), and much more. You may join and get a password, or just view some of the material. This is one interactive project on the Web to take seriously! Don't do this one with a slow modem!

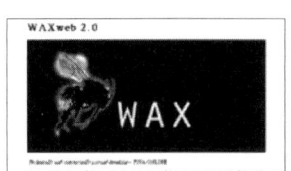

ORGANIZATIONS/GUILDS

Academy of Motion Picture Arts and Sciences
URL: http://www.ampas.org/ampas/
Rating: 3
Comments: To look at where the Oscar comes from, cruise over to this place. You can read press releases, look at the visiting artist programs, and download beautiful stills from Buster Keaton movies that have been taken from archival prints. Not many images are present here, but there is more than enough information for the curious about where the Oscar comes from and where it is going.

Organizations/Guilds

Academy of Television Arts and Sciences
URL: http://www.emmys.org/tindex.html
Rating: 4
Comments: The Academy offers a nicely designed site with all the information you would expect to see here about their organization and educational opportunities. There are some nice historical photos of people like Jack Benny and Jimmy Durante receiving Emmy awards. One of the most interesting parts was "The Making of the MCA/Universal Cyberwalk" on the Web. This is a 53–minute RealAudio presentation about the making of a commercial Web site.

Australian Film Institute
URL: http://www.vicnet.net.au/vicnet/afi/afiho.htm
Rating: 3
Comments: Established to promote Australian film culture, the Institute's WWW site is organized around its central functions: the AFI Awards (with last year's winners and nominees currently listed), exhibition (with various touring programs), distribution (yet to be filled with anything more than a brief mention), and research/information (with brief descriptions of the AFI's research services). Hopefully, soon, some actual Aussie film material will be highlighted on this site. Priscilla and Muriel, here we come!

Boston Film and Video Foundation
URL: http://www.actwin.com:80/cgi-bin/BFVF/@ab84d/index.html
Rating: 4
Comments: The opening statement at the top of the page is as follows. "The Boston Film/Video Foundation is a regional arts center whose mission is to encourage and facilitate access to and understanding of film, video and electronic media as a means of creative expression." This organization offers access to equipment and membership rates very reasonably. You can check

out their classes and even download some student work. This is a fine project and presentation of a nonprofit organization working with the community. They even have their own film and video festival in May. Start something like this in your town!

Broadcast Education Association
URL: http://www.usu.edu/~bea/
Rating: 4
Comments: The BEA is a "professional association for professors, industry professionals and graduate students who are interested in teaching and researching electronic media." Probably not much here for nonmembers, except maybe the media hotlinks. Very nicely presented.

California Film Commission
URL: http://www.ca.gov/commerce/cf_home.html
Rating: 3
Comments: This is a commercial trade services site for promoting and maintaining film work in the state of California. It gives rules on permits, information on locations, safety information and a lot more. If you are working here, read these pages to order the information on paper that you will need. Ugly, but this has informative material.

Cherokee High School Star Trek Club
URL: http://pages.prodigy.com/NJ/cstc/cstc95hp.html
Rating: 4
Comments: Now into its second year, the CSTC was established by students at Cherokee High School in Marlton, New Jersey. Read their official charter and constitution and locate their officers. I just *had* to click on the "Volleyball" link and what did I find? Oh just the rules and roster for the club's intramural volleyball team, appropriately called The Klingons! As these kids proudly boast, they are "the only Cherokee club with an Internet site!" Good work!

Cinema 16
URL: http://www.mty.itesm.mx/~dch/centros/cinema16/
Rating: 3
Comments: Cinema 16 is a film club out of Monterrey, Mexico, and has set up a Spanish language page full of film reviews, a gallery of stills from Krzysztof Kieslowski's *Three Colors* trilogy, and a calendar of their screenings. A nice-looking site with a fun feel to its design.

Director's Guild of America
URL: http://leonardo.net/dga/
Rating: 4
Comments: With more than 10,000 members worldwide, the DGA is a force to reckon with and has an informative profile on the Web. To join, one must be a director or assistant director doing work with "theatrical, industrial, educational and documentary films, as well as television live, filmed and taped radio, videos and commercials." Lots of information for joining, articles and photos of actors and directors of films nominated for awards, and an FAQ. For the director, this is the place to see. Actually they have an impressive, if very nondescriptive, set of links.

Documentary Film Group
URL: http://http.bsd.uchicago.edu/doc/
Rating: 2
Comments: The name of this group seems to imply a proletarian film approach, but in fact it is a cinema club listing their various film series at the University of Chicago. Very interesting and eclectic mix of screenings. If I lived in Chicago, I would be there! Rather short synopses of films, but for the hard to find art house screenings, it can be a good resource to see what is playing and what it is about before venturing to your local art house. The Vampire series page wasn't ready when I visited, but I look forward to coming back to see the final product. Here is a little information about them sent to me by e-mail. "The Documentary Film Group is on record with the Museum of Modern Art as the longest continuously running student film society in the nation. Founded in 1932, we have a sixty-two year

history as an all volunteer, student run organization committed to the concept of providing a low cost, high quality venue for a wide variety of films."

FAIR - Fairness & Accuracy In Reporting
URL: http://www.igc.org/fair/
Rating: 3
Comments: Established in 1986 as a national media watchdog organization, FAIR has developed into one of the most vocal supporters of anticensorship and First Amendment rights. Their WWW page includes the widely read column "Media Beat," various special reports on media bias, the magazine *Extra!*, a media contact list, and the famous "FAIR Media Bias Detector." Check this page out if you really dislike Rush Limbaugh!

Film Society Montaasi (Finland)
URL: http://otax.tky.hut.fi/.publish/montaasi/
Rating: 3
Comments: "Film Society Montage has been the place for the cinema enthusiasts in Otaniemi, Espoo, Finland since 1957." Since this is primarily in Finnish, it is difficult to understand the links and descriptions. There is a short page in English about the society and their screenings. They show 35mm films at Kino Dipoli and produce 16mm and S8mm films at Montage. Other than this information, a couple of film festivals in Finland and elsewhere are mentioned. This site deserves praise for being in its native language, but could do better with a little more info in English.

Finnish Film Foundation
URL: http://www.kaapeli.fi/~lumo/English/FFF/
Rating: 3
Comments: Established in 1969, the Finnish Film Foundation was created to finance, support and promote film production in Finland. This site suggests they are doing a great job and know how to use the Internet to further their task. Of particular interest to the general film fan is the Films from Finland section which provides annual listings of feature and documentary Finnish films, complete with credits, still photos, synopsis, and distributor.

Organizations/Guilds

Hollywood Supports
URL: http://www.datalounge.com/hsupports/
Rating: 4
Comments: *"Hollywood Supports* was launched in the fall of 1991 by leading entertainment industry figures to counter workplace fear and discrimination based on HIV status and sexual orientation." This description of this site says it all. Seminars, projects, legal help and advice all find a place here. One of the projects going is the "Day of Compassion," which places attention on stories involving HIV–infected or AIDS–plagued individuals and their daily life struggle. Many television shows, from soaps to talk shows, are involved. Find out more about this important effort in otherwise blase tinseltown. The list of board of directors is an impressive and eclectic mix.

International Federation of Television Archives
URL: http://www.nbr.no/fiat/fiat.html
Rating: 2
Comments: Still pretty much an information sheet, the FIAT/IFTA site contains copies of their newsletters (now in Adobe Acrobat format), the Recommended Standards and Procedures for Selection for Preservation of Television Material handbook, and television archivist conference details. A gold mine for those belonging to FIAT, but maybe a bit less entertaining for others. How about some QuickTime samples of TV preservation?

International Television Association
URL: http://www.itva.org
Rating: 3
Comments: The ITVA is a network of visual communicators which tries to link them up with business and development projects. They have more than 8,000 members. Conference information, job hotline, regional and chapter news, and other vital information for members is available. If you would like to join, there is information on dues, membership advantages, and discounts. Information rich for interested parties.

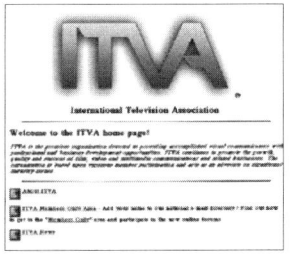

Internet Film Commissioner
URL: http://www.ibmpcug.co.uk/~scrfin/ifc/ifc.html
Rating: 3
Comments: The Internet Film Commissioner site provides useful information about shooting feature films in the UK and Europe. There's a huge listing of UK production companies which includes contact details and even descriptions. This nice-looking and growing site also has details about film financing and trade organizations.

Live Wire Youth Media
URL: http://www.iit.edu/~livewire/
Rating: 3
Comments: Now these are the kinds of Web sites we'd like to see more of. Live Wire Youth Media is a nonprofit organization out of Chicago designed to put the latest communication technology in the hands of urban kids. One of their projects, Plugged In, is comprised of teens in Chicago and East Palo Alto, California, creating an online dialogue through video, audio, text, and images to discuss urban issues. Currently this page is composed mostly of various project details, but should soon be adding more exciting content. Good work, folks.

Media Development Association
URL: http://www2.pavilion.co.uk/medianet/
Rating: 4
Comments: Titled MediaNet, this site was set up by the UK-based Media Development Association to "encourage MDA members and other media professionals to 'network', make contacts, keep up-to-date, and exploit the possibilities of new media." Event listings, news briefs and member database make this a dynamic site for those involved in the media to interact with one another. While the job board was fairly empty, the funding section had numerous good leads.

Media Watchdog
URL: http://theory.lcs.mit.edu/~mernst/media/
Rating: 4
Comments: "Media Watchdog is a collection of online media watch resources, including specific media criticism articles and information

Organizations/Guilds

about media watch groups." This is a collection of links and information that I have not seen present on other sites. How about an article and discussion group on "The Sexual Abuse Witchhunt" or articles on "Euromyths" or "Limbaugh's Lies"? International in scope though not always content, there is hope for media activists on the Web.

MediaWeb
URL: http://www.sa.ua.edu/tcf/mediaweb.htm
Rating: 3
Comments: As the front page states, "MediaWeb is a loose coalition of film/TV/video WebMasters that seeks to foster collaboration and to minimize the redundancy of materials on film/TV/video sites." But the true secret to this site is that it also contains Web links to all of the members' pages, therefore serving as an excellent jumping-off point for casual users. This site (and the informative MediaWeb discussion group) is also an essential resource for anyone thinking about setting up their own film and video WWW site.

National Film Board of Canada
URL: http://www.nfb.ca/
Rating: 4
Comments: Set up in 1939 by documentary film pioneer John Grierson, the National Film Board of Canada has established a bilingual Web site which serves as an excellent example of how such organizations can utilize the Internet. The site is divided into four sections (Information, Organization, Production, Distribution) and details the various functions of the NFB while promoting Canadian filmmaking. Check out the Canadian Cinema Address Book for a worthwhile directory of producers and distributors. You can also browse through the NFB's 9,000 film collection (not yet searchable) through tiny links hidden at the bottom of the Collection page and read their descriptions. Mr. Grierson would be ever so proud.

Norwegian Film Institute
URL: http://www.dnfi.no/
Rating: 3
Comments: It is strange that the Finnish and Norwegian Film Institutes are online, but not the Swedish. The Swedish Film Institute has traditionally been the one to lead the others in financing films and coproductions, but now the little brother of Norway has run past the slow moving behemoth. Production information, film database, and contact info for the Norwegian film industry.

Pacific Film & Television Commission
URL: http://design.net.au/pftc/
Rating: 4
Comments: The Australian Pacific Film & Television Commission concentrates on film production in Queensland. People involved in the film industry, crew rates, and other valuable info for prospective Queensland based film production proliferate here. This is a site to attract business, and is very rich in information. Some of the major movies and TV productions filmed here are *Street Fighter*—F/F Shadaloo Productions (USA); *Mighty Morphin Power Rangers* —F/F Twentieth Century Fox (USA); and *Island of Dr. Moreau*—F/F New Line Cinema (USA).

Society for the Preservation of Film Music
URL: http://www.oldkingcole.com/spfm/
Rating: 3
Comments: The SPFM site might not be the flashiest page around, but if you enjoy critical accounts of film scoring and music preservation (like the 650 members of SPFM), then this is for you. You'll find details of their annual conference, a newsletter, a collection of sound clips from previous speakers, and a decent list of WWW pages devoted to film composers. Unfortunately, no musical clips from selected films.

Squeaky Wheel
URL: http://freenet.buffALO.EDU/~wheel/
Rating: 2
Comments: Squeaky Wheel is a community media arts resource center in Buffalo, New York. Access to technology, media library, screenings, a venue for presentation of your own work, and contacts with other individuals and groups working in the field are some of the reasons for joining. This is an informational page for a valuable community resource, but not one that is that interesting for the average Internet film surfer. They do have a nice list of festivals and exhibitions, though.

Sundance Institute
URL: http://cybermart.com/sundance/institute/institute.html
Rating: 4
Comments: Robert Redford's Sundance Institute in Utah is a great initiative by a mainstream performer to support independent film. They have labs for filmmakers, screenwriters, playwrights, independent producers, and much more. They also have international programs and a film festival. There is a lot to read and a lot to apply for. Facilities are also available for independent conferences that wish to make use of the beautiful location. They even have their own catalog of mail order goods.

UK Guide to Student Film Societies
URL: http://www.warwick.ac.uk/~suaag/societies/societies.html
Rating: 3
Comments: Nicely presented directory of UK university film societies with brief descriptions of the filmsocs as well as their respective logos. Always interesting to see what's playing on the campus film circuit.

PRODUCTION & DISTRIBUTION

Arizona Film & Video Production Resources
URL: http://bensonassoc.com/bensonassoc/film/home.html
Rating: 3
Comments: For production companies seeking facilities, personnel, locations or other needs, this is a listing trying to be the definitive one for video and film production in the state of Arizona. Though not all categories are connected to any companies, they are listed. Everything from animal trainers to video digitizing services are listed.

Australian Media Facilities Directory
URL: http://www.amfd.com.au/AMFD/amfdhp.htm
Rating: 4
Comments: The Aussies do a good job on their Web sites, that is for sure. High marks go to most of the commercial sites there that I have seen, and this is no exception. All kinds of media contacts, from actors to public relations firms are listed here, and the layout is very professional. Start here for your Australian contacts.

British Actors' Register
URL: http://www.Internet-eireann.ie/power/actor/actor.htm
Rating: 3
Comments: The British Actors' Register (out of Ireland?) dubs itself as an "Internet service providing Agents, Directors and Casting companies with information on actors and actresses." You can search their database for males or females using such criteria as lead or character and by age group. Currently, there seem to be few actors actually registered with this service (around 30).

Camera Department
URL: http://www.seanet.com/Users/timtyler/film/camera.html
Rating: 4
Comments: Tim Tyler's excellent Camera Department page is a comprehensive online resource for professional motion picture camera personnel. The directory is divided into "people," "equipment," and "education" sections with well-chosen links. The jewel of this site is the "Online Camera Department Crew List" with lots of professionals listed. And this page looks good to boot!

Canadian Filmmaker's Distribution Center
URL: http://www.arena.com/film/
Rating: 2
Comments: This is an online catalog for the film distribution for a number of Canadian filmmakers. No pictures or clips are online here, but there are film descriptions, and prices for rental. Useful if you need it, but not a dynamic presentation. I would have liked to see bios on the filmmakers.

Chicago Filmmakers
URL: http://www.tezcat.com/~chifilm/homepage.html
Rating: 3
Comments: Filmmakers in the Windy City are lucky to have such a useful resource site on hand. Here you'll find a schedule of the classes and workshops offered by this 21-year-old nonprofit media arts center as well as the program for their Kino-Eye cinema exhibition. No clips and not very many images here, but a good deal of info about this group.

Cinematographer's Online Bible
URL: http://www-scf.usc.edu/~hunziker/cim/cim.htm
Rating: 3
Comments: Here's a site for all of you budding Directors of Photography put together by another budding filmmaker, Conrad Hunziker (currently a film student at USC)! Insightful information covering all aspects of cinematography (both 16 and 35mm). Most of the handy tips are useful, though a bit limited. But in order for this "Bible" to establish some credibility, those "any job offers?" buttons MUST go. Good luck!

CineWEB
URL: http://www.cineweb.com/
Rating: 3
Comments: Upon arriving at CineWeb, one is asked to give e-mail address, name, and affiliation. This is a free service which may then be entered and one may choose any of the alternatives listed. For example, CompuScout is a database of rental properties for location shooting. Reel Info has information about all aspects of film and video production. The list seems pretty long, so there is a lot of information at this site compared to others I have seen. You may also post your resume online for $69 a year. Personally, I don't like the graphics for these pages, but the information is well presented.

Delta 9 Independent Film Resource
URL: http://www.eden.com/~delta-9/
Rating: 3
Comments: This is a spot used for resources for independent film and videomakers in Austin, Texas, and around the world. This place has the coolest little film reel icons I have seen on the Web. It is soberly and minimally designed and aesthetically pleasing. Though neither the filmmaker database or script database had much in it at the moment, I am sure this site will be taking off. Good content and looks, but not enough in the fridge yet! Check out the grants page for financing that next project.

Electric Judy
URL: http://www.electric-judy.com/
Rating: 1
Comments: Electric Judy sounds like a digital Punch and Judy show but is really a site for specialists in theater, film and television lighting, and wardrobe based in the UK. This site is comprised of resumes and links. It is lacking in design and concept, though the qualifications for the company employees seem quite okay. Sometimes the Web may not be the right way to present a company.

Entertainment Law Resources
URL: http://www.laig.com/law/entlaw/
Rating: 3
Comments: Mark Litwak's excellent "Entertainment Law Resources" page not only hawks his popular books, but also provides useful legal tips related to the media: "The Film Distribution Deal: Tactics and Strategy" or "Negotiating the Electronic Publishing Agreement." And if you still have questions related to one of your projects, I assume Mr. Litwak, Esq., is always available—for a fee. This page also hosts a comprehensive film festival listing which is worth a look.

EZTV
URL: http://leonardo.net/eztv/
Rating: 3
Comments: The first page has a nightmarish purple psychedelic background reminiscent of crash pads in San Francisco, circa 1967. A presentation of this video media center and artist group lies behind some clickable graphics. They have done major work for big studios like Miramax, Polygram, Disney, and Warner. "EZTV operates a comprehensive media center with EMC non-linear editing systems, as well as several inter-formal linear video editing systems, accommodating BetaSp, 3/4"SP, H-8 and S-VHS. Macintosh, Windows and Amiga platforms are present for digital illustration, animation and special effects." It is a nice place to investigate too! They did the 90-minute documentary *Luck, Trust and Ketchup* (1994) about film director Robert Altman and *Short Cuts*. Besides the info, there is an online "Cyberspace Gallery" with some very strange pictures. Sometimes the purple writing on freaky backgrounds is hard to read, but worth the effort.

FINEcut - Video Moviemaker's Resources
URL: http://www.rmplc.co.uk/eduweb/sites/terrymen/movie1.html
Rating: 3
Comments: The who, how, and why of videomaking is here on this useful Web site. Their huge film festival listing is tremendous as is the set of book reviews centered on making videos. Getting around the pages is a bit of a task at times, but overall the site is pleasant and fulfilling. Make sure to browse through their "Video A to Z—cuts through the gobbledegook and puts it in plain English"__glossary.

Hollywood Mall
URL: http://www.HollywoodMall.com/
Rating: 2
Comments: This "Family 'OK' Internet Network" site is an average collection of links to various U.S. film profession information resources such as talent agencies (limited), casting calls (even more limited), and executive producers (still to be constructed). The best section by far is the decent listing of state by state film bureaus, although these are mostly only contact addresses. Hoping for this site to improve a bit.

Icelandic Film Production
URL: http://www.centrum.is/filmfund/
Rating: 4
Comments: These pages are part of a larger site on Iceland, and explain the history of Icelandic filmmaking and its connection to other Scandinavian countries. One of the smallest but most exciting film producing countries in the world now can release information worldwide. There is an extensive list of films produced in Iceland since 1977, including my favorite *When the Raven Flies*. This film released in 1984 and directed by Hrafn Gunnlaugsson, whose name means raven, is a bloody, violent, passionate mixture of spaghetti westerns and samurai films. Find out more about one of the best kept secrets in filmmaking, Icelandic film.

This site gets high ratings since the material is unavailable anywhere else. For researchers, film students, and cineastes curious about Iceland.

Independent Film & Video Makers Resource Guide
URL: http://www.echonyc.com/~mvidal/Indi-Film+Video.html
Rating: 4
Comments: Mike Vidal has done a wonderful and admirable work in this resource on the Web. He describes it as "a hypertext reference to resources on the Internet for the independent film and video community." No graphics, but lots of hyperlinks of value. This site is too massive to start to review. Just get there and use it. You will be busy for days just browsing.

JV III NYC Film Production Resource Locator
URL: http://www.panix.com/jviii/filmlctr/jv3film1.html
Rating:
Comments: Not as comprehensive as the New York Movie Web, the JV III site does offer some alternative resource for filmmakers. A simple scroll down list leads typically to phone numbers of a few companies. This site was an early arrival on the WWW, but is in dire need of a major facelift.

Location Online
URL: http://marvin.sedd.trw.com:1025/LOL/
Rating: 1
Comments: The blurb reads: "Your complete location department, featuring an interactive search program for international film location sites. Coming Soon: a convenient directory of all location-related services by area." I did three searches—Stockholm, Alabama, and finally Los Angeles. The first two gave no result, while the last (obviously) came up with a number of choices for properties that could be used for location shooting. Didn't work, but a good idea when it becomes implemented. This gets a 1, because maybe it does work by the time you read this.

Lucasfilm THX Home Page
URL: http://www.thx.com/thx/thx.html
Rating: 4
Comments: "The Audience is Listening…" Many of us have thrilled from the experience of watching a film in THX and here is Lucasfilm's site to show off the technology. Find out what laser discs are in THX or see what films had THX sound in 1995. See if any of your local movie theaters are hooked for THX by using the searchable database of cinemas. I guess until computer speakers are equipped with THX technology, there won't be any audio examples. Nice to see a site devoted to making soundtracks so "visually" appealing.

Mandy's Film & TV Directory
URL: http://www.mandy.com/
Rating: 3
Comments: Mandy's is a substantial film and television production resource directory that is international in scope. Published by UK-based Eurocrew, Ltd., this site makes sure that everything is covered from art directors to editors. Each entry has a little blurb with contact details. When I looked through it, though, the directory still seemed in need of more resources, but let's assume it will soon fill up its massive grid. No images.

New York Film & Video Web
URL: http://www.ios.com/nyfilm/
Rating: 4
Comments: A very comprehensive Web page for film production in the Big Apple. Directories include production companies, guilds, suppliers, and film commissions (complete with some regulation texts). Simple to navigate, this site also offers such useful information as NYC weather and a listing of hotels offering film industry discounts. Expect continued development of these pages.

Production & Distribution

North Carolina Independent Filmmakers Assoc.
URL: http://www.well.com/user/ncifa/ncifamn.htm
Rating: 4
Comments: Filmmaking is alive and well in North Carolina! The NCIFA has set up a handsome site devoted to the NC film industry. There's an excellent production resource directory (animal trainers to wardrobe), a slate of projects currently in production, and a long list of all the films made in North Carolina over the past 90 years. Easy to navigate and useful information.

Northwest FilmNet
URL: http://vvv.com/maplewood/nwhome.html
Rating: 2
Comments: I wish commercial sites would make things more readable! I can forgive college students doing their first Web page and putting purplish blue letters on black backgrounds, but people out to make money ought to know better! "Northwest FilmNet—Victoria, British Columbia—the place to find listings of Victoria area actors, technical professionals, producers, directors, screenwriters and film industry resources." Though few actors and talent agencies are listed, the other production areas were well represented. An important resource for those that need to shoot in BC, otherwise move on. Presentation was low quality but the information was fine.

Production Weekly
URL: http://users.aol.com/prodweek/pw.html
Rating: 1
Comments: PW is based in Beverly Hills, California, and offers a complimentary issue of their newsletter, which is described in the following words. "PW is a weekly breakdown of projects in pre-production, preparation and development for film, television, music videos, commercials, etc. ..." The first one is free, and then information on subscription follows. At the moment, the rest of the site is just a number of links around the Net, and not anything really new. As an information source it might be good, but as a Web site it is undeveloped so far.

Scoring Services
URL: http://www.scoring.com/
Rating: 3
Comments: New York City-based Scoring Services composes TV jingles and motion picture scores. If you are in the market for that, this is a good place to sample their talents. Listen to audio clips via RealAudio or glance over their impressive client list. They even have links to those clients with WWW sites. Fun to check out, I must admit.

Showdata Online
URL: http://www.aztec.co.za/biz/showdata/
Rating: 3
Comments: This South African list of facilities and production resources for film, TV and new media also has entertainment and educational links as well. Some of the resources are very well designed, and others just text on a colored background. Check out the AGN distance learning project for a good one.

Sony Pictures Imageworks
URL: http://spiw.com/cgi-bin/ver/index.html
Rating: 4
Comments: This is the site for Sony Pictures' visual effects division and is absolutely awesome for anyone who has ever wondered: "How did they do that?" The "Visions Achieved" section not only explains how certain special effects were created, but also gives us behind-the-scenes photos and QuickTime demo movies to show off their skills. Very cool.

Texas Film & Video Producers Resources
URL: http://waterworks.com./~tfv/
Rating: 2
Comments: Going to Texas to shoot and need a best boy in San Antonio? You can start by looking here, but I wonder if this is really a complete listing. For example, there are no Steadicam operators listed in Houston or San Antonio. Seems strange. Text only database and e-mail contact makes for fast working. No graphics whatsoever on these pages. It might help to spiff it up a little on the home page. How about a picture of each city listed?

The Guide
URL: http://theguide.gim.de/Etrans/
Rating: 2
Comments: The guide is a handbook for information on production, actors, and writers for music, TV, and cinema. This site in Germany offers a search function, but after a few searches I came to the conclusion that most of the indexed entries were for German outfits or individuals. There were some US based entries as well, but on the whole, it is lacking substance. Maybe more companies and individuals will be attracted. It is a bilingual database and at the moment only lists production facilities.

Universal Studios, Florida
URL: http://www.imeid.com/ustop.html
Rating: 2
Comments: Universal shows shots of their back lots on little tours of their Florida facility. You can look at these pretty bad digitalized photos of lookalike areas for Hollywood, Southern California, San Francisco/New England, Metropolitan, and World Exposition. You can also order a video if you want closer looks at possible location shooting areas. I am surprised that an outfit as big as this one doesn't opt for better pictures on their Web site. The cost is minimal. Amateurish at best in this presentation, but it could be valuable for content for location scouters.

VCV Stunts
URL: http://www.procom.com/~daves/vcvstunt.html
Rating: 2
Comments: And I thought I had seen everything! Yep, it's a motion picture stuntman agency with their own Web page—and I do mean page in the singular. Maybe they should call it a flyer instead. Still, since it is "Netscape 1.1 Enhanced," you can view the two photos of an actual stuntman in action or read the great descriptions: "VCV Stunts also has experts in whips, fights, knives and just plain old knock-down drag-out brawls! We also do car transfers, drags and other stunts common to the motion picture business." They also make the point that "We are not hiring new Stunt personnel at this time." Oh, how I love cyberspace!

Vidéographe
URL: http://www.connectmmic.net/videograf/
Rating: 3
Comments: This nonprofit video collective based in Quebec offers production facilities and "supports the creation of original and non-commercial videos. Videographe offers four services: production, distribution, promotion and marketing, and video archives." The presentations together with fun graphics are enjoyable and spark interest for a taste of what they are doing. Unfortunately, most of the material is in French, and I only found English on the first page. Still, it isn't that difficult to understand what is going on if you have a rudimentary command of the French language.

Virtual Film Market
URL: http://moviemarket.com/
Rating: 2
Comments: The CyberVideo Consumer Movie Previews list production info on films being released in cinemas and on video, as well as MPEG trailers for them. The list of 70 films was fair. Another area, The Virtual Film Market, is an off–limits area for the mortal types not associated with the film industry. The privileged have a password to get in. "VFM is an industry marketplace for accredited media industry personnel to facilitate the worldwide distribution of film and television rights." You may apply to join if you can prove you are an industry pro. They have the following statement on the home page. "The first Video-on-Demand server accessible worldwide via the web." What it actually is amounts to downloadable MPEG films. False advertising, and *not* the first by any means!

Virtual Headbook
URL: http://www.xmission.com/~wintrnx/virtual.html
Rating: 3
Comments: Even if you're not a casting director, this site is fun to play on. Try searching their actor profiles by plugging in desired age, gender, and union affiliation. You get dished up a headshot and bio. If you *are* a casting director, then you can receive film and sound clips of your potential models/actors.

RESEARCH AND DATABASES

Broadcast Pioneers Library
URL: http://www.itd.umd.edu/UMS/UMCP/BPL/bplintro.html
Rating: 3
Comments: The Broadcast Pioneers Library WWW site at the University of Maryland should be a required visit for all students of broadcasting. Why? Where else can you download a sound clip of the famous 1961 "Vast Wasteland" speech by FCC Chairman Newton Minow or old advertising spots from the 1950s and 60s? You can also browse through descriptions of the library's various collections as well as conduct a search of their holdings. All I have to figure out now is how to physically get to Maryland through the Net.

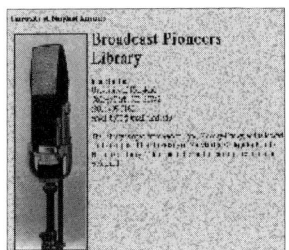

CSUOHIO Film Database
URL: gopher://trans.csuohio.edu:70/1ftp-nop:nic.funet.fi@/pub/culture/tv+film/database/
Rating: 4
Comments: The Internet Movie Database tools and files are available here for setting up the database in Amiga, MS-DOS, or UNIX environments. This admirable collaboration by many people in the UK, continental Europe, and Scandinavia includes updated files on everything from producers to release dates. Though not purely academic, this database is one of the better ones on the Internet and can be used by fans and academics (with reservations) alike.

Early Motion Pictures Home Page
URL: http://lcweb2.loc.gov/papr/mpixhome.html
Rating: 4
Comments: This area maintained by the Library of Congress has search facilities for localizing information and clips contained in the collection of early cinema. Intelligently written background information, collections featuring a number of films on a theme (like the World's Fair at San Francisco), still photographs from the original films, and downloadable digital clips are maintained online. Films from 1897 to 1916 are featured. Well done and valuable for researchers.

Eastman Kodak Company
URL: http://www.kodak.com/homePage.shtml
Rating: 4
Comments: This is a great place to catch up on the past, present, and future of one of the most influential film-stock companies. Their history of Kodak pages titled *From Glass Plates to Digital Images* is actually quite informative and you can search the entire site for anything related to Kodak's activities. Worth a quick snoop.

Film Webliography
URL: http://www.lib.lsu.edu/hum/film.html
Rating: 3
Comments: This is a good starting point for bibliographies, databases, discussion groups, and so forth, but the list is far from current. There are better ways to find out mailing lists via listservs than to look at outdated gophers as is done here. Instructions for sending requests for keywords to a listserv is better. Otherwise this could be a dynamite site for students if it was updated some more. For example, where is *Postmodern Culture* or *CTHEORY*? These electronic journals have been around for a while and deal with film quite often. Good try, but doesn't reach to the outer edge of the established media yet.

Filmleksikonet (Norwegian Movie Database)
URL: http://www.uio.no/cgi-bin/filmleksikon
Rating: 4
Comments: This database at the University of Oslo is only in Norwegian, but for the film scholar who wishes to read Norwegian reviews of the films listed, check production information on Norwegian films and films released in Norway until 1994, this is the place. No graphics, but a very good Web form based retrieval system. Any Scandinavian speaker will be able to use this one! Not of general interest, but very good.

GRAFICS Early Cinema Server
URL: http://grafics.histart.umontreal.ca/default-eng.html
Rating: 4
Comments: GRAFICS is a French acronym meaning "Research Group on the Beginnings and the Formation of the Cinema and

Theatrical Institutions." A bilingual server presentation at the University of Montreal, this excellent area for presenting research in early cinema in Quebec, Canada, has a predominantly French language content, but is worth checking out for academics in search of more contacts.

HADDON: Ethnographic Film Archive
URL: http://www.rsl.ox.ac.uk/isca/haddon/HADD_home.html
Rating: 3
Comments: "Named after Alfred Court Haddon, the early British anthropologist and pioneer in the use of film in anthropological research," the HADDON project is an online catalog of archival ethnographic film. Although the main database has yet to be connected to this WWW site (due to be online by October 1996), this very innovative project needs assistance in testing its interface (just fill out the online form). Keep an eye out for its main launch in late 1996.

Internet Movie Database
URL: http://www.cm.cf.ac.uk/Movies/welcome.html
Rating: 4
Comments: Is this an entertainment site, an academic site, or a review site? This is all of the aforementioned and more. The granddaddy of the movie databases on the Internet, this one has fully developed search facilities and links to all sections of the data. Sometimes called the Cardiff Movie Database, because the original is based in Cardiff, Wales, there are mirrors all around the world. Pick the one closest to you and spend a couple of days searching for details on movies. You can't be guaranteed that all info is correct, but it is a good place to start. According to Col Needham, their helpful WebMaster, "Hits are in the region of 750,000 per day and rising all the time."

Media History Web
URL: http://spot.colorado.edu/~rossk/history/histhome.html
Rating: 4
Comments: "The Media History Project is a collaborative effort between professional and lay media historians to provide a comprehensive guide to all online materials relevant to the study, appreciation, and understanding of media history." This opening line on the site sounds great and it seems to live up to this idea as well. This opening page has a *very* classy design look and is very pleasing to read. Nice icons for navigation make this one of the best sites I have seen for research and academic use. Courseware pages are an extra plus for educators. This is comprehensive and constantly growing. Don't miss it. All media are represented.

Museum of Broadcast Communications
URL: http://webmart.org/mbc/
Rating: 3
Comments: One of the only two museums in America for broadcasting, this site covering the museum is still very much under construction, but the informative headers for different areas make this look like a winner when it is finished. Television, radio, and files related to its study and history are available here.

Museum of Television and Radio
URL: http://www.mtr.org/
Rating: 4
Comments: A wonderful resource for students and fans alike. When you arrive, take a visual tour of the museum or pop by one of the featured exhibits (a James Dean TV show was there when I stopped by). Hopefully they'll upload some TV and radio clips in the near future to really become a museum of the 21st Century. By the way, on your way out, why not stop by the Museum Store for some TV and radio memorabilia.

National Film Preservation Board
URL: gopher://marvel.loc.gov/11/research/reading.rooms/motion.picture.nfpb
Rating: 4
Comments: The Board is in charge of choosing films deemed important on the "basis of their historical, cultural and aesthetic significance." The films must also be at least 10 years old. These films will be preserved and archived at the Library of Congress for the National Film Registry Collection. This initiative is very important for the survival of our film heritage in the United States. Public nominations are welcome. To submit, contact Steve Leggett, sleggett@mail.loc.gov

National Museum of Photography: Film and Television
URL: http://www.nmsi.ac.uk/nmpft/
Rating: 4
Comments: While this museum's physical space is located in Bradford, England, its virtual presence is right here. Thumb through their collections and see some of the holdings (I downloaded a JPEG file containing frames from the first successful motion picture film made in Britain, *Incident at Clovelly Cottage* made in 1895). Their various information sheets are also worth a look. Bonus: site is searchable!

On This Day in Movie History
URL: http://www.msstate.edu/M/on-this-day
Rating: 4
Comments: Always a hoot, the Internet Movie Database spits out birthdays and deathdays of film stars as well as films released "on this day in movie history." Many people tell me they use this page for their Netscape start-up home page. Anything for a giggle, I guess.

Pacific Film Archive
URL: http://www.uampfa.berkeley.edu/
Rating: 3
Comments: The Pacific Film Archive is located at the University of California, Berkeley, and houses a collection of over 7,000 titles. You can visit their theater through a big MPEG flick or read the film screening calendar which is accompanied by excellent film notes and short credits.

Polish Cinema Database
URL: http://info.fuw.edu.pl/Filmy/
Rating: 4
Comments: What if every country could do this? This is a national cinema database with films made after 1947 in Poland, and some by Polish directors abroad. This is a volunteer effort and the team asks for help in contributing to the facts here. A quick search of Polanski showed his *Knife in the Water*, with a synopsis and production credits. Over 1,000 films are listed, with about 300 having more detailed posts. In the future, they plan to add short films and television productions to the database. Though the authors do not guarantee all information, this is obviously a valuable resource for Polish film lovers.

Silent Movies
URL: http://www.cs.monash.edu.au/~pringle/silent/
Rating: 4
Comments: Glen Pringle's ambitious Silent Movies site is something that has been lacking previously on the Web. Silent film screenings around the country at various cinemas, home pages for a variety of silent film stars, and film preservation are the main themes of this site. As a resource for film students and academics, as well as a source of some interesting trivia and photos, the project is ideal, but even ordinary film fans will get a lot out of this one. Silent star of the

Research & Databases

month features people like Harold Lloyd or Blanche Sweet. This is also one of those sites that features primarily text, with a few photos available.

Tardis Television Database
URL: http://www.tardis.ed.ac.uk/~dave/guides/index.html
Rating: 2
Comments: More like an episode guide archive, but searchable. Currently, there are guides to about 50 US and UK TV shows with some useful information (although most are terribly out-of-date!). The search engine (for names only) doesn't seem to be functioning properly. I typed in Cleese (noting an episode guide for "Fawlty Towers"), and got back a message in tiny letters: "Sorry, actor not found." I headed straight to the Internet Movie Database and found what I was looking for.

Telemuseum, Stockholm, Sweden
URL: http://www.telemuseum.se/musinfo/telemuseng.html
Rating: 2
Comments: The Telemuseum in Stockholm is devoted to "depicting developments in telecommunications within the fields of telegraphy, telephony, radio and television." There are a few photos of the museum here and a lot of contact e-mails for various staff members. Hopefully, someday they'll fill out the site with cyberversions of their interesting exhibits. In Swedish and English.

Vanderbilt Television News Archive
URL: gopher://tvnews.vanderbilt.edu/1
Rating: 4
Comments: This archive, started in 1968, is devoted to the preservation of television newscasts for study. The recorded newscasts are cataloged and the monthly publication *Television News Index and Abstracts* is available here in electronic format. A total of 23,000 individual network evening news broadcasts were on tape as of 1994. Tapes of broadcasts are available for loan from the archive located at Vanderbilt University in Tennessee, USA. This archive is unique on the Internet. Contact: tvnews@tvnews.Vanderbilt.Edu

SCREENWRITING

BBB Movie Scripts
URL: http://pages.ripco.com:8080/~bbb/scripts.html
Rating: 3
Comments: Big Bad Barbarian has compiled a number of scripts and links to scripts for well-known movies. He has scripts for scenes cut from the final films and early and final drafts for *Total Recall*. A good resource to see what is really in the film and what didn't make it. His movie goofs document is fun for the person who wants to wow friends with trivia about continuity mistakes. Example: "*Anatomy of a Murder*—Lee Remick has a skirt when she gets up to leave a cafe. By the time she gets outside, she's wearing slacks."

Charles Deemer's Screenwriting Page
URL: http://www.teleport.com/~cdeemer/scrwriter.html
Rating: 4
Comments: Charles Deemer has created an amazing screenwriting page which provides comprehensive information about the business and the craft. The "Tips from the Pros" and "Voices of Experience" sections are particularly useful as established screenwriters share their insights. But the real goodies are within the "Nuts and Bolts" section with detailed information about writing, editing, and selling scripts. There's additionally a link to screenplay software sites as well as a wonderfully functional screenplay format page with hyperlinked descriptors. A must for all of you budding screenwriters!

Internet's Screenwriter's Network
URL: http://www.screenwriters.com/screennet.html
Rating: 3
Comments: Snappy-looking site with almost too much information for novice and acclaimed screenwriters. Part of the Hollywood Network WWW site, this page has many resources related to the art and business of screenwriting. Pose questions via e-mail to various script consultants or enter the "Screenwriter's Lounge" and chat with other budding writers. Search the Script Library for sample screenplays. Like the Hollywood Network, though, it's very easy to get lost here amongst the millions of graphics!

Writers' Computer Store
URL:
http://www.hollywoodnetwork.com:80/hn/shopping/kiosk/index.html
Rating: 2
Comments: Out of Sausalito, California, the Writers' Computer Store is an excellent place to find software programs to facilitate various forms of writing, from short stories to screenwriting. Yet I must admit, some of the products do seem a bit dubious. Take, for example, one program called IdeaFisher® which boasts that "No longer are creative thinking and your future left to accidental discovery, serendipity, or the muses. Now there is IdeaFisher, the unique computer-based innovation tool that brings ideas to your mind through a proven, focused process of association." Scary, but true.

SOUNDS

Caddyshack Movie Sounds
URL: http://www.ee.duke.edu/~ceh/caddy/caddy.html
Rating: 2
Comments: This fan page offers 11 megabytes of sounds. Hope these two guys don't have it on a university server without the systems administrator knowing! He will kill them. If you like the movie you must love this one. As they said: "We pretty much recorded the whole movie."

Plan 9 From Outer Space Soundtrack (RealAudio)
URL: http://www.w2.com/docs2/c4/p9liner.html
Rating: 4
Comments: This site, from Performance Records, was one of the first to fiddle with RealAudio - an application allowing for direct "streaming" of audio into your computer rather than timely downloading. Not only do you get the opportunity to listen to the *entire* soundtrack of the classic "bad" film by Ed Wood, Jr., there is also an image of the movie's poster as well as a fun-to-read essay by cult film critic, Danny Peary.

Princess Bride Sound Clips
URL: http://www-personal.engin.umich.edu/~cstrick/PrincessBride/sounds.html
Rating: 3
Comments: *The Princess Bride* is a great film, but does it warrant its own sound page? Obviously others think so and here's a site which offers 25 sound clips from the movie. As a bonus, there's even a copy of the script to wander your eyes over. As the page's maintainer proclaims up front, "This movie holds a special place in my heart, not only because I was in tears laughing so hard, but also because my wife and I used the theme song as the background music at our wedding." I wonder if they got the music off his page?

Seinfeld Sound Clips
URL: http://www.ifi.uio.no/~rubens/seinfeld/sounds/index.html
Rating: 4
Comments: Just imagine, an entire site devoted to audio clips from the popular TV show "Seinfeld." It's either a dream come true or a nightmare, depending on how much you like the show. The page itself is fairly simple (which is most appropriate for a show about "nothing") with close to 200 sound clips (accompanied by handy textual transcriptions) divided up by episode. The theme song and six bass riffs are also included. Weird thing about this site is that the link to "another" Seinfeld sound page is on *top* of the page. For my money's worth, there's no need to look further. Anything by Kramer makes a wonderful start-up sound.

Simpsons Sounds
URL: http://www.duke.edu/~djwitzel/Simps.html
Rating: 3
Comments: If you like Homer and Bart and the rest of the gang recreating sounds of their bodily functions—anguish, love, hate, and the frustration of being mentally deranged—cruise on over. Arranged by aired seasons, this rating depends on your taste for the Simpsons!

Sound Clip Directory
URL: http://www.eecs.nwu.edu/~jmyers/other-sounds.html
Rating: 4
Comments: This is a huge collection of sound sites all over the world, featuring sound bites of all categories. This is the biggest collection I have ever seen on the Web and ranges from reggae to classical Indian music. You will even find presidential debates here. If you don't have sound software, you can find it here too.

TV Bytes: WWW TV Themes Page
URL: http://themes.parkhere.com/themes/
Rating: 4
Comments: This is the granddaddy of TV audio pages with literally hundreds and hundreds of digitized TV theme songs. Everything from "Charlie's Angels" to "H.R. Pufnstuf." Most of the clips are arranged by genre (action, comedy, children's, etc.) and there's also a growing collection of TV commercial files. Hopefully we can get Patrick Kenny (the site's creator) to redesign the page for greater functionality and add a search capability. That is, if hordes of entertainment lawyers don't get to him first. Play on!

Twin Peaks Sounds
URL: http://www.desktop.com.au/~lwerndly/tpsound.html
Rating: 2
Comments: This page contains sounds that can be downloaded. The files are various pieces of dialogue from "Twin Peaks." For the cultists and occultists alike. There is a Windows program for playing random TP quotes (as if you had nothing better to do!). How about things like "Eureka! Dale I could kiss your pointy little head." Not for the uninitiated!

STUDIOS

Elstree - remember me?
URL: http://metro.turnpike.net/E/elstree/
Rating: 3
Comments: "Known for many years as the British Hollywood, Elstree studios have in recent times struggled to survive, but Borehamwood has a proud heritage of film and TV production, and continues today as TV production centre." The Elstree Studios site has information on the plan to save the studios, supported by the likes of Steven Spielberg, a brief history of the filmmaking that has gone on here, and a list of "bitchy" comments by various stars. Samuel Goldwyn on the funeral of Louis B. Mayer: "The reason so many people showed up at his funeral was because they wanted to make sure he was dead." Basically just information, but it is nice to see some places besides Hollywood on the Net.

Fine Line Features
URL: http://www.flf.com/
Rating: 4
Comments: Conscious of how huge graphics really slow down most of our travels through cyberspace, the folks at Fine Line have designed their site to be pleasing to the eye without the giant image maps found on other film pages. Colorful synopses, photos from premieres, and city release dates are some of the more interesting items to be found here. Unlike many of the other film companies, Fine Line is also devoted to archiving their various movie pages after the film's first run. Excellent work!

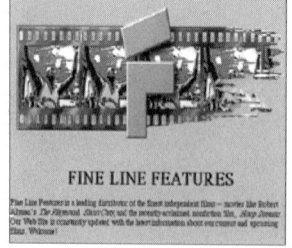

Studios

Gramercy Pictures
URL: http://www.polygram.com/polygram/Film.html
Rating: 3
Comments: Kinda cool site plugging films from this division of PolyGram. Most of the film pages attempt to replicate a movie trailer with flashing Web pages and eventually deliver the goods you are probably looking for: synopsis, credits, and star pictures. Currently a bit out-of-date, these pages need some maintenance. Thankfully, they release great movies!

MGM/UA
URL: http://www.mgmua.com/
Rating: 4
Comments: MGM's Lion's Den site was one of the first major Hollywood studios to go online and they have been at the forefront of using the Net to sell their current film slate. Typical fare of images, credits and interviews is coupled with interactive chat rooms and behind-the-scenes tidbits. Check out the MGM Top 10 for the coolest new Web sites.

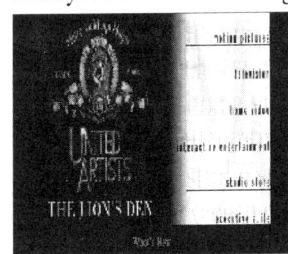

New Line Cinema
URL: http://cybertimes.com/NewLine/Welcome.html
Rating: 2
Comments: I was really psyched up about seeing New Line's Web site since they distribute one of my short films and wanted to contact them via e-mail. I was very disappointed to see just a commercial offering of images, though no downloads for films, info on stars, and the usual hype for mainstream films. A fairly detailed article about the film, including synopsis, was available for some of the films featured. I was hoping for a little more substance and even a WebMaster to turn to. No such luck. If you like their newest films, you'll like the site, but only five films were listed.

Paramount Pictures
URL: http://www.paramount.com/
Rating: 4
Comments: Enter the Paramount gate to see pages on the studio's newly released films or current TV shows. Always featuring creative pages, Paramount (along with its parent company, Viacom) is attempting to lead the field in online entertainment. And they are fun indeed, with still photos, interviews, credits, production notes, and downloadable trailers. Many of the pages have games to play or other interactive opportunities. Amazing what a little money can do to a Web site, eh?

Sony Pictures Entertainment
URL: http://www.spe.sony.com/Pictures/
Rating: 4
Comments: Just part of the gigantic Sony WWW site, the SPE pages have enough here to keep you busy for hours on end. Movie pages (clips, clips, clips), TV program pages ("Married...With Children"), and the Sony Theaters Photo Archive. Lots to look at and everchanging. Tip: Visit the *Jumanji* pages. Coming soon: the studio tour!

Troma
URL: http://www.troma.com/home/
Rating: 4
Comments: Home to such film classics as *The Toxic Avenger*, *Class of Nuke 'Em High*, and *Sgt. Kabukiman NYPD*, Troma films have launched their new WWW site, Tromaville! Like their films, this site is crass, humorous, and often in poor taste. Video clips, images, and lots of overt pitching of their films can be found here. Their "Tromatic: hotlist" is worth a look as well. Great stuff!

United International Pictures
URL: http://www.uip.com/
Rating: 4
Comments: The first thing that strikes you about the UIP site is how many languages you can read it in: English, French, German, Spanish, and Dutch! Film pages for *Apollo 13* and *Casper* reside here with loads of images to pull into your computer. Innovative new pages are always being added as well.

Universal Pictures
URL: http://www.mca.com/universal_pictures/index.html
Rating: 4
Comments: Visit one of the major Hollywood studios via the WWW. Primarily a site to market their upcoming film slate, there's still a lot to look at here which makes a stop by good value. Each featured film has downloadable stills, credits, and production notes. And what visit to Universal would be complete without a stop by their famed studio/theme parks in California and Florida. Fun.

Walt Disney Company
URL: http://www.disney.com/
Rating: 4
Comments: The most famous animation studio in the world has its own Web site catering to information seekers wanting to know about the Disney channel, videos, books, music, and of course Disneyland. This is a very comprehensive site which even covers areas for business travelers who wish to use Disneyland for conferences or corporate playground. If you can't find it here, it probably doesn't belong here! I found no merchandising area, but it will probably be forthcoming. Video clips and soundtrack bites were listed and downloadable too.

TV NETWORKS

Australian Broadcasting Corporation
URL: http://www.abc.net.au/
Rating: 4
Comments: This is a very slick-looking and informative site about Australian television and radio. You can browse, go to specific programs, look at media, science, net culture, and all with the same high quality graphics, which actually load quickly. This is a great site for everybody to look at. There is even a special section called KAM YAN for aboriginal people and projects for and about them. The combination of entertainment, culture, and technology is admirably done. This is a definite top site!

British Broadcasting Corporation
URL: http://www.bbcnc.org.uk/
Rating: 4
Comments: The BBC Web site is well done, sober, intelligent, and has all the quality that one expects of public services most respected broadcasting facility. Radio, TV, world service, education, and the Internet are the choices on the first page. You can get everything from program listings to broadcasting links. Go to it.

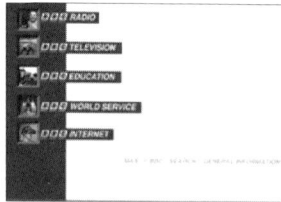

CBC (Canada)
URL: http://www.cbc.ca/
Rating: 3
Comments: A good programming guide to Canadian television, this falls short of the BBC site, but on the other hand, the financial resources are probably nowhere near the same, and the audience is a lot smaller. A good initiative by the CBC, and bilingual in relevant areas.

CBS (USA)
URL: http://www.cbs.com/
Rating: 3
Comments: CBS has a little gift on their server, a 300k screensaver made from their eye logo. "The Late Show," "Dr. Quinn," Sports, News, and other popular programs are featured with links on the main page. Specials of the day or near future are highlighted which is a good service for the TV browser/surfer. FAQ and a photo gallery are some of the extras. This is a pleasant commercial site which is tastefully done, not gaudy, and doesn't overload the graphics so much that you can move around easily.

Channel 4 (UK)
URL: http://www.cityscape.co.uk/channel4/
Rating: 4
Comments: Channel 4 has been one of the dynamic partners in British television history. They have funded Greenaway films, exciting low budget independent works like *My Beautiful Launderette*, and provided television series of high quality to Europe and abroad. There is even an extensive book about the history of TV 4 production published in the UK. This site features program titles, times, synopses, and even info about shows that were never aired, like "Sex with Paula," but that have cultural significance. This program is now being aired, incidentally, after lying dormant for nine years. This site is a gold mine of information and never-ending changes.

CNN (USA)
URL: http://www.cnn.com/index.html
Rating: 4
Comments: The news service that saves the world! You sometimes get that idea by the way their ads present CNN! There are even TV analyses of the Gulf War that use CNN as the hero, saving the UN from Iraq by giving us all the information we need. Bush once said early during the war attacks that he only knew what he had seen on CNN. This is an incredibly news-rich area, and they even offer a classroom news service by e-mail with current events and questions for teachers' use. Dense with information, but fairly easy to navigate, this is the number one news

service on the Net. You may not like their point of view, but they have most important news listed. I like to check out their technology pages when I have the time.

Deutsche Welle
URL: http://www-dw.gmd.de/
Rating: 3
Comments: One of the first major commercial multilingual sites on the WWW, the Deutsche Welle pages have current news stories uploaded as well as an excellent, calendar-based program guide for all of the network's international broadcasting. Still being developed, these pages should grow into a major information resource area on the Net.

ESPN (USA)
URL: http://espnet.sportszone.com/
Rating: 4
Comments: ESPN sports network has a good-looking commercial site with nice graphic buttons and organization. News, columnists, letters, and lots of scores for games make this the American sports lover's paradise.

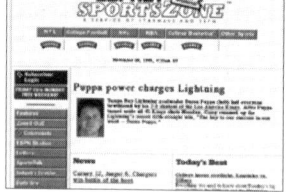

FOX (USA)
URL: http://www.foxnetwork.com/home.html
Rating: 4
Comments: Those crazy folks at Fox have put together a great site to hype their TV shows. Fox's kids, sports, and entertainment programs are featured with plenty of depth to each link. Also available is a live, telnet-based chat room which, at the time I logged in, seemed to have more in common with other chat sessions ("Are you cute?") than any of Fox's programs. More focused discussions can be found on the various show bulletin boards where fans trade information about their favorite stars or upcoming episodes. The kids section is well designed and not only includes TV schedules, but also a multitude of contests and games.

MTV (USA)
URL: http://www.mtv.com/
Rating: 4
Comments: The cable channel which defined the 1980s and 90s is now one of the Web: schedules, program pages, and MTV news headlines. Some of the pages are extra cool, like the ones featuring downloadable movies, images, and sounds from "Beavis & Butt-head." Fair warning: huge images await you, but usually worth the time spent downloading.

NBC (USA)
URL: http://www.nbc.com/
Rating: 4
Comments: As the US network covering the 1996 Summer Olympics, this site is a sure bet for your hotlist! Officially dubbed "NBC HTTV," this site has information about all of their programs (often differentiated by genre) as well as affiliated stations (easily obtained through a clickable US map). Check out the studio production facilities with stage equipment lists and QTVR tour. Always fun to browse around here!

NHK (Japan)
URL: http://www.nhk.or.jp/
Rating: 3
Comments: Japanese broadcasting giant, NHK, has a Web site largely devoted to its ongoing promotion of interactive television and HDTV. I found the English-language pages a bit difficult to navigate, but was always greeted with strange and interesting graphics. Don't bypass the section titled "Comments from the Top" featuring weekly proclamations from NHK President Mikio Kawaguchi: i.e., "NHK will change dynamically toward the 21st century!"

Nippon Television Network (Japan)
URL: http://www.ntv.co.jp/
Rating: 3
Comments: Interestingly, this Web site from one of Japan's top commercial TV broadcasters is aimed toward international TV program distributors and not viewers. Still, any ol' person can read the plot synopses and look at the fun images. Also link to news stories from leading newspaper, *The Yomiuri Shimbun*. I love the odd note placed everywhere on the site: "Programs are not available to the general public."

PBS (USA)
URL: http://www.pbs.org/
Rating: 4
Comments: As probable NEA grant cuts loom about, let's hope the PBS Online site isn't adversely affected. Now *this* is "public" service! Information on PBS programs and services as well as the informative Online NewsHour produced by MacNeil/Lehrer Productions. The scrolling program menu makes navigation a breeze on this taut WWW site. Fun activities for kids on many of the program pages.

QVC (USA)
URL: http://www.qvc.com/
Rating: 3
Comments: QVC (rival to the Home Shopping Network) has put up a site which has everything except the many goods they sell over the air. Seems like the World Wide Web would be another excellent venue for hawking their wares. Meet QVC host Donna Harfenist in the Lounge or examine the weekly program guides to make sure you don't miss the "Russian Collectibles" show or your chance to strike gold on the "Gold Hour."

Showtime (USA)
URL: http://showtimeonline.com/
Rating: 2
Comments: Showtime is a subscription commercial US cable channel featuring classic films and movies and programs made for their service. This Web site took a lot of time to load and I finally turned off the graphics since the server running it seemed a bit slow. They offer a "multimedia software gizmo" featuring what is on at Showtime. This software is available in Mac and Windows versions and is the program calendar for each month. I felt that the site was trying to be flashy with graphics but didn't come up to the standard of other commercial sites. There are a lot of amateur sites that look *much* better than this one. Hopefully, the gizmo will be cool to look at, though the download time on my 28,800 modem was about 25 minutes... It is still downloading... By the way, if you log on from outside the USA, you get a message that the site was only intended for North America. This is a *very* bad move!

Sveriges Television (Sweden)
URL: http://www.svt.se/
Rating: 4
Comments: Although primarily in Swedish, there's enough sprinkling of English on this site to get you around. STV show information as well as film & video sales (in English). The Swedish Media E-mail list might also come in handy sometime. Excellent schedule listings for Channels 1 and 2 and tele-text (lotto results!).

Swiss Broadcasting Corporation
URL: http://www.srg-ssr.ch/
Rating: 3
Comments: Enjoying "a cool new look," the SBC WWW site is quickly filling up with interesting details about its various broadcasting activities. Best bit here is a link to "Zebraworld"—pages based on the popular youth TV program "Zebra." Be sure to check out "the pretty scene of Geneva which is automatically updated every 10 minutes from a Fotoman Pixtura Camera high atop the Swiss TV tower."

Turner Broadcasting System (USA)
URL: http://www.turner.com/
Rating: 4
Comments: A late arrival onto the Net, TBS has finally made it—and with style! The grand prize goes to CNN Interactive for an up-to-date news fix, but also visit the pages devoted to TNT, TCM, and Turner Home Entertainment. "Reel-time" chat room, press releases, and easy to use program schedules. Hope you're proud, Ted!

TV3 - Televisio de Catalunya (Spain)
URL: http://www.bcn.servicom.es/TV3/
Rating: 3
Comments: Even non-Spanish speaking Webbers can enjoy this site set up by TV3 in Catalunya, Spain. Wonderful corporate tables show percentage of TV genres shown on the network and program schedules. Peek at the pages for the "Sputnik" and "Super3" programs to see what you are missing by not watching the tube in Spain.

Universal cHANnEL
URL: http://www.mca.com:80/tv/
Rating: 4
Comments: Home to such popular programs as "seaQuestDSV" and "Partners," the Universal cHANnEL site offers cast and credit details of the shows as well as sponsoring chat forums for fans to talk about their favorite programs. Nice looking with plenty of graphics to gawk at.

VH1 (USA)
URL: http://vh1.com/
Rating: 3
Comments: A spin–off from MTV, but with a more mature audience in mind, and possibly a more serious approach, this music video channel's Web site offers artist bios, images, video clips, and an e-mail discussion group. There are even jobs listed at the network and a chance for everyday people to get their 5 minutes of fame on TV. Pretty good, though far from MTV's comprehensive and labyrinthian offering.

TV PROGRAMS

Absolutely Fabulous
URL: http://online.anu.edu.au/ArtHistory/TOR/
Rating: 3
Comments: "Pass mother the vodka, will you sweetie?" Oh, just another day in the life of Edina, Patsy and Saffy from the cult BBC TV program, "Absolutely Fabulous." This home page is designed around the show's main characters and offers sound clips, memorable quotes, images, and bios of the actors. For good measure, the theme music is thrown in to boot!

All My Children
URL: http://purplenet.com/soaps/AllMyChildren.html
Rating: 2
Comments: Get behind the scenes at the ABC set of this TV soap. See comic strips mentioning the soap, such as the Family Circus. Get fan club addresses, spoilers for the coming week, and other such fan material. Collectibles for sale are also on hand. They are *pretty* tacky, though. The luscious fan pictures of such sites are missing though there are autographed black and white pictures of some of the stars.

Andy Griffith Show
URL: http://www.wInternet.com/~muff/andy-griffith.html
Rating: 3
Comments: You can almost smell Aunt Bee's cooking at this site. This *is* Mayberry on the Web with various stats ("number of steps up to the Taylors' front porch: 2"), bloopers ("the squad car's license plate is DC-269 in one episode instead of JL-327"), things Barney says wrong ("nave = naive"), and a map of America's favorite home town. Only a few links, but kooky tidbits make this site worth a quick visit.

Animaniacs
URL: http://www2.msstate.edu/~jbp3/animx/animx.html
Rating: 4
Comments: Arising from the alt.tv.animaniacs newsgroup, this Web site contains a number of interesting documents related to this hilarious cartoon series: a New Readers' Guide (NRG), an FAQ affectionately called the Nifty Animaniacs Reference File (NARF), the Cultural References Guide for Animaniacs (CRGA), the Animaniacs Future Episode List (AFPL), and the Mega-Lyrics File (no acronym!). There's even an Animaniacs Purity Test to find out just how fanatical you really are. OK.......?????

Another World
URL: http://monet.uwaterloo.ca/~eddie/aworld.html
Rating: 4
Comments: This place may look like the domain of fans, but this soap is meticulously analyzed here and broken down into all elements. Synopses and incredibly detailed breakdown of production elements make this site a must for film and TV researchers. Some scholarly articles based on the show are placed here and there is even a "Soapmud" in the works. Get into the virtual world of soaps!

Babylon 5
URL: http://www.hyperion.com/lurk/
Rating: 4

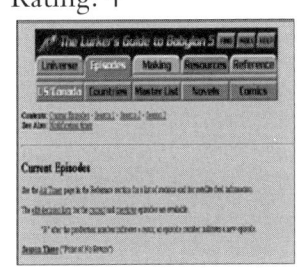

Comments: "The Lurker's Guide to Babylon 5" is an excellently designed site devoted to this popular sci-fi TV series. Included here is a season-by-season breakdown of the show, episode list, country-specific schedules (automatically generated by way of your IP address!), cast and credits, as well as a million other items of interest. So many items, in fact, that they are broken down in terms of ftp, mailing lists, www, etc. A huge plus for the option of preloading all of the images into your browser's cache for quicker movement through the pages. Very nice site!

Baywatch
URL: http://baywatch.compuserve.com/
Rating: 3

Comments: Read the *official* "Baywatch" page on Compuserve, with its own gossip rag, the *Baywatch Insider*. The issue I looked at had the inside story on Pamela Anderson's four-day courtship and marriage to Motley Crue's drummer Tommy Lee. Interviews, behind the scenes photos and stories. Basically the typical fan mag, only online. They even have an e-mail interface so you can send fan mail to anybody listed in the cast on this site. There is also a forum for discussion where teenage boys fight over who is the most beautiful babe to have graced the set of "Baywatch." This is heaven for the "Baywatch" fans, and *People* magazine for others.

Beavis & Butt-head
URL: http://calvin.hsc.colorado.edu/
Rating: 3

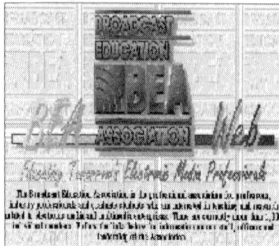

Comments: Chris Wallner's homage to his heroes, the surly lads of MTV's postmodern generation, features links to many "Beavis and Butt-head" areas on the WWW. Chris also has a lot of hate e-mail he has received protesting other shows that are pushing our lads off the MTV scheduling. Some of the most adamant media coverage has been given this obnoxious duo, while mass murderers become superheroes. Where is fiction and real life meeting?

Brady Bunch
URL: http://www.teleport.com/~btucker/bradys.htm
Rating: 4

Comments: "It's the Story...." Wonderful site with Brady FAQs, Brady scripts, Brady bios, Brady pix, Eve Plumb's birth certificate (!?!), and Brady sounds (and Alice, too!). One of the easiest sites to navigate on the Web. A groovy must for any true Brady Bunch follower also resides here: the blueprints of the Brady's house! Very impressive!

Cheers
URL: http://s9000.furman.edu/~treu/cheers.html
Rating: 3
Comments: "Cheers" has maintained a fan group all over the world and here you can find black and white publicity stills of medium quality, sounds—like the "Cheers" theme, comprehensive episode guide, "Normisms," and much more. This is not a gigantic resource, but rather a clever little one with just that thing you might be looking for. My favorite is the lyric to Woody's absolutely hideous "Kelly Song" with the following dialogue after—Kelly: Woody that was beautiful. Woody: You really liked it? Kelly: Oh, I liked it more than anything. Woody: Thanks, Kelly. So, where's my gift?

CHiPs
URL: http://underground.Internet.com/CHiPs/CHiPs.html
Rating: 4
Comments: So, you don't know what "CHiPs" is? "CHiPs is a television program which ran on NBC from 1977 to 1983. It starred Erik Estrada and Larry Wilcox as California Highway Patrol officers Ponch and Jon." You have the FAQ, episode synopses, guest stars, images, sounds, QT movies, and all the rest. They even have a discussion group! A 1970s cop show as cult series? Well, if Beastie Boys can do a video like a 1970s cop show, why not see the real thing? Not as bloody or realistic as "Cops" and therefore suitable for the squeamish. Not my cup of tea, but great for the fan.

Court TV
URL: http://www.courttv.com/
Rating: 4
Comments: This channel describes itself like this: "Court TV is a 24-hour-a-day, 7-day-a-week, cable legal news network and cable programmer dedicated to reporting on the U.S. legal and judicial systems." Court TV broadcasts trials and an updated TV picture every two minutes on the "What's Hot" page. Their site of the week is a link page to various judicial agencies or firms that are important in the law in the US. An online glossary is available for the uninitiated, with legal terms indicated in hypertext documents. It has a nice design and easy maneuverability with an interesting use tables and layout on the first page. We are all in need of legal advice now and then and this might be an interesting place to start looking.

Doctor Who
URL: http://zen.btc.uwe.ac.uk/~n2-ellis/DWID.html
Rating: 4
Comments: The "Doctor Who in Detail" pages are organized around each of the show's 25 seasons and provide a wealth of information about this classic cult program. And "details" is indeed the key word here! Each episode page lists working title, cast, original air date and time, studios, locations, and other notes (i.e. episode #653 had no script editor!!). A must visit for all of you "Doctor Who" fans out there (if you haven't been here already, that is!).

Due South
URL: http://duke.usask.ca/~turner/duesouth.html
Rating: 3
Comments: Appropriately housed in Saskatchewan, this Web page titled "Just Due It" features lots of stuff about this popular comedy program. FAQs, episode guides (three versions), image archives, sound clips, art by fans, and drinking games. Not too bad for a show only in its second season. Also link to "Other Things Canadian."

Earth2
URL: http://www.best.com/~ftmexpat/e2/earth2.html
Rating: 4
Comments: This site, "by Billy Ray & Michael Duggan & Carol Flint & Mark Levin" is an attractive resource center for sci-fi TV program "Earth2" and offers up various credit listings, an episode guide, discussion & chat groups, as well as a number of other pointers. Favorite section is titled "Earth2 Support" which features various pleas to bring back the now-canceled show. The choice between Netscape and non-Netscape versions is always appreciated. And all of this is searchable as well!

EastEnders
URL: http://galt.cs.nyu.edu/students/beads/ee/
Rating: 3
Comments: The long running BBC series is one of the most loved programs of all time in the UK. You can find info about where and when it is being shown around the world, trivia pages, FAQ files, and a discussion of soap opera and the criteria for being a soap. The graphics didn't load when I logged on. Text-rich and graphic-poor. Some of the links do offer pictures though.

TV Programs

Fawlty Towers
URL: http://cathouse.org/BritishComedy/FawltyTowers/
Rating: 4
Comments: As with most of the pages on this server, there are no graphics, but a few links to WWW episode guides for the series, selected quotes, and the *Touch of Class* script. There are a number of good quality black and white pictures ready for downloading, though these files are from about 80k to almost 150k, taking a bit of time to load. The links to the Tardis and Cardiff databases add possibilities for finding out which actors worked on a particular episode and the transmission date. Good informational connections, but low on glitz. And fun screen savers abound for downloading for the "Fawlty Towers" crowd.

Frasier
URL: http://www.umich.edu/~messina/frasier/
Rating: 2
Comments: Low-tech page for fans of "Frasier." Typical fare of FAQ, pictures, sounds, and episode guide. Funny list of Niles and Maris trivia ("Niles has $400.00 Bruno Magglis—with tassels").

Friends
URL: http://www-personal.umich.edu/~geena/friends.html
Rating: 3
Comments: Humorously called the "Not Another Friends Page!," this site is full of "Friends" stuff. But beware—this page is graphic intensive (as is mentioned when you arrive: "Hey Kids! Guess what's coming your way? A whole slew of pictures for your viewing pleasure!"). Cute, but slow. Other than a million and one images, there's an episode guide, QuickTime flicks, and sounds ("to hear the theme song, click on the cast photo above..."). With some reorganization, this site can be top-notch.

General Hospital
URL: http://www.cts.com/~jeffmj/GeneralHospital.html
Rating: 4
Comments: Soap of soaps. This one has been showing since I was a kid in the sixties and it seems to be still going strong. This volunteer-supported site seems to be one of the best I have seen on this kind of effort. It is well designed and has a lot of interesting and well-written information. If I was going to write on a soap, I would come here to look. This is for fans, because of the sheer detail, but that is also one of the attractions for a person doing a soap analysis. The jpeg photos are of high quality, and the links to other soap sites and related groups is extensive. This is a must for the television soap person.

Gilligan's Island
URL: http://www.epix.net/~jabcpudr/gilligan.html
Rating: 1
Comments: This TV show which saved many a boring afternoon in my teenage days would deserve a place in memory on the Web as one of the worst shows ever made, and therefore one of the best. This is the same case as our dear Ed Wood... Unfortunately, this page is not very structured or interesting, and the few pictures and links are of minimal interest. Only for the totally devoted.

Gladiators
URL: http://dspace.dial.pipex.com/town/square/fm71/index.html
gladiator@dial.pipex.com
Rating: 4
Comments: Love 'em or hate 'em, there's no denying that the "Gladiators" TV programs have touched a nerve with audiences around the world. Dubbed "Gladnet," this site highlights information about the show including an insightful explanation of the games they play ("Duel, a game with action where a contender gets attacked by a Gladiator using Pugel sticks while standing atop a tower") and interviews with the Gladiators themselves. Be sure to also check out the guide to country-based Gladiator programs

TV Programs

(in Russia, two of the Gladiators are named Dynamite and Spartak). Let the games begin!

Hawaii Five-O
URL: http://www.chapman.edu/students/tkrell/hawaii/five-o/
Rating: 3
Comments: "Tim's Five-O Fun Page" is a cute narrative based on the cult TV program. Lots of images from the show (I assume) and funny comments. Sample: "It's on the top floor of this hotel that Jack Lord can be seen at the beginning of each episode." Several episodes contained scenes which were filmed on-site at the Ilikai—most notably "Bomb, Bomb, Who's Got the Bomb?" Is this page for real?

Highlander
URL: http://www.rust.net/~cmarco/high.htm
Rating: 3
Comments: *huge* print guides you through this site devoted to the popular TV series, "The Highlander." Hypertext FAQ, transcribed AOL interviews with the show's actors, and a few big pictures are the main features of this page. Part of a larger site called Sci-Fi Central maintained by Charlie Marracco.

Home Improvement
URL: http://www.canuck.com/~marauder/homeimpr.html
Rating: 3
Comments: More favorite TV shows on the Web. There is a lot of trivia and gossip available here, and links to a calendar by star Debbe Dunning for all the tool types in the home. The show has won a lot of awards and these are listed. Some pictures are online, but best on site are the bios and information about the cast.

Kids in the Hall
URL: http://wwwvms.utexas.edu/~barbcarr/index.html
Rating: 3
Comments: This page is centered on the popular Canadian TV show, "Kids in the Hall," and features plenty of "Kithy" downloadables: sounds, QuickTime flicks, and FAQs. Best link, though, leads to a Queens University honour thesis on comedy and the "Kids in the Hall"! I sure do miss the show.

Land of the Lost
URL: http://www.execpc.com/~nolsen/lotl/lotl.html
Rating: 3
Comments: The author of this Web site argues that this show in its first season was one of the best children's sci-fi programs done for TV. The following season began a decline that ended in a catastrophical third season. The episode listings are quite detailed, so that anyone missing an episode can easily check up on what went on and see if the localization of the program is worth the effort. The lyrics for the opening song and various credits are here, but the most interesting is the grammar and language of the Pakuni, the ape-men in this land in some time vortex. This may remind you of the excitement about the fictive Klingon language for Trekkies. If you like this show, this is a fine place, though there are few images and no clips or sounds.

Late Show with David Letterman
URL: http://www.cbs.com/lateshow/
Rating: 4
Comments: Dave's Top Ten Lists like "Other Ways President Clinton Has Insulted Newt Gingrich," photos, FAQ from CBS, and ordering T-shirts are just some of the things present at this commercial CBS site. The FAQ will tell you how to send away for tickets for Letterman shows, give you addresses for fan mail to CBS TV shows, and much more. Calvert DeForest, who introduced Dave on the first "Late Night with David Letterman" show in 1982 and has played numerous characters, has his own home page linked to the Letterman show page.

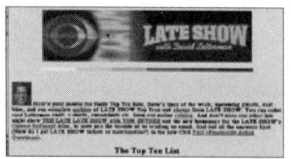

Lost in Space
URL: http://www.galcit.caltech.edu/~joe/lis/episode.html
Rating: 3
Comments: "Warning, Will Robinson, Warning!" Cable TV has ensured that camp classic "Lost in Space" is never forgotten and to help you follow the show is this handy episode list. Cast, credits, and brief synopses of every episode aired during its three-year stint is what you get here. Nothing fancy, just precise details.

TV Programs

M*A*S*H
URL: http://www.best.com/~dijon/tv/mash/
Rating: 2
Comments: This well-loved TV show has never lost a following in the US. It is pretty popular in other areas of the world as well. FAQ, episode guide, images, sounds, and little more is present here. This is rather meager fare for such a topic and the images aren't particular good either.

Mad About You
URL: http://www.alumni.caltech.edu/~witelski/may.html
Rating: 2
Comments: This Web site's author, Tom Witelski, is mad about this TV program as well, and definitely about Helen Hunt, one of the stars, since you can maneuver around to various Hunt pages via this one. There is an FAQ, episode guide, a few pictures of varying quality and a lot of links to the Internet Movie Database. I personally didn't want to see the show after seeing this one. The font sizes were rather ugly. If you like the show, check it out.

Married…With Children
URL: http://www.zmall.com/misc/bundyland/
Rating: 4
Comments: "Welcome to Bundyland." FAQs, bios, episode guides, clips, and fanzine, "Bundy Quarterly." There's even info on how to get tickets to watch the show! But the item which really strikes me here is the message posted on the cover page which airs a fear felt by many little home page maintainers, "Note to FOX Network: If there is any problem with (us) freely promoting 'Married…With Children,' please let us know and the contents will be removed immediately." I wonder when the honeymoon will end. Well, until then, enjoy!

Melrose Place
URL: http://melroseplace.com/
Rating: 2
Comments: TV will never be the same after the Web. All fans who can't get enough of their favorites, and who are tired of looking at

reruns and videotapes, can explore the adulatory texts and graphics of such sites as this one. Let's see what Alison has to say about herself here. "Hey, I am Alison Parker. Originally from Wisconsin but now a true L.A. girl. Advertising is my game, but that's not all I do. I like to travel, exercise, and 'let loose' every once in a while. I have the best time hanging out with my friends." Heavy duty! If you are a fan, get over here quick, but I get turned off by captions underneath photos that read "Studly Billy" and "Doesn't Matt look hot?"

Mighty Morphin' Power Rangers
URL: http://kilp.media.mit.edu:8001/power/homepage.html
Rating: 3
Comments: TRIVIA ALERT! This program was being shown on Swedish and Norwegian television when a murder occurred in Britain, committed by two small boys. Mass media hysteria about TV violence causing aberrant behavior in children resulted in the Power Rangers show being pulled off the air for a few weeks. Manuel Perez, a fan of the show, created this site, which even has a disclaimer to ward off the attorneys for copyright suits. The usual resources abound, with one exception, you may become a Web Ranger and get your own page. Check out the "The Mighty Morphin Power Rangers Cultural References Guide" for intertextual references. Graphically, this is a pretty nice site.

Mister Rogers' Neighborhood
URL: http://www.pbs.org:80/rogers/mrr_home.html
Rating: 4
Comments: "Won't You Be My Neighbor?" You gotta love a page which welcomes you with greetings by Mister Rogers and King Friday (sound clips of this also available)! Not just a place for the kids ("Plan & Play Activities"), but also a great place to possibly rekindle many of your own Mister Roger memories (with the lyrics to many of the songs sung on the program available to help you out). Enough pictures of Mister Rogers gushing into the camera to keep any hard-core fan satisfied. And remember, this is the "official" site for the show

TV Programs

Monty Python's Flying Circus
URL: http://bau2.uibk.ac.at/sg/python/monty.html
Rating: 4
Comments: This is the site for the diehard Monty Python fan! A number of the scripts for the TV show are available here, like "Big Nose" and "Nudge Nudge, Know What I Mean." Images, sounds, lyrics, chords to songs, and search abilities within the scripts make this one of the funniest resources going. Some home pages for the members are also listed. For those North Americans who may have missed this show, it is the comedy cult show of Europe, though it only ran on BBC from Oct. 5, 1969, to Dec. 5, 1974. John Cleese and Terry Gilliam are the most famous members of the group.

Mystery Science Theater 3000
URL: http://www.rain.org/~roryh/mst3k/index.html
Rating: 4
Comments: Also known as MST3K, this show has inspired a number of Web pages devoted to talking about the TV show which makes fun of old, cheesy movies. This page is one of the best, featuring a very well-organized FAQ, an episode guide, and a guide to shorts with a built-in checklist to keep track of what episodes you've seen already. Now *that's* cult TV viewing!

Northern Exposure
URL: http://www.netspace.org/~moose/moose.html
Rating: 4
Comments: Fans of this quirky TV show will love this humorously titled site, "The Moose's Guide to 'Northern Exposure.'" There is an amazing worldwide schedule of the show, episode lists, sound clips, images, program credits, scripts written by fans, a random quote generator, and a bibliography of the show. And all of these resources are searchable! Best is the link to all the information one would ever want or need about, well, mooses! An A+ site for fans or soon-to-be fans.

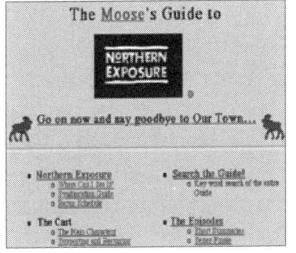

Prisoner
URL: http://www.ling.uu.se/~bengt/tp.html
Rating: 3
Comments: Originally aired between 1967 to 1992, "The Prisoner" continues to garner fans from around the world and this site is there to serve them. Dishing out healthy helpings of FAQs, episode guides, and interviews, the real treats of this site are the downloadable movies and sound clips. If you can look past the rather clumsy configuration of backgrounds and images of this site from Sweden, you'll find something mildly stimulating to look at and listen to.

Ren & Stimpy
URL: http://www.cris.com/~lkarper/rands.html
Rating: 3
Comments: Happy, Happy, Joy, Joy! Ren and Stimpy's very own home page of the WWW! Browse through the image and sound files or join the alt.tv.ren-n-stimpy newsgroup. Links to various episode guides and FAQs. Obviously this is a love of labor for page maintainer Larry Karper, who states that "Although I am at an age at which most people consider themselves to be adults, I'm not so sure. I like to keep on hand a picture of Stimpy (150k) just in case I forget about my childlike nature."

Saturday Night Live
URL: http://www.best.com/~dijon/tv/snl/
Rating: 3
Comments: These "Saturday Night Live" archives consist primarily of FAQs about the show and information about various members of the cast, including small photos of each person. The FAQs are pretty good, but the presentation with more images and scripts would have been much better. Why are there no links to related sites?

Scooby Doo
URL: http://hubcap.clemson.edu/~jsikes/scooby.html
Rating: 4
Comments: Hey it's Shaggy, Velma, Daphne, Fred and Scooby Doo on the WWW! There's a "Scooby Doo" TV schedule, pictures & sounds, and even a Scooby Snack Recipe Contest! Favorite outbound

link on this wonderful site: "The Scooby Do Coloring Book." (http://www.cs.odu.edu/~johns_d/scooby/coloringbook/color.shtml) "Hey Scoooooooby!"

seaQuest DSV
URL: http://www.phoenix.net/~leigh/seaQuest/
Rating: 4
Comments: Calling all "Questies!" This is the Web's best page devoted to the popular TV series, "seaQuest DSV." Not only is the page very nice looking, it also has links to everything about the program, from episode guides to quotable quotes. When I clicked on the "Birthdays" link, I thought I was going to find out when the show's star, Roy Scheider, was born, but instead found a list of people I didn't recognize. Alas, they are folks from the alt.tv.seaquest discussion group. Now that's true fan culture!

Seinfeld
URL: http://www.engr.wisc.edu/~heinj/seinfeld.html
Rating: 3
Comments: This is a fan page for this show, and has a lot of information on the characters for the show. The pictures are of good quality, though as always, screen shots are of lesser resolution. Episode guides, newsgroups, mailing lists, FAQ, Seinquestions, and other Web pages are featured here.

Simpsons
URL: http://yarrow.wt.com.au/~sjackson/simpsons/
Rating: 4
Comments: Gigantic WWW site devoted to America's favorite dysfunctional family, the Simpsons! Image, movie and audio clips galore, FAQs, and fan info. Play "Guess the Voice" or check out the links to some sites that might be related to the Simpsons (i.e. "that O.J. guy, Nuclear Reactors and Springfield information"). There's even a link to a sound clips of Homer dubbed in French. "Le D'oh!"

Star Trek
URL: http://www-iwi.unisg.ch/~sambucci/scifi/startrek/index.html
Rating: 4
Comments: No other TV program rules the Internet like "Star Trek" with literally hundreds of Web sites devoted to all facets of Trek life. But for my money, there's none more comprehensive and well organized as Luca Sambucci's site from St. Gallen, Switzerland. It's all here, Trekkies, with every link annotated, rated and country of origin identified! Look at the section titled "Country Statistics" to see which countries have the largest number of "Star Trek" home pages? It's mind-boggling!

Tick
URL: http://www.prairienet.org/~phyber/tickpage.html
Rating: 4
Comments: Gavin Suntop's cool "Tick" page has everything Tick-related: FAQ, picture archive (20 GIFs), episode guide (with his own ratings), and character guide. I got a chuckle reading some of the items in the "Tick News and Rumor section." Sample item: "Source: Gavin Suntop, Subject: The Tick Home Video, Status: CONFIRMED Good news for all you Tick fans! The long awaited Tick Home Video is out..." More stuff coming online soon!

Unsolved Mysteries
URL: http://www.unsolved.com/
Rating: 4
Comments: Of course it's not just a TV show, it's a phenomenon! Sections titled "Lost Love," "Missing," and "Fugitives" guide you through the cases. Read bulletins about bank robbers, like the "Red Dye Robber," but remember, he is considered armed and dangerous. If you don't want to use the special 1-800 number to get updates on any of the "unsolved mysteries," you can always check this Web site's update page.

X-Files
URL: http://duggy.extern.ucsd.edu/~linny/index.html
Rating: 4
Comments: This wildly popular sci-fi TV series currently has over 50 Web sites devoted to it and my favorite one of the lot is this snappy site by 19-year-old Jenifer Linville. Categories of info include "Media Surveillance" (with transcribed online chats with the show's stars), "Wire-Tap" (lots of sound files), and "Humor" (with essay titled "You Know You're an X-Phile When. . ."). If Jenifer isn't hired right out of college by one of the big WWW sites, I'll be very surprised!

VIDEO INFO/SALES

Art & Trash Video
URL: http://www.io.org/~imp/athome.htm
Rating: 3
Comments: As their name suggests, this Toronto-based vendor sells art and trash videos. Look through their inventory of 7,500 titles by way of various topic, genre or country listings. Nothing terribly special about these pages except the ability to order many difficult-to-find videos.

Austrian Video Archive
URL: http://austria-info.at/ava/
Rating: 3
Comments: This service offers a database of video footage on Austria for purchase. Search, visit, and order videos. This one is primarily for production companies. Instead of going there and hanging out in coffeehouses and visiting their company you can browse online. Think I'd rather go there, but this saves time and money! Here is a sample listing. Index: Code   Location   Season   Settings   Motifs   Themes 4094: Z4H   Salzburg   Winter   snowbunny with glasses; type; People 4096.

Best Video
URL: http://www.bestvideo.com
staff@bestvideo.com
Rating: 4
Comments: Featuring over 24,000 titles ("accumulating at a rate of 125 per week"), Best Video offers an easy way to search their inventory via either name search or through 250 different topic categories. Super image collections, monthly video reviews, and little informative tidbits. Emphasis seems to be on classical Hollywood and cult films.

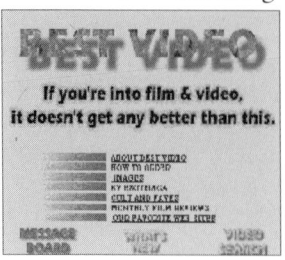

Big Lizard Video
URL: http://www.well.com/user/bigliz/
Rating: 3
Comments: All the way from Columbia, Missouri, comes Big Lizard Video, "the best source for eclectic, cult, hard-to-find, and downright weird videos and laser discs." And they aren't kidding! Their budget text-only catalog lists everything from *And Now the Screaming Starts* to *Witchcraft Through the Ages*. Simple site, but great videos to order by mail.

Blockbuster
URL: http://pwr.com/blockbuster/
Rating: 3
Comments: This is a great place for purchase of NTSC (US system) videos and laser discs as well as paraphernalia for movie fans. News and previews for new and old releases. Some of the material is also in Spanish. A great plus for the multilingual Americas. You can't order online but you can write them via e-mail for more information on ordering. This chain has stores everywhere in the US.

Carpel Video
URL: http://www.peakcom.com/carpel/
Rating: 2
Comments: No cult or classic videos for sale here. "Welcome to Carpel Video...sellers of blank recycled and brand new, brand name video tapes in all formats." I remember an old "Saturday Night Live" skit featuring the Scotch tape store ("...nope, don't have it. Nothing but Scotch tape here") and this site is frighteningly similar. No e-mail address, no online ordering, just a 1-800 phone number. Well, what are you waiting for?

CINEVISTA Video
URL: http://www.gayweb.com/112/112home.html
Rating: 3
Comments: CINEVISTA Films got its start distributing German gay film, *Taxi Zum Klo*, and this site highlights their video sales. Specializing in independent, gay-themed videos such as *Grief* and *Caravaggio*, this site provides an easy-to-use order form to purchase videos via the Internet with a credit card. This is a great way to get some of these hard-to-find films.

Classic TV Commercials Video
URL: http://www.webscope.com/commercials/
Rating: 2
Comments: For just $14.95, you too can get a one-hour video full of those wonderful old TV commercials. Although I must admit, if reading the sales pitch on this page is supposed to convince me to buy the damn thing, it might not even be worth the $14.95 (plus $3.50 shipping). Read on: "Imagine watching 'I Love Lucy' *without* the Philip Morris Commercials??? Some people do though the Commercials are an intrinsic part of the experience of watching an old favorite, thus ruining the enjoyment of a great piece of history." Please!

Family Home Video
URL: http://www.iea.com/~fhv/
Rating: 4
Comments: Very inexpensive videos can be purchased over the Net through Family Home Video. Use their search engine to browse through 25,000 titles. I must admit I was a bit worried about the name of this company at first, but when I searched for some John Waters films and was successful, my mind was put to rest. Each found film is linked to the Internet Movie Database for further information (although this automated script often searches the database for titles never to be found, such as "Charlie Chaplin, Volume I"). Still, the cheap prices and ability to order online makes this site a very seductive source for purchasing videos.

Flicks on Discs
URL: http://www.teleport.com/~gilbert/flicks/public_html/index.html
Rating: 2
Comments: Pretty basic WWW page from this Portland, Oregon, laser disc retailer. Lots of lists of titles and a fairly decent newsletter with future laser disc release dates. I like their name, though.

Guide to Video Distributors
URL: gopher://marvel.loc.gov/00/research/reading.rooms/motion.picture/mopic.tv/vidguide
Rating: 3
Comments: This gopher bibliography document, published by the Library of Congress, is "intended to help users of video materials locate feature films, documentaries, and educational programs available for purchase and/or rental." The date published was 1993, so it is probably a bit out-of-date, though a good starting point for searches.

HBO Home Video Online
URL: http://hbohomevideo.com/
Rating: 2
Comments: Yes, the eternal VCR play button even exists in this virtual world of Home Box Office Video Online on the first page. Information about HBO productions released in video stores after their premiere on this pay entertainment channel seems to be the major point of interest. Scanned video boxes, sounds, video clips, images of stars and synopses are all here, but the time needed to load seems hardly worth it in the long run. I may be cynical, but most of this material would never make it to the local cinema, so do we want it that badly in our homes? The layout of the site is fine, but the content seems second–rate.

Ken Crane's Laser Disc Super Store
URL: http://www.kencranes.com/laserdiscs/
Rating: 2
Comments: Boasting that they are the "Largest Laserdisc Mail Order Retailer in the U.S.," this is a great place to pick up virtually any laser disc title. Browse their catalog by category or title and order your laser discs online. Some graphics are available for downloading as well.

Picture Palace
URL: http://www.ids.net/picpal/index.html
Rating: 3
Comments: Quite the "chatty" home page selling old film videos, laser discs, and CD-ROMS. Their 36,000+ online catalog makes searching for titles or stars a breeze. The Picture Palace's prices are competitive and should be one of the first resources you turn to when looking to purchase an old flick on video. These folks also maintain excellent information pages about Buster Keaton and Jonas Mekas. A little redesigning of this site (ridding it of huge background gifs and long, text–heavy pages) will make it first-rate one day.

Rocket Video
URL: http://www.rocketvideo.com/
Rating: 4
Comments: Here's a Web site by one of Hollywood's hottest video stores! Its searchable 15,000 title database is quick and efficient. Online ordering form brings the store to wherever you are. Subscribe to their "Rocket Science" e-zine for "the latest news, views and reviews from Hollywood and beyond."

Science Fiction Continuum
URL: http://www.sfcontinuum.com/sjvideo/
Rating: 2
Comments: Sci-fi and cult videos for sale here by this New Jersey company. Not just lists, here, but in-depth descriptions and video cover images throughout. Is this the only place where you can get such classics as *Crawling Eye* ("giant eyeballs with tentacles descend on the Earth from inside a radioactive fog!")?

Universal Entertainment Videos
URL: http://www.dva.com/
Rating: 2
Comments: Universal Entertainment Videos does not seem affiliated with Universal Pictures but does have their own video outlet and all the movies are under $10. They offer online or phone orders, and the online Web form offers choices for films, CDs or games. The choice of films was not enormous, but will cater to some tastes leaning toward the old mainstream hits, bizarre, schlock, or playboy calendar crowd. Varied, but they might have that one you want like *Boris and Natasha—The Movie*.

LISTSERV Discussion Lists & USENET Newsgroups

LISTSERV discusssion lists and USENET newsgroups are listed in this section in alphabetical order. We do not review these groups because it would involve being subscribed for months at a time to follow the discussion threads in order to evaluate them on a fair basis. Instead, we provide you with a helpful list to get you started. Since subscription to these groups and lists are free, you can't lose anything by trying them out for a while. The groups vary greatly, from the academically oriented to the totally mainstream. Be forewarned that members of some groups can be arrogant and antagonistic. You won't normally find that at the academic sites, though, if you stick to those. Lurk for a while before putting your two cents in, or your foot in your mouth!

LISTSERV LISTS
The site address for writing to the discussion list is given, but remember that you must first subscribe. For more details on how to do that, see the "Shots in Cyberspace" chapter of this book. Do not send subscription requests to the addresses given because they will appear as messages that are distributed to all the subscribers!

CINEMA-L   CINEMA-L@AMERICAN.EDU
Discussions on All Forms of Cinema

CJMOVIES   CJMOVIES@UACSC2.ALBANY.EDU
Journal of Criminal Justice and Popular Culture

CTHEORY   CTHEORY@VM1.MCGILL.CA
Canadian Cultural Theory E-zine

DGTLCLAS DGTLCLAS@VM1.MCGILL.CA
Discussion on Digital Media and Multi Media for Instructional

FILM-L   FILM-L@ITESMVF1.RZS.ITESM.MX
Filmmaking and Reviews List.

FILMUS-L   FILMUS-L@IUBVM.UCS.INDIANA.EDU
Film Music Discussion List

FRAMEWORKS
FRAMEWORKS@LISTSERV.AOL.COM
Experimental Film Discussion List

H-FILM   H-FILM@MSU.EDU
H-NET List for Scholarly Studies and Uses of Media

H-FILM@UICVM.UIC.EDU
An H-Net List for Film History and Studies

H-MMEDIA H-MMEDIA@MSU.EDU
H-Net List for Multimedia and New Technologies in Humanities

HORROR   HORROR@IUBVM.UCS.INDIANA.EDU
Horror in Film and Literature

ILLTV   ILLTV@VM1.MCGILL.CA
illTV is the McGill University Student Television Network

MCJRNL   MCJRNL@UBVM.CC.BUFFALO.EDU
Media Journal Distribution List

MEDCC-L   MEDCC-L@UAFSYSB.UARK.EDU
Issues Related to the Study of Media, Culture, & Curriculum

MEDIA-L   MEDIA-L@BINGVMB.CC.BINGHAMTON.EDU
Media in Education

MEDIAWEB MEDIAWEB@VM.TEMPLE.EDU
Film/Video Web Sites Discussion

MMEDIA-L MMEDIA-L@ITESMVF1.RZS.ITESM.MX
Multimedia Discussion List

MIT-TV-L MIT-TV-L@MITVMA.MIT.EDU
MIT Cable Television Schedule

ROSEBUD   ROSEBUD@SEARN.SUNET.SE
International Discussion List for Film Students

SCREEN-L SCREEN-L@UA1VM.UA.EDU
Film and TV Studies Discussion List

VIDNET-L
VIDNET-L@UGA.CC.UGA.EDU
Video Network Discussion List

Other discussion groups that don't use LISTSERV software:

KIDMEDIA
Discussions between people interested in, or involved in, the creation, production, distribution and/or consumption of media whose primary target audience is children.

To get on the list send request to:
kidmedia-request@airwaves.chi.il.us

EXHIBITIONISTS
Purpose: Primarily for managers and/or projectionists, but open also to anyone working in a cinema or film society, etc.

To get on the list send request to:
exhibitionists-request@jvnc.net

SOUNDTRACKS
Discussions/reviews film and television soundtracks.

To get on the list send request to:
soundtracks-request@ifi.unizh.ch (Michel Hafner)

FILM THEORY
The purpose of the list is to discuss film aesthetics, cultural critique of cinema, the theory of film practice, the practice of film theory, and non-mainstream movies.

To subscribe, send an e-mail message to:
majordomo@world.std.com

In the body of the message, write:
subscribe film-theor
MOVIES-SEIVOM

Movies-seivoM, the Self-Referential Movies Mailing List, recommends and discusses movies that "break the 4th wall" and display a more-overt- than-usual awareness of themselves as movies.

To join the list, send an e-mail with "Subscribe" as the Subject to: Movies-seivoM@kinexis.com.

USENET GROUPS

The newsgroups listed here vary in content and the amount of volume. Some of them are very technical, while others are chatty and informal. The subjects covered range from technical satellite dish information all the way to characters in specific television programs. You will need newsgroup reader software and availability to the newsgroups via a server that stores them. If you are unsure if they can be accessed from your Internet service provider, just give them a call and ask how you should do it. If you use Netscape, you may configure it to access the news server directly under the OPTIONS section in the menu, under PREFERENCES then MAIL AND NEWS and write in the address for the server where there is a space marked NEWS (NNTP) SERVER. After you have done this, then click on the NEWS-GROUPS button near the top of the NETSCAPE program and you will be able to use the site specified.

Here are some WWW sites that may be valuable for you while getting started on USENET newsgroups.

Everything You Always Wanted To Know About
Usenet - By Daniel Akst
http://techweb.cmp.com/techweb/ng/issues/025issue/usenet.htm

Usenet Info Center FAQ
http://www.lib.ox.ac.uk/internet/news/faq/archive/usenet.info-center-faq.html

USENET Newsgroups sorted by section:

alt.asian-movies
alt.binaries.sounds.movies
alt.binaries.sounds.tv
alt.cable-tv.re-regulate
alt.cd-rom.reviews
alt.cult-movies
alt.cult-movies.evil-deads
alt.cult-movies.rhps
alt.cult-movies.rocky-horror
alt.dcom.catv
alt.fan.jackie-chan
alt.fan.quentin-tarantino
alt.movies.branagh-thmpsn
alt.movies.joe-vs-volcano
alt.movies.kubrick
alt.movies.monster
alt.movies.scorcese
alt.movies.silent
alt.movies.spielberg
alt.movies.tim-burton
alt.movies.visual-effects
alt.movies.visual-effects
alt.satellite.tv.europe
alt.sex.movies
alt.tv.animaniacs
alt.tv.babylon-5
alt.tv.bakersfield-pd
alt.tv.barney
alt.tv.beakmans-world
alt.tv.beavis-n-butthead
alt.tv.bh90210
alt.tv.brady-bunch
alt.tv.brisco-county
alt.tv.brothers.grunt.sucks
alt.tv.comedy-central
alt.tv.commercials
alt.tv.dinosaurs
alt.tv.dinosaurs.barney.die.die.die
alt.tv.forever-knight

alt.tv.game-shows
alt.tv.hbo
alt.tv.hermans-head
alt.tv.highlander
alt.tv.infomercials
alt.tv.kids-in-hall
alt.tv.kungfu
alt.tv.liquid-tv
alt.tv.lois-n-clark
alt.tv.mad-about-you
alt.tv.mash
alt.tv.max-headroom
alt.tv.melrose-place
alt.tv.mst3k
alt.tv.muppets
alt.tv.mwc
alt.tv.nickelodeon
alt.tv.northern-exp
alt.tv.nypd-blue
alt.tv.prisoner
alt.tv.public-access
alt.tv.real-world
alt.tv.red-dwarf
alt.tv.ren-n-stimpy
alt.tv.robocop
alt.tv.robotech
alt.tv.rockford-files
alt.tv.roseanne
alt.tv.saved-bell
alt.tv.seaquest
alt.tv.seinfeld
alt.tv.simpsons
alt.tv.snl
alt.tv.talkshows.late
alt.tv.time-traxx
alt.tv.tiny-toon
alt.tv.tiny-toon.fandom
alt.tv.tv-nation
alt.tv.twin-peaks
alt.tv.x-files
alt.tv.x-files.creative

Listserv/Usenet

alt.video.laserdisc

au.twin-peaks

aus.films
aus.sf.star-trek
aus.tv
aus.tv.community

bit.listserv.cinema-l
bit.listserv.film-l
bit.listserv.movie.memorabilia
bit.listserv.screen-l

bln.medien

cl.gruppen.ig_medien
cl.medien.aktionen

cl.medien.allgemein
cl.medien.datenbanken
cl.medien.diskussion
cl.medien.funk
cl.medien.text
cl.medien.vernetzung
finet.freenet.mediateekki.leffat
misc.writing.screenplays

no.film

rec.arts.movies
rec.arts.movies.current-films
rec.arts.movies.lists+surveys
rec.arts.movies.misc
rec.arts.movies.movie-going
rec.arts.movies.past-films
rec.arts.movies.people
rec.arts.movies.production
rec.arts.movies.reviews
rec.arts.movies.tech
rec.arts.sf.movies

rec.arts.sf.reviews
rec.arts.sf.tv
rec.arts.sf.tv.babylon5
rec.arts.sf.tv.quantum-leap
rec.arts.tv
rec.arts.tv.mst3k
rec.arts.tv.soaps
rec.arts.tv.soaps.abc
rec.arts.tv.soaps.cbs
rec.arts.tv.soaps.misc
rec.arts.tv.uk
rec.music.movies
rec.video
rec.video.cable-tv
rec.video.desktop
rec.video.production
rec.video.releases
rec.video.satellite.tvro

sci.engr.advanced-tv

ucb./digital-video
ucb.film-program
ucb.org.filmstuds

uk.media

APPENDIX & CROSS-REFERENCES

RESOURCES AND SITES:

E-MAIL ADDRESSES
bert.deivert@hks.se	Bert Deivert
dharries@afionline.org	Dan Harries
cyberprof@igc.apc.org	Howard Frederick, ask about obtaining course materials he uses for course *Cyberresearch and Global Internetworking*
nightdave@aol.com	You can order the INTERNET video here
comserve@vm.its.rpi.edu	Comserve communications research net, send message HELP for information
movie@ibmpcug.co.uk	send message HELP for database info

FINGER addresses- use any finger gateway
finger ivan@carroll1.cc.edu	Ivan's plan is interesting...
finger lunch@think.com	Lunch menu at this site
finger nasanews@space.mit.edu	Latest news from NASA
finger weather@cirrus.mit.edu	Latest weather for Boston area
finger barlow@well.sf.ca.us	Grateful Dead's lyricist
finger help@dir.su.oz.au	Query databases

CROSS-REFERENCES for sites in this book
Sub-category headings

Academic
Animation Journal
URL: http://www.chapman.edu/animation
Category: Animation

Shizuoka University Animation Page
URL: http://www.lib.shizuoka.ac.jp/animaw1.html
Category: Animation

Griffith, David Wark
URL: http://ernie.bgsu.edu/~pcharle/gish/dwg.html
Category: Directors

Kubrick, Stanley
URL: http://www.lehigh.edu/~pjl2/kubrick.html
Category: Directors

Marker, Chris
URL: http://www.ss.rmit.edu.au/miles/marker/Marker.html
Category: Directors

American Film Institute
URL: http://www.afionline.org/
Category: Film & Media Schools

Art Center College of Design (Pasadena, CA)
URL: http://www3.artcenter.edu/
Category: Film & Media Schools

Australian Film Television and Radio School
URL: http://www.usyd.edu.au/~graham/aftrs.html
Category: Film & Media Schools

Bowling Green State University- Dept. of Telecommunications
URL: http://www.bgsu.edu/departments/tcom/
Category: Film & Media Schools

Brown University- Department of Modern Culture and Media
URL: http://www.modcult.brown.edu/
Category: Film & Media Schools

California Institute of the Arts- School of Film/Video
URL: http://itchy.calarts.edu/FV.html
Category: Film & Media Schools

Chapman University- Department of Film and Television
URL: http://www.chapman.edu/comm/ftv/index.html
Category: Film & Media Schools

Florida State University- Film School
URL: http://www.fsu.edu/~film/
Category: Film & Media Schools

Appendix & Cross-References

Johns Hopkins University- Dept. of Film and Media Studies
URL: http://www.jhu.edu/~english/film_media/film_media.html
Category: Film & Media Schools

Minneapolis College of Art & Design- Media Arts
URL: http://www.mcad.edu/academic/mediaArts/mediaArts.html
Category: Film & Media Schools

New York University- Cinema Studies
URL: http://www.nyu.edu/gsas/dept/cinema/
Category: Film & Media Schools

Northwestern University- Dept. of Radio/TV/Film
URL: http://www.rtvf.nwu.edu/info/Info.html
Category: Film & Media Schools

Queen's University- Film Studies
URL: http://www.film.queensu.ca/
Category: Film & Media Schools

Radio & Television Institute- Finland
URL: http://www.yle.fi/rti/rtiengl/rtihome.htm
Category: Film & Media Schools

San Francisco State University- Cinema Department
URL: http://www.cinema.sfsu.edu/
Category: Film & Media Schools

Temple University- Film and Media Arts
URL: http://blue.temple.edu:80/~fma/
Category: Film & Media Schools

University of Barcelona - Centre for Cinematic Research
URL: http://www.swcp.com/~cmora/cine.html
Category: Film & Media Schools

University of Copenhagen- Department of Film & Media Studies
URL: http://www.media.ku.dk/
Category: Film & Media Schools

University of Iowa- Film Studies
URL: http://www.lib.uiowa.edu/proj/film/
Category: Film & Media Schools

University of Karlstad- Film Studies
URL: http://www.hks.se/~bertd/toc.html
Category: Film & Media Schools

University of Texas at Austin- Department of Radio, Television, Film
URL: http://www.utexas.edu/coc/rtf/
Category: Film & Media Schools

University of Toronto- Cinema Studies
URL: http://www.utoronto.ca:80/innis/cinema/
Category: Film & Media Schools

University of Waterloo- Film Studies
URL: http://arts.uwaterloo.ca/FINE/juhde/film.htm
Category: Film & Media Schools

Vancouver Film School
URL: http://www.multimedia.edu/
Category: Film & Media Schools

York University- Dept. of Film & Video
URL: http://www.yorku.ca/faculty/finearts/fv/fvhome.htm
Category: Film & Media Schools

Contemporary Chinese Cinema
URL: http://www.citri.edu.au:8888/ccc/index.html
Category: Film & TV Assorted

Film Censorship Archive
URL: http://fileroom.aaup.uic.edu/FileRoom/documents/Mfilm.html
Category: Film & TV Assorted

Lumo - Finnish Film Page
URL: http://www.kaapeli.fi/~lumo/English/
Category: Film & TV Assorted

U.S. National Film Registry - Titles
URL: http://www.cs.cmu.edu:80/afs/cs.cmu.edu/user/clamen/misc/movies/NFR-Titles.html
Category: Film & TV Assorted

Vampyrs Film List
URL: http://ubu.hahnemann.edu/Misc/Vamp-Mov.html
Category: Film & TV Assorted

Appendix & Cross-References

WWW.FilmMusic.Com
URL: http://www.filmmusic.com/
Category: Film & TV Assorted

Broadcasting Link
URL: http://www.algonet.se/~nikos/broad.html
Category: Film & TV Indices

Cinema Sites
URL: http://www.webcom.com/~davidaug/Movie_Sites.html
Category: Film & TV Indices

CineMedia
URL: http://www.afionline.org/CINEMEDIA/CineMedia.home.html
Category: Film & TV Indices

GEWI Film Page
URL: http://gewi.kfunigraz.ac.at/~puntigam/
Category: Film & TV Indices

Guide to Film & Video Resources
URL: http://http2.sils.umich.edu/Public/fvl/film.html
Category: Film & TV Indices

OMNIBUS-EYE
URL: http://www.rtvf.nwu.edu/
Category: Film & TV Indices

Queer Media Resources
URL: http://abacus.oxy.edu/qrd/media/
Category: Film & TV Indices

SCREENSite
URL: http://www.sa.ua.edu/TCF/welcome.htm
Category: Film & TV Indices

Critical Inquiry
URL: http://www.uchicago.edu:80/u.scholarly/CritInq/
Category: Magazines & Journals

CTHEORY
URL: http://www.freedonia.com/ctheory/
Category: Magazines & Journals

Federal Communications Law Journal
URL: http://www.law.indiana.edu/fclj/fclj.html
Category: Magazines & Journals

fps: The Magazine of Animation on Film and Video
URL: http://www.cam.org/~pawn/fps.html
Category: Magazines & Journals

Journal of Norwegian Media Research
URL: http://macmedia19.uio.no/Prosjekt/nmt/index.english.html
Category: Magazines & Journals

KINEMA
URL: http://arts.uwaterloo.ca/FINE/juhde/kinemahp.htm
Category: Magazines & Journals

Millennium Film Journal
URL: http://www.sva.edu/MFJ/
Category: Magazines & Journals

Postmodern Culture
URL: http://jefferson.village.virginia.edu/pmc/contents.all.html
Category: Magazines & Journals

|T|E|L|E|C|I|N|E|
URL: http://omnibus-eye.rtvf.nwu.edu/telecine/
Category: Magazines & Journals

Weltwunder der Kinematographie
URL: http://www.snafu.de/~dgfk/WDK_Iverz.html
Category: Magazines & Journals

!PIXIN(*)COMPENDIUM! Project
URL: http://omnibus-eye.rtvf.nwu.edu/compendium/
Category: Movies

Howard Rheingold
URL: http://www.well.com/user/hlr/
Category: New Media

San Francisco Digital Media Center
URL: http://www.well.com/user/sfdmc/
Category: New Media

Appendix & Cross-References

WAXweb
URL: http://bug.village.virginia.edu/
Category: New Media

Boston Film and Video Foundation
URL: http://www.actwin.com:80/cgi-bin/BFVF/@ab84d/index.html
Category: Organizations/Guilds

UK Guide to Student Film Societies
URL: http://www.warwick.ac.uk/~suaag/societies/societies.html
Category: Organizations/Guilds

Broadcast Pioneers Library
URL: http://www.itd.umd.edu/UMS/UMCP/BPL/bplintro.html
Category: Research and Databases

CSUOHIO Film Database
URL: gopher://trans.csuohio.edu:70/1ftp-nop:nic.funet.fi@/pub/culture/tv+film/database/
Category: Research and Databases

Early Motion Pictures Home Page
URL: http://lcweb2.loc.gov/papr/mpixhome.html
Category: Research and Databases

Eastman Kodak Company
URL: http://www.kodak.com/homePage.shtml
Category: Research and Databases

Film Webliography
URL: http://www.lib.lsu.edu/hum/film.html
Category: Research and Databases

Filmleksikonet (Norwegian Movie Database)
URL: http://www.uio.no/cgi-bin/filmleksikon
Category: Research and Databases

GRAFICS Early Cinema Server
URL: http://grafics.histart.umontreal.ca/default-eng.html
Category: Research and Databases

HADDON: Ethnographic Film Archive
URL: http://www.rsl.ox.ac.uk/isca/haddon/HADD_home.html
Category: Research and Databases

Media History Web
URL: http://spot.colorado.edu/~rossk/history/histhome.html
Category: Research and Databases

Museum of Broadcast Communications
URL: http://webmart.org/mbc/
Category: Research and Databases

Museum of Television and Radio
URL: http://www.mtr.org/
Category: Research and Databases

National Film Preservation Board
URL: gopher://marvel.loc.gov/11/research/reading.rooms/motion.picture/nfpb
Category: Research and Databases

National Museum of Photography: Film and Television
URL: http://www.nmsi.ac.uk/nmpft/
Category: Research and Databases

Pacific Film Archive
URL: http://www.uampfa.berkeley.edu/
Category: Research and Databases

Polish Cinema Database
URL: http://info.fuw.edu.pl/Filmy/
Category: Research and Databases

Silent Movies
URL: http://www.cs.monash.edu.au/~pringle/silent/
Category: Research and Databases

Telemuseum, Stockholm, Sweden
URL: http://www.telemuseum.se/musinfo/telemuseng.html
Category: Research and Databases

Vanderbilt Television News Archive
URL: gopher://tvnews.vanderbilt.edu/1
Category: Research and Databases

Another World
URL: http://monet.uwaterloo.ca/~eddie/aworld.html
Category: TV Programs

Guide to Video Distributors
URL:gopher://marvel.loc.gov/00/research/reading.rooms/motion.picture/mopic.tv/vidguide
Category: Video Info./Sales

Commercial Products
animation usa
URL: http://www.usa.net/ausa/
Category: Animation

Cartoon Factory
URL: http://www.cartoon-factory.com/
Category: Animation

As Seen on TV
URL: http://www.asontv.com/
Category: Film & TV Assorted

Cult Film Page
URL: http://sepnet.com/rcramer/index.htm
Category: Film & TV Assorted

Nielsen Media Research
URL: http://www.nielsenmedia.com/
Category: Film & TV Assorted

Samuel French Theatre and Film Bookshops
URL: http://www.hollywoodnetwork.com:80/hn/shopping/bookstore/sfbook.html
Category: Film & TV Assorted

Ticket Booth
URL: http://www.cipsinc.com/spot/
Category: Film & TV Assorted

Movie Poster Web Page
URL: http://www.musicman.com/mp/mp.html
Category: Images

Addresses of the Rich and Famous
URL: http://www.infohaus.com/access/by-seller/Addresses_of_the_Rich_Famous
Category: Memorabilia

Aspen Moon Grafika (Polish Posters)
URL: http://www.mjwebworks.com/webworks/amg/
Category: Memorabilia

C*stars Cinemagic Art
URL: http://www.3i.com/cstars/cinemagic/cinemagic_top.html
Category: Memorabilia

CBS Store Online
URL: http://www.cbs.com/blackrock/store.html
Category: Memorabilia

Hollywood Shopping Network
URL: http://www.hollywoodnetwork.com:80/hn/shopping/index.html
Category: Memorabilia

Hollywood Toy and Poster Company
URL: http://www.hollywdposter.mb.ca/hollywdposter/
Category: Memorabilia

Iconographics: Movie Poster Gallery
URL: http://www.newmexico.com/icon/
Category: Memorabilia

Jess and Carl's Theater Posters
URL: http://www.atw.fullfeed.com/~huster/
Category: Memorabilia

Movie Madness
URL: http://www.moviemadness.com/
Category: Memorabilia

Movie Poster Warehouse
URL: http://www.io.org/~mpw/
Category: Memorabilia

Nightmare Factory
URL: http://www.io.com/~nightime/trek.html
Category: Memorabilia

Warner Bros. Studio Stores
URL: http://batmanforever.com/welcome/stores.html
Category: Memorabilia

Appendix & Cross-References

Movie Link
URL: http://www.movielink.com/
Category: Movie Theaters

Adobe Systems
URL: http://www.adobe.com/
Category: New Media

Apple Computers
URL: http://www.apple.com/
Category: New Media

Apple Multimedia Program
URL: http://www.amp.apple.com/
Category: New Media

Edge Interactive Media
URL: http://www.well.com/user/edgehome/
Category: New Media

Interactive Systems Inc.
URL: http://www.teleport.com/~isi/
Category: New Media

LucasArts Entertainment
URL: http://www.lucasarts.com/menu.html
Category: New Media

Microsoft Corp.
URL: http://www.microsoft.com/
Category: New Media

Nintendo
URL: http://www.nintendo.com/
Category: New Media

Philips Media On-Line
URL: http://spider.media.philips.com/media/
Category: New Media

QuickTime Continuum
URL: http://quicktime.apple.com/
Category: New Media

Sega Online
URL: http://www.segaoa.com/
Category: New Media

Silicon Graphics' Silicon Surf
URL: http://www.sgi.com/
Category: New Media

Voyager Co.
URL: http://www.voyagerco.com/
Category: New Media

Canadian Filmmaker's Distribution Center
URL: http://www.arena.com/film/
Category: Production & Distribution

CineWEB
URL: http://www.cineweb.com/
Category: Production & Distribution

Lucasfilm THX Home Page
URL: http://www.thx.com/thx/thx.html
Category: Production & Distribution

Writers' Computer Store
URL: http://www.hollywoodnetwork.com:80/hn/shopping/kiosk/index.html
Category: Screenwriting

Art & Trash Video
URL: http://www.io.org/~imp/athome.htm
Category: Video Info./Sales

Best Video
URL: http://www.tagsys.com:80/ads/BestVideo/
Category: Video Info./Sales

Big Lizard Video
URL: http://www.well.com/user/bigliz/
Category: Video Info./Sales

Blockbuster
URL: http://pwr.com/blockbuster/
Category: Video Info./Sales

Appendix & Cross-References

Carpel Video
URL: http://www.peakcom.com/carpel/
Category: Video Info./Sales

CINEVISTA Video
URL: http://www.gayweb.com/112/112home.html
Category: Video Info./Sales

Classic TV Commercials Video
URL: http://www.webscope.com/commercials/
Category: Video Info./Sales

Family Home Video
URL: http://www.iea.com/~fhv/
Category: Video Info./Sales

Flicks on Discs
URL: http://www.teleport.com/~gilbert/flicks/public_html/index.html
Category: Video Info./Sales

HBO Home Video Online
URL: http://hbohomevideo.com/
Category: Video Info./Sales

Ken Crane's Laser Disc Super Store
URL: http://www.kencranes.com/laserdiscs/
Category: Video Info./Sales

Picture Palace
URL: http://www.ids.net/picpal/index.html
Category: Video Info./Sales

Rocket Video
URL: http://www.rocketvideo.com/
Category: Video Info./Sales

Science Fiction Continuum
URL: http://www.sfcontinuum.com/sjvideo/
Category: Video Info./Sales

Universal Entertainment Videos
URL: http://www.dva.com/
Category: Video Info./Sales

Critique

Allen, Woody
URL: http://www.idt.unit.no/~torp/woody/
Category: Directors

Cameron, James
URL: http://www.soton.ac.uk/~pdc194/cameron/
Category: Directors

Hitchcock, Alfred
URL: http://www.primenet.com/~mwc/
Category: Directors

Tarantino, Quentin
URL: http://www.GANet.Net/~pg0/quentin/greatbig.htm
Category: Directors

Tarantino, Quentin
URL: http://www.webcom.com/~kbilly/
Category: Directors

100+ Movie Reviews by Joan Ellis
URL: http://movie.infocom.net/
Category: Film Reviews

As the Reel Rolls
URL: http://www.fcs.net/maclark/
Category: Film Reviews

Entertainment Extra!
URL: http://www.ddc.com/extra/
Category: Film Reviews

Film.com Reviews
URL: http://www.film.com/film/reviews/
Category: Film Reviews

Mandel & Patrick's Movie Corner!
URL: http://www.fyi.net/~andre/mand&pat.htm
Category: Film Reviews

Middlesex News Film Reviews
URL: gopher://ftp.std.com:70/11/periodicals/Middlesex-News/movies
Category: Film Reviews

Appendix & Cross-References

Movie Mom's Guide to Films and Videos
URL: http://pages.prodigy.com/VA/rcpj55a/moviemom.html
Category: Film Reviews

Movie Review Query Engine
URL: http://www.cinema.pgh.pa.us/movie/reviews
Category: Film Reviews

Out Magazine Movie Reviews
URL: http://www.out.com/out/entertainment/movies.html
Category: Film Reviews

Pathfinder Movie Reviews
URL: http://pathfinder.com/@@N4f1msEDRQIAQPdo/pathfinder/hitcity/movies.html
Category: Film Reviews

San Francisco Chronicle Film Reviews
URL: http://www.sfgate.com/chronicle/pink-section/film.html
Category: Film Reviews

Teen Movie Critic
URL: http://www.skypoint.com/members/magic/roger/teencritic.html
Category: Film Reviews

The Third Thumb
URL: http://www.ganesa.com/ganesa/~pat/movies/movrev.html
Category: Film Reviews

Video & Movie Review Database
URL: gopher://isumvs.iastate.edu/1~db.VIDEO
Category: Film Reviews

Women Studies Film Reviews
URL: http://www.inform.umd.edu:8080/EdRes/Topic/WomensStudies/FilmReviews
Category: Film Reviews

Bright Lights Film Journal
URL: http://www.crl.com/~gsamuel/bright.html
Category: Magazines & Journals

Cosmic Landscapes: Film & Video Review
URL: http://users.aol.com/cosmicland/cl1.htm
Category: Magazines & Journals

Film International
URL: http://gpg.com/film/
Category: Magazines & Journals

Filmmaker Magazine
URL: http://found.cs.nyu.edu/CAT/affiliates/filmmaker/filmmaker.html
Category: Magazines & Journals

GLAAD Newsletter
URL: http://www.digitopia.com/glaad/news/news-index.html
Category: Magazines & Journals

Inquisitor Magazine
URL: http://www.inquisitor.com/
Category: Magazines & Journals

Media 3
URL: http://www.deakin.edu.au/arts/VPMA/Media3.html
Category: Magazines & Journals

Media Magazine
URL: http://www.adelaide.edu.au/5UV/MM/
Category: Magazines & Journals

Multimedia World Online
URL: http://www.mmworld.com
Category: New Media

FAIR - Fairness & Accuracy In Reporting
URL: http://www.igc.org/fair/
Category: Organizations/Guilds

Live Wire Youth Media
URL: http://www.iit.edu/~livewire/
Category: Organizations/Guilds

Media Watchdog
URL: http://theory.lcs.mit.edu/~mernst/media/
Category: Organizations/Guilds

Entertainment
Anderson, Gillian
URL: http://gpu3.srv.ualberta.ca/~mlwalter/GAHP.html
Category: Actors

Appendix & Cross-References

Applegate, Christina
URL: http://www.ifi.uio.no/~steinbo/applegate.html
Category: Actors

Bacon, Kevin
URL: http://www.mindspring.com/~mab/kevin/kevin.html
Category: Actors

Barrymore, Drew
URL: http://www.wfu.edu/~david/drew/
Category: Actors

Brooks, Louise
URL: http://www.escape.ca/~ianmcc/LB-index.html
Category: Actors

Carter, Helena Bonham
URL: http://www.io.com/~mjf/helena.html
Category: Actors

Cates, Phoebe
URL: http://pages.prodigy.com/AL/kellerra/Phoebe.html
Category: Actors

Dangerfield, Rodney
URL: http://www.rodney.com/rodney/index.html
Category: Actors

Ford, Harrison
URL: http://www.mit.edu:8001/people/lpchao/harrison.ford.html
Category: Actors

Foster, Jodie
URL: http://weber.u.washington.edu/~jnorton/jodie/jodie.html
Category: Actors

Grant, Hugh
URL: http://ucsub.colorado.edu/~kritzber/new/hugh/hugh.html
Category: Actors

Harris, Ed
URL: http://www.fishnet.net/~decadent/edharris.html
Category: Actors

Hepburn, Audrey
URL: http://grove.ufl.edu/~flask/Hepburn.html
Category: Actors

Herman, Pee Wee
URL: http://www.seanet.com/Users/weazel/peewee.html
Category: Actors

Hopkins, Anthony
URL: http://www.mit.edu:8001/people/douglas/sirtony.html
Category: Actors

Kilmer, Val
URL: http://www.tc.cornell.edu/~cat/pages/
Category: Actors

Lewis, Juliette
URL: http://netspace.net.au/~tpropert/jl.html
Category: Actors

Locklear, Heather
URL: http://uptown.turnpike.net/garyfs/index.htm
Category: Actors

Martin, Steve
URL: http://www.dundee.ac.uk/~dcyork/steve.htm
Category: Actors

McNichol, Kristy
URL: http://coos.dartmouth.edu/~elnitsky/Kristy.html
Category: Actors

Monroe, Marilyn
URL: http://ux1.cso.uiuc.edu/~jarrett/marilyn.html
Category: Actors

Monroe, Marilyn
URL: http://www.ionet.net/~jellenc/marilyn.html
Category: Actors

Pitt, Brad
URL: http://web2.airmail.net/~jimhoffa/bradpitt.html
Category: Actors

Appendix & Cross-References

Reeves, Keanu
URL: http://www.users.interport.net/~eperkins/
Category: Actors

Ricci, Christina
URL: http://login.dknet.dk:80/~klaus/ricci/
Category: Actors

Ryan, Meg
URL: http://web.cs.ualberta.ca/~davidw/MegRyan/meg.cgi
Category: Actors

Ryder, Winona
URL: http://www.auburn.edu/~harshec/WWW/Winona.html
Category: Actors

Shearer, Harry
URL: http://pobox.com/harry/
Category: Actors

Thompson, Scott
URL: http://204.225.234.1/
Category: Actors

Van Damme, Jean Claude
URL: http://www.shef.ac.uk/uni/union/susoc/cass/homes/pm/pm933303/van-damme.html
Category: Actors

W.C. Fields
URL: http://www.louisville.edu/~kprayb01/WCBinder.html
Category: Actors

Walken, Christopher
URL: http://www.brunel.ac.uk:8080/~mapgsat/movies/walken/
Category: Actors

Weaver, Sigourney
URL: http://www.pt.hk-r.se/student/di94vno/ripley.html
Category: Actors

@cme Page (WB Cartoons)
URL: http://www.io.com/~woodward/@cme/
Category: Animation

Felix the Cat
URL: http://wso.williams.edu/faculty/psci335/gerstein/felix.html
Category: Animation

Almodóvar, Pedro
URL: http://www.netpoint.be/abc/pedro/
Category: Directors

Hartley, Hal
URL: http://www.best.com/~drumz/Hartley/
Category: Directors

Hitchcock, Alfred (French)
URL: http://hitchcock.alienor.fr/
Category: Directors

Kieslowski, Krzysztof
URL: http://www-personal.engin.umich.edu/~zbigniew/Kieslowski/kieslowski.html
Category: Directors

Lynch, David
URL: http://web.city.ac.uk/~cb157/Dave.html
Category: Directors

Ray, Satyajit
URL: http://math.umbc.edu/~arghya/satyajit.html
Category: Directors

Woo, John
URL: http://underground.net/~koganuts/Galleries/jw.main.html
Category: Directors

Wood, Ed
URL: http://garnet.acns.fsu.edu/~lflynn/edwood.html
Category: Directors

AFI Los Angeles International Film Festival (USA)
URL: http://www.afionline.org/SCREEN/AFIFEST/index.html
Category: Festivals/Events

Berlin Film Festival
URL: http://fub46.zedat.fu-berlin.de:8080/~frs/bff-index.html
Category: Festivals/Events

Appendix & Cross-References

Cannes International Film Festival (France)
URL: http://franceweb.fr/Cinc/Cannes/
Category: Festivals/Events

Chicago International Film Festival (USA)
URL: http://www.ddbn.com/filmfest/
Category: Festivals/Events

Chicago Lesbian and Gay International Film Festival
URL: http://videos.com/gandl/
Category: Festivals/Events

Denver International Film Festival
URL: http://www2.csn.net/DenverFilm/
Category: Festivals/Events

Filmfest München
URL: http://filmfest.spacenet.de/
Category: Festivals/Events

London Film Festival
URL: http://www.ibmpcug.co.uk/lff.html
Category: Festivals/Events

Montreal World Film Festival
URL: http://www.ffm-montreal.org/
Category: Festivals/Events

Oberhausen Short Film Festival (Germany)
URL: http://www.uni-duisburg.de/HRZ/IKF/home.html
Category: Festivals/Events

Portland International Film Festival (USA)
URL: http://www.film.com/film/filmfests/portland.95.html
Category: Festivals/Events

Rotterdam International Film Festival
URL: http://www.luna.nl/~iffr/home.html
Category: Festivals/Events

San Sebastián International Film Festival
URL: http://sarenet.es/iffss/
Category: Festivals/Events

Seattle International Film Festival
URL: http://www.siff.film.com/
Category: Festivals/Events

Stockholm Film Festival
URL: http://www.filmfestivalen.se/
Category: Festivals/Events

Sundance Film Festival
URL: http://plaza.interport.net/festival/intro.html
Category: Festivals/Events

Sydney Film Festival
URL: http://www.ozemail.com.au/~sff/
Category: Festivals/Events

Toronto International Film Festival
URL: http://www.bell.ca/toronto/filmfest/
Category: Festivals/Events

Vancouver International Film Festival
URL: http://www.viff.org/viff/
Category: Festivals/Events

Venice Film Festival
URL: http://www.portve.interbusiness.it/wetvenice/biennale/cinema/cinema.html
Category: Festivals/Events

Detroit News Movie Page
URL: http://www.detnews.com/SHOWTIME/movies/index.html
Category: Film Reviews

Mr. Showbiz
URL: http://web3.starwave.com:80/showbiz/
Category: Film Reviews

Tucson Weekly's Film Vault
URL: http://desert.net/tw/film/index.htm
Category: Film Reviews

Amazing Clickable Beavis
URL: http://freedom.nmsu.edu/~jlillibr/ClickableBeavis.html
Category: Film & TV Assorted

Appendix & Cross-References

Australian Television Guide
URL: http://www.sofcom.com.au/TV/index.html
Category: Film & TV Assorted

Bagpipes Go To The Movies
URL: http://www.ems.psu.edu/~fraser/PipesMovies.html
Category: Film & TV Assorted

Balcony
URL: http://balcony.com/
Category: Film & TV Assorted

Cathouse British Comedy Pages
URL: http://cathouse.org/BritishComedy/
Category: Film & TV Assorted

Celebrity Pages
URL: http://emporium.turnpike.net/~daniel/Alicia/celebs.html
Category: Film & TV Assorted

CNN Showbiz News
URL: http://www.cnn.com/SHOWBIZ/index.html
Category: Film & TV Assorted

Cosmo's TV Guide
URL: http://home.ptd.net/~cosmo/
Category: Film & TV Assorted

Cult Shop
URL: http://lasarto.cnde.iastate.edu/Movies/CultShop/
Category: Film & TV Assorted

Cult TV Episode Guide
URL: http://www.ee.ed.ac.uk/~jmd/CultTV/
Category: Film & TV Assorted

Drew's Script-O-Matic
URL: http://home.fish.net.au/~drew/scripts.htm
Category: Film & TV Assorted

Film Personality Deaths
URL: http://catless.ncl.ac.uk/Obituary/movies.html
Category: Film & TV Assorted

Flicker
URL: http://www.sirius.com/~sstark/
Category: Film & TV Assorted

Gay-Lesbian Themed Film & TV Projects
URL: http://www.datalounge.com/hsupports/development-projects.html
Category: Film & TV Assorted

Great Comedy Movies
URL: http://www.sccs.swarthmore.edu/~dansac/movies/comedy.html
Category: Film & TV Assorted

Grolsch filmpagina
URL: http://www.riv.nl/grolsch/film.htm
Category: Film & TV Assorted

Hans Zimmer Worship Page
URL: http://www.ugcs.caltech.edu/~btman/hanszimmer/
Category: Film & TV Assorted

Hong Kong Movies
URL: http://www.mdstud.chalmers.se/hkmovie/
Category: Film & TV Assorted

Martial Arts Films
URL: http://www.digiweb.com/webm/chris/
Category: Film & TV Assorted

Marvin the Martian
URL: http://eeisun2.city.ac.uk/~ftp/maw/marvin.html
Category: Film & TV Assorted

MORSE: Movie Recommendation System
URL: http://www.labs.bt.com/innovate/multimed/morse/morse.htm
Category: Film & TV Assorted

Movie Cliches List
URL: http://www.well.com/user/vertigo/cliches.html
Category: Film & TV Assorted

Science Fiction Film Archive
URL: http://www.primenet.com/~laurus/scifi/sffilm/sffilm.htm
Category: Film & TV Assorted

Appendix & Cross-References

Soundtrack Web
URL: http://alfred.uib.no/People/midi/soundtrackweb/
Category: Film & TV Assorted

TV1
URL: http://www.TV1.com
Category: Film & TV Assorted

VCR Q&A
URL: http://bradley.bradley.edu/~fil/vcr.html
Category: Film & TV Assorted

Weekend Box Office Report
URL: http://cellini.leonardo.net/aasen/topbox.html
Category: Film & TV Assorted

World TV Standards Guides
URL: http://www.ee.surrey.ac.uk/Contrib/WorldTV/
Category: Film & TV Assorted

AIRWAVES Television Page
URL: http://radio.aiss.uiuc.edu/~rrb/tv.html
Category: Film & TV Indices

Cinema Connection
URL: http://www.webcom.com/~3e-media/TMC/cineprax.html
Category: Film & TV Indices

Clamen's Movie Information Collection
URL: http://www.cs.cmu.edu/afs/cs.cmu.edu/user/clamen/misc/movies/
Category: Film & TV Indices

Film.com
URL: http://www.film.com/film/
Category: Film & TV Indices

Hollywood Online
URL: http://www.hollywood.com/
Category: Film & TV Indices

Media-Link
URL: http://www.dds.nl/~kidon/media.html
Category: Film & TV Indices

RML's Movie Page
URL: http://netspace.net.au/~haze/
Category: Film & TV Indices

Take TWO
URL: http://www.webcom.com/~taketwo/
Category: Film & TV Indices

Television Pointers
URL: http://www.cs.cmu.edu/afs/cs.cmu.edu/user/clamen/misc/tv/README.html
Category: Film & TV Indices

TV Net
URL: http://www.tvnet.com/
Category: Film & TV Indices

WebOvision
URL: http://www.catalog.com/cgibin/var/media/index.html
Category: Film & TV Indices

Yahoo Entertainment
URL: http://www.yahoo.com/Entertainment/
Category: Film & TV Indices

Basketball Diaries
URL: http://underground.net/BDiaries/
Category: Films

Batman Forever
URL: http://batmanforever.com/
Category: Films

Blade Runner
URL: http://kzsu.stanford.edu/uwi/br/off-world.html
Category: Films

Bloodlust
URL: http://www.ozemail.com.au/~jswjon/
Category: Films

Blues Brothers
URL: http://matahari.tamu.edu/bluesbrothers
Category: Films

Appendix & Cross-References

Casablanca
URL: http://users.aol.com/VRV1/index.html
Category: Films

Cry the Beloved Country
URL: http://os2.iafrica.com/ve/cry_menu.htm
Category: Films

Desperado
URL: http://cinemascape.comtecmedia.com/chris/desperado.html
Category: Films

Dr. No
URL: http://www.dur.ac.uk/~dcs3pjb/jb/drno.html
Category: Films

Dune
URL: http://www.princeton.edu/~cgilmore/dune/
Category: Films

Fast Times at Ridgemont High
URL: http://wizvax.net/truegger/fast-times.html
Category: Films

Godfather Trilogy
URL: http://www.exit109.com/~jgeoff/godfathr.html
Category: Films

Godzilla
URL: http://www.ama.caltech.edu/users/mrm/godzilla.html
Category: Films

Hoop Dreams
URL: http://www.well.com/user/srhodes/hoopdreams.html
Category: Films

Indiana Jones
URL: http://dialin.ind.net/~msjohnso/
Category: Films

Jeffrey
URL: http://www.digitopia.com/jeffrey/
Category: Films

Leon
URL: http://www.ltm.com/dinan/leon/html/leon.html
Category: Films

Lion King
URL: http://www.ugcs.caltech.edu/~btman/lionking/
Category: Films

Monty Python and the Holy Grail
URL: http://cathouse.org/BritishComedy/MontyPython/HolyGrail/
Category: Films

Phantasm
URL: http://www.phantasm.com/
Category: Films

Psycho
URL: http://www.geopages.com/Hollywood/1645/
Category: Films

Rocky Horror Picture Show
URL: http://www.nforce.com/~rhps/
Category: Films

Sex, Drugs & Democracy
URL: http://www.cc.columbia.edu/~arb33/
Category: Films

Star Wars
URL: http://www.princeton.edu/~nieder/sw/sw.html
Category: Films

TRON
URL: http://www.aquila.com/guy.gordon/tron/tron.htm
Category: Films

Dystopian Visions Image Galleries
URL: http://underground.net/~koganuts/Galleries/
Category: Images

Hollywood Sign Live
URL: http://www.rfx.com:80/hollywood/index.html
Category: Images

Appendix & Cross-References

Hong Kong Movies Picture Library
URL: http://kaarna.cc.jyu.fi/~tjko/hkmpl/
Category: Images

Image Finder
URL: http://arachnid.cs.cf.ac.uk/Misc/wustl.html
Category: Images

Spanish Movie Flyers
URL: http://eliza.netaxis.com/~cbird/spain/spantext.html
Category: Images

Three Colors - Pictures
URL: http://www.mty.itesm.mx/~dch/centros/cinema16/tres_colores/texto/tres_colores.html
Category: Images

Twin Peaks Pictures
URL: http://www.uaep.co.uk/pages/tpph1.html
Category: Images

Buzz
URL: http://www.buzzmag.com/
Category: Magazines & Journals

CONNECT Magazine
URL: http://www.connectmag.com/connect/
Category: Magazines & Journals

Dis 'n' Dat Newsletter
URL: ftp://ftp.wang.com/pub/lar3ry/dnd/dnd-HOME.html
Category: Magazines & Journals

Entertainment Weekly
URL: http://pathfinder.com/ew/
Category: Magazines & Journals

HotWired
URL: http://www.hotwired.com/
Category: Magazines & Journals

London Calling
URL: http://www.demon.co.uk/london-calling/filmmus.html
Category: Magazines & Journals

Mediamatic
URL: http://www.mediamatic.nl/Magazine/
Category: Magazines & Journals

Premiere
URL: http://www.premieremag.com/
Category: Magazines & Journals

Time Out
URL: http://www.timeout.co.uk./
Category: Magazines & Journals

TV Guide
URL: http://www.delphi.com/tvgo/
Category: Magazines & Journals

Amsterdam Film Guide
URL: http://www.dds.nl/~filmhuis/ladder.htm
Category: Movie Theaters

Atlanta WWW Movie Guide
URL: http://www.echonyc.com/~mvidal/atlanta-movies.html
Category: Movie Theaters

Berlin Cinema Guide
URL: http://www.netcs.com/Kino/
Category: Movie Theaters

BigScreen Cinema Guide
URL: http://www.execpc.com/~sjentsch/cinema/PCG.html
Category: Movie Theaters

Boston Local Movie Listings
URL: http://www.actwin.com/movies/index.html
Category: Movie Theaters

CINEASC - UK Internet Film Guide
URL: http://www.gold.net/users/ae37/cineasc/index.html
Category: Movie Theaters

Dublin Cinema Guide
URL: http://www.maths.tcd.ie/pub/films/dublin_cinemas.html
Category: Movie Theaters

Appendix & Cross-References

Hawaii Movie Page
URL: http://aloha.com/~ia/wallace.html
Category: Movie Theaters

Los Angeles Webstation Online Movie Guide
URL: http://198.147.111.7/movies/
Category: Movie Theaters

Manchester Cinemas
URL: http://www.U-net.com/manchester/cinemas/home.html
Category: Movie Theaters

Metro Movie Guide (Halifax-Canada)
URL: http://www.isisnet.com/mm/movieguide/
Category: Movie Theaters

Movienet (Goldwyn/Landmark Theaters)
URL: http://www.movienet.com/
Category: Movie Theaters

Movietimes.com
URL: http://www.movietimes.com/
Category: Movie Theaters

Mr. Woof's Drive-In Theater Information
URL: http://www.wInternet.com/~mrwoof/driveman.html
Category: Movie Theaters

Nederlands Filmmuseum
URL: http://shaman.dds.nl/~nfm/index.html
Category: Movie Theaters

Rocky Horror Theater List
URL: http://www.cis.ohio-state.edu/hypertext/faq/usenet/movies/rocky-horror-theaters/faq.html
Category: Movie Theaters

Toronto Movie Guide
URL: http://www.hype.com/toronto/movies/home.htm
Category: Movie Theaters

Vancouver Movie Listings
URL: http://www.iceonline.com/icedocs/resources/icemovie.html
Category: Movie Theaters

Comedy Central Flicks
URL: http://www.comcentral.com/loads.htm
Category: Movies

Movies on the Net
URL: http://www.el-dorado.ca.us/~homeport/Internet_movies.html
Category: Movies

MPEG Movie Archive
URL: http://w3.eeb.ele.tue.nl/mpeg/index.html
Category: Movies

MTV Animation
URL: http://www.mtv.com/animation/
Category: Movies

News Reels Archive
URL: http://192.253.114.31/D-Day/News_reels/News_reels_contents.html
Category: Movies

webdog's Movies
URL: http://www.webdog.com/movies.html
Category: Movies

TeleCircus San Francisco
URL: http://www.well.com/user/tcircus/
Category: New Media

Cherokee High School Star Trek Club
URL: http://pages.prodigy.com/NJ/cstc/cstc95hp.html
Category: Organizations/Guilds

Cinema 16
URL: http://www.mty.itesm.mx/~dch/centros/cinema16/
Category: Organizations/Guilds

Documentary Film Group
URL: http://http.bsd.uchicago.edu/doc/
Category: Organizations/Guilds

Film Society Montaasi (Finland)
URL: http://otax.tky.hut.fi/.publish/montaasi/
Category: Organizations/Guilds

Appendix & Cross-References

Sony Pictures Imageworks
URL: http://spiw.com/cgi-bin/ver/index.html
Category: Production & Distribution

Internet Movie Database
URL: http://www.cm.cf.ac.uk/Movies/welcome.html
Category: Research and Databases

On This Day in Movie History
URL: http://www.msstate.edu/M/on-this-day
Category: Research and Databases

Tardis Television Database
URL: http://www.tardis.ed.ac.uk/~dave/guides/index.html
Category: Research and Databases

Caddyshack Movie Sounds
URL: http://www.ee.duke.edu/~ceh/caddy/caddy.html
Category: Sounds

Plan 9 From Outer Space Soundtrack (RealAudio)
URL: http://www.w2.com/docs2/c4/p9liner.html
Category: Sounds

Princess Bride Sound Clips
URL: http://www-personal.engin.umich.edu/~cstrick/PrincessBride/sounds.html
Category: Sounds

Seinfeld Sound Clips
URL: http://www.ifi.uio.no/~rubens/seinfeld/sounds/index.html
Category: Sounds

Simpsons Sounds
URL: http://www.duke.edu/~djwitzel/Simps.html
Category: Sounds

Sound Clip Directory
URL: http://www.eecs.nwu.edu/~jmyers/other-sounds.html
Category: Sounds

TV Bytes: WWW TV Themes Page
URL: http://themes.parkhere.com/themes/
Category: Sounds

Twin Peaks Sounds
URL: http://www.desktop.com.au/~lwerndly/tpsound.html
Category: Sounds

Elstree - remember me?
URL: http://metro.turnpike.net/E/elstree/
Category: Studios

Fine Line Features
URL: http://www.flf.com/
Category: Studios

Gramercy Pictures
URL: http://www.polygram.com/polygram/Film.html
Category: Studios

MGM/UA
URL: http://www.mgmua.com/
Category: Studios

New Line Cinema
URL: http://cybertimes.com/NewLine/Welcome.html
Category: Studios

Paramount Pictures
URL: http://www.paramount.com/
Category: Studios

Sony Pictures Entertainment
URL: http://www.spe.sony.com/Pictures/
Category: Studios

Troma
URL: http://www.troma.com/home/
Category: Studios

United International Pictures
URL: http://www.uip.com/
Category: Studios

Universal Pictures
URL: http://www.mca.com/universal_pictures/index.html
Category: Studios

Appendix & Cross-References

Walt Disney Company
URL: http://www.disney.com/
Category: Studios

Australian Broadcasting Corporation
URL: http://www.abc.net.au/
Category: TV Networks

British Broadcasting Corporation
URL: http://www.bbcnc.org.uk/
Category: TV Networks

CBC (Canada)
URL: http://www.cbc.ca/
Category: TV Networks

CBS (USA)
URL: http://www.cbs.com/
Category: TV Networks

Channel 4 (UK)
URL: http://www.cityscape.co.uk/channel4/
Category: TV Networks

CNN (USA)
URL: http://www.cnn.com/index.html
Category: TV Networks

Deutsche Welle
URL: http://www-dw.gmd.de/
Category: TV Networks

ESPN (USA)
URL: http://espnet.sportszone.com/
Category: TV Networks

FOX (USA)
URL: http://www.foxnetwork.com/home.html
Category: TV Networks

MTV (USA)
URL: http://www.mtv.com/
Category: TV Networks

NBC (USA)
URL: http://www.nbc.com/
Category: TV Networks

NHK (Japan)
URL: http://www.nhk.or.jp/
Category: TV Networks

Nippon Television Network (Japan)
URL: http://www.ntv.co.jp/
Category: TV Networks

PBS (USA)
URL: http://www.pbs.org/
Category: TV Networks

QVC (USA)
URL: http://www.qvc.com/
Category: TV Networks

Showtime (USA)
URL: http://showtimeonline.com/
Category: TV Networks

Sveriges Television (Sweden)
URL: http://www.svt.se/
Category: TV Networks

Swiss Broadcasting Corporation
URL: http://www.srg-ssr.ch/
Category: TV Networks

Turner Broadcasting System (USA)
URL: http://www.turner.com/
Category: TV Networks

TV3 - Televisio de Catalunya (Spain)
URL: http://www.bcn.servicom.es/TV3/
Category: TV Networks

Universal cHANnEL
URL: http://www.mca.com:80/tv/
Category: TV Networks

Appendix & Cross-References

VH1 (USA)
URL: http://vh1.com/
Category: TV Networks

Absolutely Fabulous
URL: http://online.anu.edu.au/ArtHistory/TOR/
Category: TV Programs

All My Children
URL: http://purplenet.com/soaps/AllMyChildren.html
Category: TV Programs

Andy Griffith Show
URL: http://www.wInternet.com/~muff/andy-griffith.html
Category: TV Programs

Animaniacs
URL: http://www2.msstate.edu/~jbp3/animx/animx.html
Category: TV Programs

Babylon 5
URL: http://www.hyperion.com/lurk/
Category: TV Programs

Baywatch
URL: http://baywatch.compuserve.com/
Category: TV Programs

Beavis & Butt-head
URL: http://calvin.hsc.colorado.edu/
Category: TV Programs

Brady Bunch
URL: http://www.teleport.com/~btucker/bradys.htm
Category: TV Programs

Cheers
URL: http://s9000.furman.edu/~treu/cheers.html
Category: TV Programs

CHiPs
URL: http://underground.Internet.com/CHiPs/CHiPs.html
Category: TV Programs

Court TV
URL: http://www.courttv.com/
Category: TV Programs

Doctor Who
URL: http://zen.btc.uwe.ac.uk/~n2-ellis/DWID.html
Category: TV Programs

Due South
URL: http://duke.usask.ca/~turner/duesouth.html
Category: TV Programs

Earth2
URL: http://www.best.com/~ftmexpat/e2/earth2.html
Category: TV Programs

EastEnders
URL: http://galt.cs.nyu.edu/students/beads/ee/
Category: TV Programs

Fawlty Towers
URL: http://cathouse.org/BritishComedy/FawltyTowers/
Category: TV Programs

Frasier
URL: http://www.umich.edu/~messina/frasier/
Category: TV Programs

Friends
URL: http://www-personal.umich.edu/~geena/friends.html
Category: TV Programs

General Hospital
URL: http://www.cts.com/~jeffmj/GeneralHospital.html
Category: TV Programs

Gilligan's Island
URL: http://www.epix.net/~jabcpudr/gilligan.html
Category: TV Programs

Gladiators
URL: http://www.gold.net/users/ak90/index.html
Category: TV Programs

Hawaii Five-O
URL: http://www.chapman.edu/students/tkrell/hawaii/five-o/
Category: TV Programs

Highlander
URL: http://www.rust.net/~cmarco/high.htm
Category: TV Programs

Home Improvement
URL: http://www.canuck.com/~marauder/homeimpr.html
Category: TV Programs

Kids in the Hall
URL: http://wwwvms.utexas.edu/~barbcarr/index.html
Category: TV Programs

Land of the Lost
URL: http://www.execpc.com/~nolsen/lotl/lotl.html
Category: TV Programs

Late Show with David Letterman
URL: http://www.cbs.com/lateshow/
Category: TV Programs

Lost in Space
URL: http://www.galcit.caltech.edu/~joe/lis/episode.html
Category: TV Programs

M*A*S*H
URL: http://www.best.com/~dijon/tv/mash/
Category: TV Programs

Mad About You
URL: http://www.alumni.caltech.edu/~witelski/may.html
Category: TV Programs

Married...With Children
URL: http://www.zmall.com/misc/bundyland/
Category: TV Programs

Melrose Place
URL: http://melroseplace.com/
Category: TV Programs

Mighty Morphin' Power Rangers
URL: http://kilp.media.mit.edu:8001/power/homepage.html
Category: TV Programs

Mister Rogers' Neighborhood
URL: http://www.pbs.org:80/rogers/mrr_home.html
Category: TV Programs

Monty Python's Flying Circus
URL: http://bau2.uibk.ac.at/sg/python/monty.html
Category: TV Programs

Mystery Science Theater 3000
URL: http://www.rain.org/~roryh/mst3k/index.html
Category: TV Programs

Northern Exposure
URL: http://www.netspace.org/~moose/moose.html
Category: TV Programs

Prisoner
URL: http://www.ling.uu.se/~bengt/tp.html
Category: TV Programs

Ren & Stimpy
URL: http://www.cris.com/~lkarper/rands.html
Category: TV Programs

Saturday Night Live
URL: http://www.best.com/~dijon/tv/snl/
Category: TV Programs

Scooby Doo
URL: http://hubcap.clemson.edu/~jsikes/scooby.html
Category: TV Programs

seaQuest DSV
URL: http://www.phoenix.net/~leigh/seaQuest/
Category: TV Programs

Seinfeld
URL: http://www.engr.wisc.edu/~heinj/seinfeld.html
Category: TV Programs

Appendix & Cross-References

Simpsons
URL: http://yarrow.wt.com.au/~sjackson/simpsons/
Category: TV Programs

Star Trek
URL: http://www-iwi.unisg.ch/~sambucci/scifi/startrek/index.html
Category: TV Programs

Tick
URL: http://www.prairienet.org/~phyber/tickpage.html
Category: TV Programs

Unsolved Mysteries
URL: http://www.unsolved.com/
Category: TV Programs

X-Files
URL: http://duggy.extern.ucsd.edu/~linny/index.html
Category: TV Programs

Professional
CartooNet
URL: http://www.pavilion.co.uk/cartoonet/
Category: Animation

London International Film School
URL: http://www.tecc.co.uk/lifs/index.html
Category: Film & Media Schools

Cable Online
URL: http://www.aescon.com/cableonline/
Category: Film & TV Assorted

Norwegian Films 1995
URL: http://www.dnfi.no/nf/nf-indx.html
Category: Films

Biz
URL: http://www.bizmag.com/
Category: Magazines & Journals

Fade In
URL: http://www.best.com/~market/fadein/
Category: Magazines & Journals

Videomaker Magazine
URL: http://www.videomaker.com/
Category: Magazines & Journals

Digital Planet
URL: http://www.digiplanet.com/
Category: New Media

Director Web
URL: http://www.mcli.dist.maricopa.edu/director/
Category: New Media

Academy of Motion Picture Arts and Sciences
URL: http://www.ampas.org/ampas/
Category: Organizations/Guilds

Academy of Television Arts and Sciences
URL: http://www.emmys.org/tindex.html
Category: Organizations/Guilds

Australian Film Institute
URL: http://www.vicnet.net.au/vicnet/afi/afiho.htm
Category: Organizations/Guilds

Broadcast Education Association
URL: http://www.usu.edu/~bea/
Category: Organizations/Guilds

California Film Commission
URL: http://www.ca.gov/commerce/cf_home.html
Category: Organizations/Guilds

Director's Guild of America
URL: http://leonardo.net/dga/
Category: Organizations/Guilds

Finnish Film Foundation
URL: http://www.kaapeli.fi/~lumo/English/FFF/
Category: Organizations/Guilds

Hollywood Supports
URL: http://www.datalounge.com/hsupports/
Category: Organizations/Guilds

Appendix & Cross-References

International Federation of Television Archives
URL: http://www.nbr.no/fiat/fiat.html
Category: Organizations/Guilds

International Television Association
URL: http://www.itva.org
Category: Organizations/Guilds

Internet Film Commissioner
URL: http://www.ibmpcug.co.uk/~scrfin/ifc/ifc.html
Category: Organizations/Guilds

Media Development Association
URL: http://www2.pavilion.co.uk/medianet/
Category: Organizations/Guilds

MediaWeb
URL: http://www.sa.ua.edu/tcf/mediaweb.htm
Category: Organizations/Guilds

National Film Board of Canada
URL: http://www.nfb.ca/
Category: Organizations/Guilds

Norwegian Film Institute
URL: http://www.dnfi.no/
Category: Organizations/Guilds

Pacific Film & Television Commission
URL: http://design.net.au/pftc/
Category: Organizations/Guilds

Society for the Preservation of Film Music
URL: http://www.oldkingcole.com/spfm/
Category: Organizations/Guilds

Squeaky Wheel
URL: http://freenet.buffALO.EDU/~wheel/
Category: Organizations/Guilds

Sundance Institute
URL: http://cybermart.com/sundance/institute/institute.html
Category: Organizations/Guilds

Arizona Film & Video Production Resources
URL: http://bensonassoc.com/bensonassoc/film/home.html
Category: Production & Distribution

Australian Media Facilities Directory
URL: http://www.amfd.com.au/AMFD/amfdhp.htm
Category: Production & Distribution

British Actors' Register
URL: http://www.Internet-eireann.ie/power/actor/actor.htm
Category: Production & Distribution

Camera Department
URL: http://www.seanet.com/Users/timtyler/film/camera.html
Category: Production & Distribution

Chicago Filmmakers
URL: http://www.tezcat.com/~chifilm/homepage.html
Category: Production & Distribution

Cinematographer's Online Bible
URL: http://www-scf.usc.edu/~hunziker/cim/cim.htm
Category: Production & Distribution

Delta 9 Independent Film Resource
URL: http://www.eden.com/~delta-9/
Category: Production & Distribution

Electric Judy
URL: http://www.electric-judy.com/
Category: Production & Distribution

Entertainment Law Resources
URL: http://www.laig.com/law/entlaw/
Category: Production & Distribution

EZTV
URL: http://leonardo.net/eztv/
Category: Production & Distribution

FINEcut - Video Moviemaker's Resources
URL: http://www.rmplc.co.uk/eduweb/sites/terrymen/movie1.html
Category: Production & Distribution

Appendix & Cross-References

Hollywood Mall
URL: http://www.HollywoodMall.com/
Category: Production & Distribution

Icelandic Film Production
URL: http://www.centrum.is/filmfund/
Category: Production & Distribution

Independent Film & Video Makers Resource Guide
URL: http://www.echonyc.com/~mvidal/Indi-Film+Video.html
Category: Production & Distribution

JV III NYC Film Production Resource Locator
URL: http://www.panix.com/jviii/filmlctr/jv3film1.html
Category: Production & Distribution

Location Online
URL: http://marvin.sedd.trw.com:1025/LOL/
Category: Production & Distribution

Mandy's Film & TV Directory
URL: http://www.mandy.com/
Category: Production & Distribution

New York Film & Video Web
URL: http://www.ios.com/nyfilm/
Category: Production & Distribution

North Carolina Independent Filmmakers Assoc.
URL: http://www.well.com/user/ncifa/ncifamn.htm
Category: Production & Distribution

Northwest FilmNet
URL: http://vvv.com/maplewood/nwhome.html
Category: Production & Distribution

Production Weekly
URL: http://users.aol.com/prodweek/pw.html
Category: Production & Distribution

Scoring Services
URL: http://www.scoring.com/
Category: Production & Distribution

Showdata Online
URL: http://www.aztec.co.za/biz/showdata/
Category: Production & Distribution

Texas Film & Video Producers Resources
URL: http://waterworks.com./~tfv/
Category: Production & Distribution

The Guide
URL: http://theguide.gim.de/Etrans/
Category: Production & Distribution

Universal Studios, Florida
URL: http://www.imeid.com/ustop.html
Category: Production & Distribution

VCV Stunts
URL: http://www.procom.com/~daves/vcvstunt.html
Category: Production & Distribution

Vidéographe
URL: http://www.connectmmic.net/videograf/
Category: Production & Distribution

Virtual Film Market
URL: http://moviemarket.com/
Category: Production & Distribution

Virtual Headbook
URL: http://www.xmission.com/~wintrnx/virtual.html
Category: Production & Distribution

BBB Movie Scripts
URL: http://pages.ripco.com:8080/~bbb/scripts.html
Category: Screenwriting

Charles Deemer's Screenwriting Page
URL: http://www.teleport.com/~cdeemer/scrwriter.html
Category: Screenwriting

Internet's Screenwriter's Network
URL: http://www.screenwriters.com/screennet.html
Category: Screenwriting

Austrian Video Archive
URL: http://austria-info.at/ava/
Category: Video Info./Sales

BIBLIOGRAPHY

Dickson, William, & Engst, Adam. (1994). *Internet Explorer Kit for Macintosh.* Indianapolis: Hayden Books (comes with diskette).

Hahn, Harley, & Stout, Rick. (1994). *The Internet Complete Reference.* Berkeley: Osborne McGraw-Hill.

Landow, George P. (1992). *Hypertext: The Convergence of Contemporary Critical Theory and Technology.* Baltimore: Johns Hopkins University Press.

VIDEOGRAPHY

The Video Guide to the Internet Overoye, Dave. (1994). *The Video Guide to the Internet.* E-mail: nightdave@aol.com

RECOMMENDED READING

At the moment, there are over 350 books about the Internet. On a recent visit to a major book store in Berkeley, California, I spied about 15 brand new titles on the bookstands. It is impossible for me to keep up on the Internet publishing sphere, since much of it occurs in periodicals and books that do not wholly deal with the Internet, but incorporate it in their writings. Many of the mainstream magazines now have sections devoted to the Internet and cyberspace. Some of the books and magazines I have read or carefully looked at and can recommend are:

Gilster, Paul, (1994). *Finding It On the Internet.* New York: John Wiley & Sons, Inc.

Hahn, Harley & Stout, Rick. (1995). *The Internet Yellow Pages, Second Edition* Berkeley: Osborne McGraw-Hill.

Kehoe, Brendan. (1994). *Zen and the Art of Internet.* New Jersey: Prentice Hall (also available online for ftp downloads).

Rheingold, Howard (1994) *Virtual Community* London: Secker and Warburg

Rucker, R, Sirius, R.U., & Mu, Queen. (1993). *The Mondo 2000 User's Guide To the New Edge.* New York: Harper Collins.

Wired magazine

FREE NEW EDITION, IF WE USE YOUR REVIEW

So now, we open up the process to you, dear reader, and invite you to tell us about sites you've discovered (and like–forget the ones you don't). Here is a form for you to write your own review. If the site is new to use or we use your comments and pithy review **we will send you FREE a copy of the next edition of *Film & Video On The Internet*.** You may send in as many reviews as you like but only one book will be given out per person. Thank you for participating.

READER REVIEW FORM

Site Name:

URL:
e-mail address:

Rating: (1-4)
Description and Comments:

Reader's Name:

Address:
City, State, Zip
e-mail address
phone

Read the Hottest Book in Hollywood!!!

THE WRITER'S JOURNEY
MYTHIC STRUCTURE FOR
STORYTELLERS &
SCREENWRITERS
by Christopher Vogler

Find out why this book has become an industry wide best-seller and is considered **"required reading"** by many of Hollywood's top studios! THE WRITER'S JOURNEY reveals how master storytellers from Hitchcock to Spielberg have used mythic structure to create powerful stories which tap into the mythological core which exists in us all.

Writer's will discover a set of useful myth-inspired storytelling paradigms (i.e. *The Hero's Journey*) and step-by-step guidelines for plotting and character development. Based on the work of **Joseph Campbell**, THE WRITER'S JOURNEY is a **must** for writers, producers, directors, film/video students, and Joseph Campbell devotees.

Vogler is a script consultant who has worked on scripts for "The Lion King," "Beauty and the Beast" and evaluated over 6000 others.

"This book should come with a warning: You're going to learn about more than just writing movies–you're going to learn about life! The Writer's Journey is the perfect manual for developing, pitching, and writing stories with universal human themes that will forever captivate a global audience. It's the secret weapon I hope every writer finds out about."
                                        - Jeff Arch,
Screenwriter, *Sleepless in Seattle*

$22.95 paper, ISBN 0-941188-13-2,
200 pages, 6 x 8

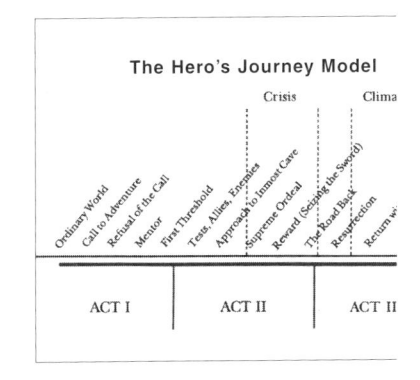

Another BEST-SELLER !
The most sought after book in Hollywood by top directors!!

FILM DIRECTING SHOT BY SHOT
by Steven Katz

This best-seller is filled with visual techniques for filmmakers and screenwriters to expand their stylistic knowledge. With beautiful illustrations and expertly written directions, *Shot by Shot* has been used as a reference tool **"on the set"** by many of Hollywood's directors.

Shot by Shot is a must for both seasoned and novice filmmakers. Includes **never before published** storyboards from Spielberg (*Empire of the Sun*), Orson Welles (*Citizen Kane*), and Hitchcock (*The Birds*).

Katz is an award-winning filmmaker with over 20 years of experience in the fields of writing, directing, and editing.

$24.95, ISBN 0-941188-10-8, 370 pages, 7 x 10, 750+ illus.

THE DIGITAL VIDEOMAKER'S GUIDE
by Kathryn Shaw Whitver

Digital video is a hot topic. The jargon is new and it's difficult to sort out what's real, what's likely to be achieved, and what's just hype.

Digital video (including Video CD) is expected to revolutionize the film and video industry in the same ways that audio CDs changed the face of the recording industry. Understanding digital video technology and taking advantage of its uniqueness is the foundation on which success in this industry will be defined.

The Digital Videomaker's Guide explores the creation of digital videos from concept to finished product.

Kathryn Shaw Whitver is an award-winning technical writer specializing in digital technologies. She currently works for OptImage, a leading multimedia and software design company.

$24.95, ISBN 0-941188-21-3, Approx 300 pages, 5 1/2 x 8 1/4

SHAKING THE MONEY TREE
How To Get Grants and Donations for Film & Video
by Morrie Warshawski

Dazed and confused by the frustrating world of grants and donations? This book demystifies the entire maze of grant world hustling and provides easy-to-follow guidelines.

Warshawski is a leading fundraising consultant for media artists. His clients include The National Endowment for the Arts, The MacArthur Foundation, and the Center for New Television.

"Put it on your shelf, under your pillow, give it to your trustees, and always have your copy handy. You'll be using it a lot."
- Brian O'Doherty, Director, Media Arts Program
          National Endowment for the Arts

$24.95, ISBN 0-941188-18-3, 188 pages, 6 x 8 1/4

FILM & VIDEO FINANCING
by Michael Wiese

Praised as **the** book that prepares producers to **get the money**! A complete "palette" of creative strategies for the independent producer looking to finance their feature films and video projects.

Contents include information on current attitudes and approaches to finding investment through limited partnerships, equity investments, banking issues, split-rights deals, debt equity deals, blocked funds, foreign pre-sales, and much more. Plus insider's tips from independent producers and money-raisers for such films as *"sex, lies & videotape,"* *"A Trip to Bountiful,"* and *"Terminator 2."*

This book will give you the ideas and strategies you need to get the job done!

$22.95, ISBN 0-941188-11-6, 300 pages, 6 x 8 1/4

FILM DIRECTING: Cinematic Motion
by Steven Katz

"...a valuable and relevant guide...(features) interesting interviews with film professionals." — *3D Artist*

This is a practical guide to common production problems encountered when staging and blocking film scenes. It includes discussions of scheduling, staging without dialogue, staging in confined spaces, actor and camera choreography in both large and small spaces, sequence shots, and much more. Interviews with well-known professionals–a cinematographer, a director, a production manager, a continuity person, and an actor–enhance this comprehensive study of stylistic approaches to camera space as they address the requirements of the production manager.

Katz is an award-winning filmmaker with over 20 years of experience in the fields of writing, directing, and editing.

$24.95, ISBN 0-941188-14-0, 200 pages, 7 x 10, illus.

PRODUCER TO PRODUCER
by Michael Wiese

"This book is like having a private consultation with Wiese. Invaluable information presented in a clear, concise manner."

Straight one-on-one talk from one of America's leading independent media producers. In 26 knockout chapters, you'll hear Wiese's latest thoughts on everything from program development, financing and production, to marketing, distribution and new media. Articles include: "Self-Distribution," "Infomercials: Where's the Info?," "Where Do You Get the Money?" and much more.

$19.95, ISBN 0-941188-15-9, 175 pages, 6 x 8, illus.

FREE CATALOG for all our books.
CALL 1-800-379-8808
ORDER FORM

To order these products please call 1-800-379-8808 or fax (818) 986-3408 or mail this order form to:

MICHAEL WIESE PRODUCTIONS
11288 Ventura Blvd., Suite 821
Studio City, CA 91604
1-800-379-8808

BOOKS:
_____
_____
_____

Subtotal $_____
Shipping $_____
8.25% Sales Tax (Ca Only) $_____

TOTAL ENCLOSED_____

Please make check or money order payable to *Michael Wiese Productions*
(Check one) ____ Master Card ____ Visa ____ Amex
Company PO#_____

Credit Card Number_____
Expiration Date_____
Cardholder's Name_____
Cardholder's Signature_____

SHIP TO:

CREDIT CARD ORDERS

CALL 1-800-379-8808

OR **FAX** 818 986-3408

OR E-MAIL
WIESE@EARTHLINK.NET

SHIPPING

1ST CLASS MAIL
One Book - $5.00
Two Books - $7.00
For each additional book, add $1.00.

AIRBORNE EXPRESS
2nd Day Delivery
Add an additional
$11.00 per order.

OVERSEAS (PREPAID)
Surface - $7.00 ea. book
Airmail - $15.00 ea. book

Name_____
Address_____
City_____State_____Zip_____
Country_____Telephone_____

(F&V I)

PN 1998.A1 D36 1996